*Here is your*

# 1981-82 Trademark Law Handbook

## Volume 1

*1981–82 Trademark Law Handbook* will be published in two volumes, of which this is Volume 1.

This procedure is a one-time adjustment to bring to date the United States Trademark Association's annual review of trademark law developments which has fallen behind schedule. Volume 2 will be published in the spring of 1982. Thereafter the *Handbook* will be published annually on a timely basis.

Among the subjects highlighted in this volume are: trademark ownership and use; registrability; supplemental registration; confusing similarity; procedure; infringement and unfair competition; Section 43(a) of the Lanham Act; state court decisions; and antitrust problems in the trademark area.

The preceding volume in this series, *1980–81 Trademark Law Handbook,* should be retained for future reference. This series in time will comprise a comprehensive library of current developments in the trademark law field.

Clark Boardman Company, Ltd.
435 Hudson Street
New York, New York 10014

*1981–82 Trademark Law Handbook*

*Volume 1*

# 1981-82 Trademark Law Handbook

Volume 1

The United States Trademark Association

Clark Boardman Company, Ltd.
New York, New York 1981

Copyright © 1981 by The United States Trademark Association.
All rights reserved. Printed in the United States of America.

A version of this material appeared in The Trademark
Reporter ®, Volume 70, Number 6.

ISBN: 0-87632-402-2

# *Contributors*

**Anthony L. Fletcher:** Conboy, Hewitt, O'Brien & Boardman, New York, New York. (Chapters 1-6)

**Jerre B. Swann:** Kilpatrick & Cody, Atlanta, Georgia. (Chapter 7, §7.01)

**Allan Zelnick:** Weiss Dawid Fross Zelnick & Lehrman, New York, New York. (Chapter 7, §7.02)

**Martin R. Greenstein:** Baker & McKenzie, Chicago, Illinois. (Chapters 8 and 9)

**Albert Robin:** Law Offices of Albert Robin, New York, New York. (Chapter 10)

# Preface

*1981–82 Trademark Law Handbook* will be published in two volumes, of which this is Volume 1. This procedure will be a one-time adjustment to bring to date the USTA's annual review of trademark law developments which has fallen behind schedule. Volume 2 will be published in the spring of 1982. It is anticipated that the *Handbook* will thereafter be published annually on a timely basis.

Trademark professionals are faced with the formidable task of keeping abreast of rapidly changing developments in trademark case and regulatory law and PTO practice. The *Trademark Law Handbook* series has been designed to provide a comprehensive overview of the quickly evolving law. Practitioners and intellectual property professionals will have available in convenient reference form the significant trademark developments of the year in softcover format.

In time the *Trademark Law Handbook* series will provide a convenient reference library of the important events in the trademark field, easily retrievable by year. This annual should be retained in your library for future use.

*1981–82 Trademark Law Handbook* focuses on the entire area of trademark practice, leading to insights that are helpful in discerning trends and furnishing guides to what courts and the PTO may find persuasive. *1981–82 Trademark Law Handbook* handily serves as the first point of reference and immediate way to the current law. Volume 1 of this year's handbook provides quick facts and answers to trademark law questions as of mid-1980. Future volumes will survey succeeding twelve-month periods.

According to Anthony L. Fletcher, one of the several authors of this year's *Handbook,* by far the most significant development in United States trademark practice during the period surveyed was the deterioration of the trademark registration system.

## Trademark Law

Mr. Fletcher furnishes statistics indicating that registrations dropped during 1979 to 20,450, down one-third from 32,174 the previous year. Nearly 50,000 applications were filed. The Official Gazette fell behind schedule, contained glaring inaccuracies, and even ceased publication briefly. According to Mr. Fletcher, it does not appear possible at present to register a trademark in the United States in less than one year, and applications can take two years or more to mature to registration.

Gerald J. Mossinghoff, new Commissioner of Patents and Trademarks, has extensive plans for speeding up trademark operations. In a recent address to the American Bar Association, he announced a goal of reducing the pendency time to three months for first action in trademark matters, and thirteen months to disposition. Developments in the progress of PTO operations will be monitored in future *Handbooks*.

The publisher welcomes Robin A. Rolfe as Executive Director of The United States Trademark Association, and looks forward to collaborating with her on future USTA publishing projects.

Clark Boardman Company, Ltd.

# Table of Contents

PART I
**Interpretation of the Lanham Act by the Court of Customs and Patent Appeals and in the Patent and Trademark Office**

CHAPTER 1
**Introductory Note**  *3*

CHAPTER 2
**Trademark Ownership and Use**  *5*

§2.01  Adoption and Use  *5*
§2.02  Use by Assignees or Related Companies  *12*
§2.03  Concurrent Use  *13*
§2.04  Effect of False Statements in Applications or Affidavits or on Goods  *15*
§2.05  Abandonment  *16*
§2.06  Effect of Registration  *19*
§2.07  Collateral References  *19*

CHAPTER 3
**Registrability**  *21*

§3.01  What Are Trademarks?  *21*
    [1]  Configuration of the Goods  *21*
    [2]  Ornamentation  *22*
    [3]  Miscellaneous  *23*
§3.02  Generic Names and "Merely Descriptive" Marks  *23*
§3.03  Geographic Marks  *31*
§3.04  Surnames  *33*
§3.05  Foreign Equivalents  *34*
§3.06  Mutilation of Marks  *34*
§3.07  Service Marks  *35*
§3.08  Collateral References  *36*

**Trademark Law**

CHAPTER 4
**Supplemental Registration** *39*

CHAPTER 5
**Confusing Similarity** *41*

§5.01  False Suggestion of Connection with Persons or Institutions—Section 2(a)  *41*
§5.02  Confusing Similarity with Previously Used or Registered Marks—Section 2(d)  *43*
    [1]  CCPA Decisions  *43*
    [2]  TTAB Decisions—Reported  *45*
        [a]  Alcoholic Beverages  *45*
        [b]  Design Marks  *47*
        [c]  The Tuxedo Monopoly Case  *50*
        [d]  Vitamin and Mineral Marks Including PLUS  *51*
        [e]  Health Care Marks  *53*
        [f]  The Barber Pole Case  *54*
        [g]  Actual Confusion Not Determinative  *55*
        [h]  The "Reaction Factor" Test  *56*
        [i]  Refusal to Register Marks that Can Be Used  *57*
        [j]  Magazine Trademarks  *58*
        [k]  Carpet Cleaning Products  *59*
        [l]  Food Products  *61*
        [m]  Health and Beauty Aids  *65*
        [n]  The Automotive After-Market  *67*
        [o]  Store Names  *69*
        [p]  Discriminating Consumers  *69*
        [q]  Miscellaneous  *70*
    [3]  TTAB Decisions—Reported in Digest  *73*
§5.03  Letters of Consent  *76*

CHAPTER 6
**Procedure** *79*

§6.01  Inter Partes Proceedings  *79*
    [1]  Res Judicata  *79*

Table of Contents

      [2] Summary Judgment  *84*
      [3] Equitable Defenses  *85*
      [4] Oppositions  *90*
      [5] Cancellations  *94*
      [6] Concurrent Use  *100*
      [7] Evidence  *100*
      [8] Proving Priority of Use  *102*
      [9] Proving Registrations  *102*
      [10] Third Party Registrations  *104*
      [11] Affirmative Defenses Must Be Proven  *105*
      [12] Notices of Reliance  *106*
      [13] Ignoring Requests to Admit  *109*
      [14] When to Submit Evidence  *110*
      [15] Objecting to Evidence  *111*
      [16] Methods of Proof  *111*
      [17] Sufficiency of Evidence to Establish Particular Points  *112*
      [18] Surveys  *115*
      [19] Miscellaneous Matters  *116*
      [20] Rehearing and Reopening  *117*
      [21] Scope of Review  *118*
§6.02 Ex Parte Appeals  *121*
§6.03 Applications  *122*
      [1] Description of Goods  *122*
      [2] Drawings  *124*
      [3] Miscellaneous  *125*
§6.04 Post-Registration Occurrences  *126*
      [1] Affidavits, Renewals, Assignments, etc.  *126*
§6.05 Collateral References  *128*

PART II
**Trademark Infringement and Unfair Competition**

CHAPTER 7
**Infringement and Unfair Competition  131**

§7.01 Appellate Federal Court Decisions  *131*
      [1] Descriptiveness and Genericism  *133*

**Trademark Law**

      [2] Standards of Review  *136*
      [3] Intent  *140*
      [4] Actual Confusion  *141*
      [5] Damages, Accounting and Attorneys' Fees  *141*
      [6] Color Combinations  *142*
      [7] Miscellaneous  *144*
§7.02  Federal District Court Decisions  *146*
      [1] Misappropriation Doctrine and Preemption  *146*
      [2] Protection of Developing Secondary Meaning  *150*
      [3] Incontestability Affidavits  *152*
      [4] Miscellaneous Likelihood of Confusion Cases  *153*
      [5] Misrepresentation  *163*
      [6] Confusion of Sponsorship  *163*
      [7] Owner's Right to Restrict Distributor's Use of Trademark  *168*
      [8] Personal Names  *171*
      [9] Use of Another's Trademark  *172*
      [10] National Bank Name Preemption  *173*
      [11] Trademark "Fair Use" Defense  *175*
      [12] Section 43(a) of the Lanham Act  *177*
      [13] Ownership of Entertainment Group Names  *178*
      [14] Pharmaceutical Product Simulation  *179*
      [15] Functionality  *180*
      [16] Former Licensee's Duties  *183*
      [17] Genericism  *184*
      [18] Related Goods  *187*
      [19] Irreparable Harm  *187*
      [20] Res Judicata  *188*
      [21] Collateral Estoppel  *190*
      [22] Jurisdiction and Venue  *191*
      [23] Bankruptcy Transfers  *193*
      [24] Assignment of Infringement Claims  *194*
      [25] Exhaustion of Administrative Remedies  *195*

# Table of Contents

[26] Laches Defense  *196*
[27] Adoption of Trademarks  *196*
[28] Post-Registration Procedures  *197*
[29] Abandonment  *198*
[30] Expansion of Trade Area  *200*
[31] Damages, Profits and Attorneys' Fees  *204*

CHAPTER 8
**Section 43(a) of the Lanham Act**  *209*

CHAPTER 9
**State Court Decisions**  *221*

CHAPTER 10
**Trademarks and the Antitrust Laws**  *225*

**Index**  *229*

PART I

# Interpretation of the Lanham Act by the Court of Customs and Patent Appeals and in the Patent and Trademark Office

CHAPTER 1

# Introductory Note

An alteration of the format of this annual Review has been made with the current edition, for three reasons: (1) Opinions today are so long, and involve such a diversity of points, that assigning them to any section is difficult. (2) Correlatively, it seems that this Review can be more usable as a research and reference tool if all authority bearing on a single subject (or area) is collected together. (3) There is more emphasis on the procedural than previously because the decisions of the Board indicate that evidentiary and procedural techniques often are mishandled; if we learn by mistakes of others, there is education aplenty buried in footnotes to Board opinions.

CHAPTER 2

# Trademark Ownership and Use

## §2.01 Adoption and Use

An occasionally sticky issue is: When does use actually commence?

When both opposer and applicant adopted and used LIQ-WACON for collection, solidification and disposal of liquid wastes, the issue was priority.[1] The controlling principles of law were: the right to use a mark accrues to the first user in trade, not necessarily to the first to adopt. This use in trade may be intrastate, as opposed to interstate, and need not rise to the dignity of technical trade (or service) mark use:

> A prior open and public use of a term as a salient feature of a trade name in connection with a viable business entity or use in advertising or promoting goods or services may be sufficient for this purpose. This "nontechnical use" or "use analagous to technical use" has been defined as encompassing, inter alia, use in advertising, use as a grade mark or as a process, per se, use as the distinguishing feature of a name, and any other use of a designation in a manner calculated to attract the attention of potential customers or customers in the applicable field of trade and to create thereby an association of the term, an exclusive one, with the product or service of a single, albeit anonymous, source.[2]

[1] Liqwacon Corp. v. Browning-Ferris Indus., Inc., 203 USPQ 305 (TTAB 1979). See also infra fns 42 and 145 in Ch. 6.
[2] Id at 308 (citation omitted).

§2.01 / Trademark Law

The "tacking" of such earlier "non-technical" use to the period of technical use is permitted for determining priority of ownership.

In deciding who was prior, the Board was bedeviled by the fact that neither party's self-serving testimony was supported by documenting exhibits or even by third party corroboration; each simply testified that it operated under the name LIQWACON. Opposer was the first to adopt LIQWACON as its corporate name and in connection with studies and arrangements for building necessary facilities to operate its business. Applicant, however, prevailed because it was the first actually to engage in business under the name. Its use, evidently, comprised oral solicitations for business under the name by salesmen. At that point in time, opposer was still seeking approvals and planning its factory, though it was so doing under the name LIQWACON. Applicant was, indeed, already in the business when it adopted the name; opposer was still in the long, laborious process of preparing to enter the business.

Opposer did win a modest victory when it argued that applicant's use appeared to be for its process, not its services. The Board remanded for the Examiner to ascertain whether LIQWACON had been used as a service mark, as well as for the process that was essential to the service, as early as the application date. Whatever that determination, however, it would not appear to alter the priority of the parties or to defeat applicant's eventual right to register.

When one who makes several products cannot show early enough priority of use for one, it is always possible to argue the doctrine of natural expansion, if facts permit. The theory is that use of a mark on certain goods protects against use by another on closely related goods because such use would confuse the public. The doctrine, in effect, reserves to a mark owner the right to enter business under the mark in certain areas of "natural expansion." It must, however, be shown that the new activity has evolved from pre-existing manufacturing and marketing activities, not from acquisi-

## CCPA and PTO Interpretations / §2.01

tion of a new business by a diversifying company.[3]

Another case held that use and sale of such accessories as belts and buckles as part of clothing sold under a trademark did not, necessarily, constitute use of the mark for the accessory items.[4]

Probaby the most interesting case involving priority, "tacking" and related goods was the *Amica* case.[5] AMICA was long used for insurance services, and promoted by means of such giveaways (manufactured by others) as paperweights, pens and keychains, for some of which it was registered. When the insurer opposed registration of AMICA for perfume, the applicant attacked the non-insurance registrations vigorously. The Board held the goods registrations valid; the insurer was a merchant, and use of AMICA with insurance adequately created a sufficiently distinct commercial impression to justify registration, even though most such giveaways also bore the manufacturer's mark. AMICA was a distributor's mark for the goods, even though the distribution was gratis for purposes of promoting the primary insurance business.

Well, then, said applicant, he had used AMICA before it was used for any of the goods for which it was registered, so the registrations should be canceled. Not so, said the Board. Basically AMICA was a service mark, which could be used by advertising. Use on promotional goods was considered to be advertising use, and such use commenced on goods for which the mark was not registered (and on magazines, etc.) before use for perfume commenced. The use of AMICA on the registered goods, though sufficient to support separate registrations of the mark for such goods, was simply a continuation of the advertising use which long predated applicant's use of AMICA on perfumes, so the insurer had priority of use of the mark for the goods. The insurer did not prevail,

---

[3] Sheller-Globe Corp. v. Scott Paper Co., 204 USPQ 329, 333 (TTAB 1979). See also infra fns 47 in Ch. 3, 78 in Ch. 5 and 87 in Ch. 6.

[4] Lee Byron Corp. v. H.D. Lee Co., Inc., 203 USPQ 1097 (TTAB 1979). See also infra fn 147 in Ch. 6.

[5] Amica Mutual Insurance Co. v. R. H. Cosmetics Corp., 204 USPQ 155 (TTAB 1979). See also infra fns 36 in Ch. 5 and 28 in Ch. 6.

§2.01 / Trademark Law

however; the goods were held sufficiently different to make confusion unlikely.

The logical conclusion of this constructive "tacking" of earlier insurance use onto the use of the mark on goods used to promote the insurance services, seems to be that the insurer also could distribute AMICA perfume, which plainly seems wrong. That eventuality, though, appears to be covered by the principle that controlled another case.

While adoption and use of a mark normally entitles the owner to extend its use to all goods within the normal expansion of his business, it does not justify expansion to different goods as to which someone else has acquired intervening (or, one supposes, even prior) rights in the mark.[6] A pasta maker thus was barred from extending his mark to wine.

Token use was held still permissible for application purposes, provided that it was followed by activities or circumstances indicating continuing intent to market the product under the mark on a commercial scale.[7] This was so in view of the expense of introducing a new product on any scale and "the risk" of so doing "prior to the screening practice involved in seeking federal registration."[8] While the use could be token, however, it had to be "bona fide"—that is the goods identified in the application had to exist, and be directed to a customer or potential customer openly and with a purpose of establishing good will, recognition and association of the mark with its owner. The at-least-one-open-and-notorious-sale requirement evidently stemmed from the requirement that such sale or shipment not be "contrived or fabricated."[9]

Prior trade name, grade mark or advertising use, while not trademark use, may prevent another's registration of the term as a trademark. Such earlier use, however, also

[6] Gio. Buton & C. S.p.A. v. Buitoni Foods Corp., 205 USPQ 477, 478 (TTAB 1979). See also infra fns 10 this chapter, 17 in Ch. 5, 52 and 91 in Ch. 6.

[7] Times Mirror Magazines, Inc. v. Sutcliffe, 205 USPQ 656 (TTAB 1979). See also infra fns 45 in Ch. 5, 92 and 157 in Ch. 6.

[8] Id at 662.

[9] Ibid.

## CCPA and PTO Interpretations / §2.01

must be (1) open and public to potential purchasers and (2) of such nature as to be reasonably calculated to create an association of the term with the user of his goods.[10]

Token use, however, will only carry one so far—to the point of initial application. When the Board granted a petition to cancel registration of INSTANT SPRING feminine hygiene douche, the record showed that the registrant had never sold products under the mark, had never advertised the mark, and did not currently manufacture a product for sale under the mark.[11] The registration was only fifteen months old at the time of decision, but evidently had only been the subject of four shipments each month to four different locations in four different states. In granting petitioner's motion for summary judgment, Board Member Rice set forth the controlling principles of law quite clearly:

> While adoption and a single bona fide use of the mark may be sufficient to secure a registration . . . more is required to sustain the mark against a charge of non usage. . . . To prove bona fide usage, respondent must demonstrate that its use of the mark has been deliberate and continuous with an intention to create a commercial impact on the mark, and not sporadic, casual or transitory. In view of respondent's admissions in its answer, it is incumbent upon respondent to show trademark rights in the "INSTANT SPRING" mark. The affidavit of respondent's employee and accompanying shipping papers show a miniscule amount of "INSTANT SPRING" product shipped to the same pharmaceutical companies without any indication that this product has ever reached the general public. These shipments do not have the color of bona fide transactions and are not accompanied by any activities or cir-

[10] Gio. Buton & C. S.p.A. v. Buitoni Foods Corp., 205 USPQ 477, 481 (TTAB 1979). See also supra fn 6 this chapter and infra fns 17 in Ch. 5, 52 and 91 in Ch. 6.

[11] Block Drug Co., Inc. v. Morton-Norwich Products, Inc., 202 USPQ 157 (TTAB 1959). See also infra fn 17 in Ch. 6.

## §2.01 / Trademark Law

> cumstances which would tend to establish a continuing effort or intent to continue use of the mark and place the product so shipped on the market on a commercial scale . . . It would appear that respondent's efforts under the mark "INSTANT SPRING" have been merely an attempt to maintain rights in the mark without ever attempting to establish a trade in the "INSTANT SPRING" product. Registrable rights cannot flow from these activities.[12]

This warning to other would-be "token" users of registered marks is loud and clear, albeit hardly unprecedented. Many, no doubt, will ignore it, and we will see similar decisions in the years to come.

What constitutes technical trademark use became an issue in several cases.

A comprehensive review of prior decisional law persuaded the Board that package inserts could never serve as specimens of trademark use (contrary to the provisions of TMEP 808.07).[13] If such use can qualify as trademark use at all, it must be as a "display associated with the goods." Such displays, within the contemplation of Section 45,

> . . . [comprise] essentially point-of-sale material such as banners, shelf-takers, window displays, menus, or similar devices which are designed to catch the attention of purchasers and prospective purchasers as an inducement to consummate a sale and which prominently display the mark in question and associate it or relate it to the goods in such a way that an association of the two is inevitable even though the goods may not be placed in close proximity to the display or, in fact, even though the goods may not physically exist at the time a purchaser views the display.[14]

[12] Id at 159.
[13] In re Bright of America, Inc., 205 USPQ 63 (TTAB 1974).
[14] Id at 71.

## CCPA and PTO Interpretations / §2.01

When registration of HOT WAX in assertedly distinctive form was sought, and the record showed use of the term in ordinary type on drums of the product, and in the allegedly distinctive form only on car wash advertising display signs and price lists, the Board questioned whether there was trademark use at all.[15]

A magazine entitled WORLD CONSTRUCTION bore the small legend on its cover "The Global Magazine Including Ingenieria Internacional Construccion and Engineering Construction World"; a similar legend appeared in the list of staff, publisher, etc. While the Board did not completely rule out the possibility that such use of ENGINEERING CONSTRUCTION WORLD could be trademark use, it did hold that it could not be so considered on a bare record showing only such use.[16]

Restaurant pre-opening activities, such as erecting signs at their sites and infrequent local newspaper stories, were not considered to vest proprietary rights in the service mark.[17]

While use of PROFESSIONAL ECONOMIC SERVICES as part of a corporate name was trade name, not service mark, use, reference in copy in the same ad to "Professional Economic Services" sufficed to constitute service mark use.[18]

Unlawful use—that is use not in compliance with applicable statutory or regulatory requirements—creates no rights. There are, however, limits to the PTO's ability to pursue this issue. When it was argued that a pill maker had not complied with applicable requirements, the Board observed that "neither the [Examining] Trademark Attorney nor the Board possesses the expertise necessary to determine the technical

[15] In re Behre Industries, Inc., 203 USPQ 1030, 1033 (TTAB 1979). See also infra fns 20 in Ch. 3 and 156 in Ch. 6.
[16] In re Dun-Donnelley Publishing Corp., 205 USPQ 575 (TTAB 1979).
[17] Arby's, Inc. v. Abby's Pizza Inns, 205 USPQ 762, 765 (TTAB 1980). See also infra fns 42 in Ch. 5, 47, 63, 157 and 164 in Ch. 6.
[18] Professional Economics Inc. v. Professional Economic Services, Inc., 205 USPQ 368, 375 (TTAB 1979). See also infra fns 7 in Ch. 3, 2 in Ch. 4, 38 in Ch. 5 and 8 in Ch. 6.

nuances and requirements of these statutes."[19] Indeed, there appeared to be a question of primary jurisdiction. The Board seemed content to accept the use as legal, despite numerous FDA inquiries and investigations, in the absence of some proper authority's determination of a violation. The Board's candid humility is refreshing. If there is a pending proceeding that will resolve the question, suspension might be in order; but for the Board to attempt to unravel complexities of requirements that baffle experts in other fields seems to be well beyond the scope of its mission.

## §2.02 Use by Assignees or Related Companies

The Diamond Sunsweet case presented a novel situation that might arise again.[20] The producers of DIAMOND walnuts and SUNSWEET dried fruits, both of which owned registrations of their own marks, decided to sell gift packs of both their produce under DIAMOND/SUNSWEET with a pinwheel logo. To do so they formed a jointly owned corporation, licensed it to use the mark for this purpose, and enforced rigid quality control. Both applied, as joint applicants, to register the DIAMOND/SUNSWEET and logo mark for gift packs, claiming use of the jointly owned mark by a related company, and consenting to such registration. Registration was refused on the ground that the joint applicants were a different entity from either, and that since each owned prior registrations of its own mark, registration was forbidden by Section 2(d). The Board reversed, quite rightly, it seems.

The reasoning was that joint ownership of marks is permitted in unusual circumstances, and by definition, joint owners are not a single, new entity. The purpose of Section 2(d) is to preclude registration of conflicting marks to ad-

---

[19] Medical Modalities Associates, Inc. v. ARA Corp., 203 USPQ 295, 300 (TTAB 1979). See also infra fns 1 in Ch. 4, 30 in Ch. 5, 56, 66, 103 and 127 in Ch. 6.

[20] In re Diamond Walnut Growers, Inc., and Sunsweet Growers, Inc., 204 USPQ 507 (TTAB 1979).

CCPA and PTO Interpretations / §2.03

verse parties and thus to avoid confusion. Here the parties were not adverse, the marks were not conflicting, and in practice the arrangement would not create confusion. Section 2(d) was held inapplicable. Those planning anything similar would do well to study the opinion. It offers a blueprint for structuring such arrangements, which seem fraught with potential pitfalls for the unwary.

Two other cases reiterated elementary principles.

When it appeared that an applicant had permitted use of its mark, by others, without control, the Board observed that such uncontrolled licensing might deprive the applicant of any registrable rights in the mark.[21]

An assignee of a registration naturally took it subject to equitable defenses by others that the assignor's conduct may have created.[22]

## §2.03 Concurrent Use

The Court of Customs and Patent Appeals had the fourth bite of the Wiener King case, after a District Court, the Third Circuit and TTAB had chewed over this new classic of concurrent use.[23] WEINER KING (EI) opened one hot dog restaurant in Flemington, New Jersey in 1962, another in the same town in 1967, and still another in 1975, after opening one in Beach Haven, New Jersey in 1973. WIENER KING (IE), intending to launch a nationwide chain of fran-

[21] Plak-Shack, Inc. v. Continental Studios of Georgia, Inc., 204 USPQ 242, 247 fn 9 (TTAB 1979). See also infra fns 73 in Ch. 5, 40, 47, 136 and 169 in Ch. 6.

See also William M. Borchard, Trademark Sublicensing and Quality Control, 70 TMR 99 (1980).

[22] CBS Inc. v. Man's Day Publishing Co., Inc., 205 USPQ 470, 476-77 (TTAB 1980). See also infra fns 43 in Ch. 5, 20 and 47 in Ch. 6.

[23] Weiner King, Inc. v. Wiener King Corp., 204 USPQ 820 (CCPA 1980), modg 201 USPQ 894 (TTAB 1979), discussed in 69 TMR 574 fn 151. See also infra fns 33 this chapter, 68 and 143 in Ch. 6 and 5 in Ch. 7. For prior cases see: Weiner King, Inc. v. The Wiener King Corp., 407 F Supp 1274, 190 USPQ 469 (D NJ 1976), modf 546 F2d 421, 192 USPQ 353 (CA 3 1976), cert denied 193 USPQ 183 (US 1977), discussed in 67 TMR 538 fn 206.

§2.03 / Trademark Law

chised hot dog restaurants, opened its first restaurant, innocently, in North Carolina in 1970. By May, 1972, IE was a registrant of its mark, owning eleven restaurants. In July, IE first learned of EI. IE continued to expand, reaching one hundred locations in twenty states by 1975; EI subsequently opened shops in Warminster, Pennsylvania and White House, New Jersey.

The court held that concurrent use issues must be solved by a comprehensive factual analysis that seemed to weigh equities, good faith and a policy of encouraging prompt federal registration by rewarding it. It refused to rule that a subsequent user, at least one who first registered, had to curtail expansion when he learned of the prior user (since the subsequent user simply continued previous, good faith, expansion plans) or that the prior user could not expand from one town to the other side of the state after the second had registered. The latter was upheld because Beach Haven was considered to be in EI's "natural zone" of expansion from Flemington, where it had operated for eleven years. That seems somewhat dubious, but not as dubious as the court's failure to consider Section 22 (constructive notice eliminates the defense of innocent adoption) and Section 33(b)(5) which would seem to freeze EI to its area of business at the date of IE's registration.

The eventual outcome was that by concurrent registrations, IE obtained the entire United States except a fifteen mile radius of Flemington, White House (within that radius) and Beach Haven.

In another case, proof that there were eighty-four chartered Home Federal Savings & Loan Associations scattered about the country, of which a number used HOME FEDERAL or HOME FEDERAL SAVINGS, sufficed to defeat territorially unrestricted registration of HOME FEDERAL SAVINGS by one of them.[24] Such registration, obviously, would have been prejudicial to the rights of others to use.

[24] Home Federal Savings & Loan Ass'n v. Home Federal Savings & Loan Ass'n of Chicago, 205 USPQ 467 (TTAB 1979). See also infra fns 19,86 and 171 in Ch. 6.

## CCPA and PTO Interpretations / §2.04

Concurrent registration seems to be a theoretical, if mind-boggling, possibility.

### §2.04 Effect of False Statements in Applications or Affidavits or on Goods

Analagous to unclean hands is the charge that your opponent has somehow lied in connection with his registration or goods. As is the case with unclean hands, often nothing good comes from the accusation.

The Board restated that there is a significant difference between false statements and fraudulent ones in a case involving BLUE NUN.[25] Fraud, it said, only exists when there is a demonstrated intent by applicant to deceive the Office by withholding facts or material information which would result in disallowance. The applicant had alleged use in interstate commerce, which plainly did not exist, and had failed to disclose use by a related company. Without actually characterizing these irregularities as false statements, the Board found no disproof of applicant's proffered explanation that these resulted from attorney's inadvertence, and declined to find fraud. While fraud is a drastic sanction for such sloppiness, the result seems to sanction all too prevalent inadequate investigation by applicants' attorneys.

A dental floss holder case raised several charges of impropriety, none of which succeeded.[26] (1) Use of a registration symbol next to an unregistered word, which was voluntarily moved on the label to abut registered marks, was held to be inadvertent and not to preclude registration. (2) Submission of old specimens, which used the mark in the same manner current ones did, was not sufficient to invalidate the resulting registration. (3) While use of the legend "Patent Pending" on a product should be discontinued when the patent

---

[25] H. Sichel Sohne, GmbH v. Michel Monzain Selected Wines, Inc., 202 USPQ 62, 64 (TTAB 1979). See also infra fns 14 in Ch. 5, 164 and 168 in Ch. 6.

[26] Floss Aid Corp. v. John O. Butler Co., 205 USPQ 274 (TTAB 1979). See also infra fns 23 and 51 in Ch. 3, 54, 102 and 17 in Ch. 6.

§2.05 / Trademark Law

application is refused or abandoned, removing the words when molds or plates next were made met this requirement.

## §2.05 Abandonment

Products bearing well-known trademarks are beginning to turn up under both national brand and private supermarket labels, often on adjoining shelves. Assuming that this is done with the consent of the mark owner, it still raises the possibility that the mark has ceased to serve as an indication of origin and thus, has been abandoned. When the owner of CRAZY for ice cream cones and cups dealt with Safeway, who distributed PANTRY PRIDE CRAZY cones, such an argument was made—unsuccessfully.[27] The mark owner did license the mark to Safeway, controlling quality by doing the manufacturing. The Board pointed out that products could bear multiple marks, and simply relying on the packages, under the circumstances (presumably meaning the license), was insufficient to demonstrate abandonment.

One can wonder, however, what surveys might show to be the effect of such practices in consumers' minds.

In PTO proceedings, registrations are prima facie evidence of use of the registered mark commencing on the filing dates of the applications resulting in those registrations.[28] Another case stressed that such registrations are evidence of continuous use since the filing date of the application.[29] Such presumptions may, of course, be overcome by proof to the contrary.

As noted supra §2.01, token use is still viable for purposes of securing registration. Two years later, however, the question of abandonment can arise. For when evidence shows nonuse of a mark for two consecutive years, abandonment

---

[27] Safe-T Pacific Co. v. Nabisco, Inc., 204 USPQ 307, 314–15 (TTAB 1979). See also infra fns 26 in Ch. 3, 160 in Ch. 5, 51 and 124 in Ch. 6.

[28] Jules Berman & Associates, Inc. v. Consolidated Distilled Products, Inc., 202 USPQ 67, 68 (TTAB 1979). See also infra fns 46 in Ch. 3, 16 in Ch. 5 and 102 in Ch. 6.

[29] Jean Patou, Inc. v. Aristocrat Products Corp., 202 USPQ 130, 131 (TTAB 1979). See also infra fns 61 in Ch. 5, 7, 100 and 157 in Ch. 6.

is presumed.[30] The registrant then must assume the burden of rebutting the inference by "a convincing demonstration of 'excusable nonuse' that would negate any intent not to resume use of the mark."[31]

That presumption was rebutted with respect to one of the marks in two cases involving hand lotion. The history was this: August 26, 1971—one shipment of six units worth $4.50; February 6, 1973—registration obtained; August 26, 1974—product panel testing requested; October 10, 1974—request approved; late 1974—two panels of two-hundred-fifty women each were furnished the hand lotion, evidently under the mark, to test, one panel receiving a squeeze bottle, one a pump bottle; January 30, 1975—product manager recommended squeeze bottle, sought information as to available six and ten ounce sizes, recommended product development cease since the product was in test, and recommended that an agency be assigned to "refine the concept/name of this product for further testing"; February 3, 1975—another squeeze bottle memo indicated that needed quantities "on a national basis" would be about four million of each size; March 25, 1976—cancellation proceedings initiated. The testing purportedly cost about $16,600, and over the years about eleven hundred labels were printed, one hundred at a time at first use, and five hundred of two different ones after the test (which causes one to wonder how the product was identified to the test panelists). The Board held this sufficient to negate the inference of nonuse. The other mark, which had been subject only to the initial sale, was held abandoned.

While the record evidently was closed more than two years after the registrant's last use, the interrogatory answers disclosing the facts were filed less than two years subsequent to the testing and the Board drew no inferences.

[30] Lanham Act §45, 15 USC §1127.
[31] Burroughs Wellcome Co. v. Warner-Lambert Co., 203 USPQ 191, 198 (TTAB 1979) (see also infra fns 63 in Ch. 5, 21 and 102 in Ch. 6); Burroughs Wellcome Co. v. Warner-Lambert Co., 203 USPQ 201 (TTAB 1979) (see also infra fns 64 in Ch. 5, 21, 45 and 102 in Ch. 6).

## §2.05 / Trademark Law

If the facts had materially changed, the registrant would seem to have had a duty to supplement its earlier interrogatory answers; certainly if it was not a duty under FRCP 26(e), it was in its own self-interest. Pendency of a cancellation petition, however, could have been sufficient reason for suspending product development or marketing plans.

In another case New Zealand immigrant Ernest V. Berry started a machine shop business in Los Angeles in the 1930s. It came to specialize in repair, reconditioning and sale of locomotive parts and generators, and expanded to shops in Mt. Vernon, Illinois, Waco, Texas and Clark's Summit, Texas.

Successors eventually leased rebuilt diesel locomotives. Mr. Berry was generous, perhaps to a fault, with his trademark, PRECISION, in design form. He encouraged and helped friends in Sacramento, Seattle and Denver to use the same mark for essentially the same services. Berry and the Sacramento business even exchanged jobs on occasion, though Berry never made any effort to control the quality of his friends' work or their use of the mark. Not surprisingly, this led to some confusion.

Board Member Kera's reconstruction of the confused history reflected apparent loving care.[32] The ultimate conclusion was that Berry abandoned his mark for machine shop services and, consequently, for the goods that the shops repaired (and sold), but not for leasing locomotives which none of the others ever did and which seemed quite remote from the repair, reconditioning and parts services. Berry's successors could rise no higher than the wellspring of their rights, and thus could not register PRECISION for goods, from the sale (or repair) of which they had no right to exclude others operating under the mark.

WEINER KING was held not abandoned in a seaside resort when the store owner lost its lease for a season.[33] Resort

---

[32] Electro-Coatings, Inc. v. Precision National Corp., 204 USPQ 410 (TTAB 1979). See also infra fns 111, 146 and 161 in Ch. 6.

[33] Weiner King, Inc. v. Wiener King Corp., 204 USPQ 820, 832 (CCPA 1980). See also supra fn 23 this chapter and infra fns 68 and 143 in Ch. 6 and 5 in Ch. 7.

CCPA and PTO Interpretations / §2.07[2]

business was seasonal, loss of lease was beyond the lessee's control and one year was not too long a hiatus.

## §2.06 Effect of Registration

One case noted that registration of a mark attacked as weak at best "is prima facie evidence that it serves as a trademark in and of itself" to identify and distinguish the registrant's products.[34] Presumably such evidence is subject to rebuttal, although if the registration is incontestable, the attack seems limited to arguing that the "mark" is generic.[35]

## §2.07 Collateral References

### [1] Adoption and Use

On use requirements generally, see Carol V. Calhoun, "Use in Commerce After Silenus: What Does It Mean?" 70 TMR 47 (1980).

### [2] Use by Assignees or Related Companies

When you think you understand the difference between a license and an assignment, read: Carol H. Sapakie, "Federal Income Taxation—I.R.C. Section 1253(b)(2)(F)—Transfer of a Trademark Constitutes a License Rather than a Sale When Royalties Are Sole Consideration," 10 Rut-Cam L.J. 489 (Winter 1979).

---

[34] Michelin Tire Corp. v. General Tire & Rubber Co., 202 USPQ 294, 298 (TTAB 1979). See also infra fns 5 in Ch. 3, 70 in Ch. 5 and 165 in Ch. 6.

See also the back-to-basics discussion of the benefits of registration in Richard L. Osborne, "When Should a Mark Be Registered" 26 Prac Law 81 (1980).

[35] See Lanham Act §33(b), 15 USC §1115(b).

CHAPTER 3

# Registrability

### §3.01 What Are Trademarks?

Occasionally the question arises whether that which is sought to be registered is a trademark at all. Slogans, color and style or grade designations all raise such questions. None of these issues arose this year, but three others did.

### [1] Configuration of the Goods

According to the Trademark Trial and Appeal Board, product configurations, while necessarily merely descriptive, are registrable if (i) they are not, in essence, utilitarian or functional, and (ii) they are either inherently distinctive, or have acquired secondary meaning.[1] (The inherently distinctive, merely descriptive trademark, be it a shape or otherwise, is a difficult concept to grasp.) The Board considered a curved edge ROLODEX index card configuration to be functional. The card's flat bottom and rail notches plainly were functional. Its rounded corners were thought by the Board to better resist wear than would square corners. The curved edges of the card were functional because they "make it visually more appealing, harmonize better than the standard card with the curved lines of applicant's ... card holders, and add to the saleability of the card and card holder."[2]

One can question that attractiveness, which enhances saleability, is functional, though some cases seem to say so.

---

[1] Oxford Pendaflex Corp. v. Rolodex Corp., 204 USPQ 249 (TTAB 1979). See also infra fns 103, 110 and 120 in Ch. 6.

[2] Id at 256.

## §3.01[2] / Trademark Law

Most trademarks, word, design and configuration, are intended to be attractive; and since normally pretty outsells ugly, that promotes saleability. That, however, is not functionality. The "function" to be protected by the rule is that something that promotes the utility of a product ought not to be registered, since it should be available to all. To rule that every would-be trademark that is attractive is functional seems to raise an unnecessary obstacle to registration of successful marks.

(The Board also held the new card shape not to be inherently distinctive and considered evidence of secondary meaning insufficiently proven. That ground seems legally sound, and at worst, only factually arguable.)

Less debatable was an ex parte appeal in which registration was denied on the Supplemental Register of a container, from which sinkers could be selected by fishermen, with SINKER SELECTOR printed thereon.[3] The appearance of the container, which was sought to be registered, seemed to be dictated primarily by utilitarian considerations.

### [2] Ornamentation

Common basic shapes used to display a word trademark are not considered inherently distinctive, so they can be registered only if secondary meaning is shown.[4] Unique or distinctive background displays are registrable without such a showing. Since applicant was unable to persuade the Board that an oval within a rectangle was inherently distinctive, it faced the problem of demonstrating that its backdrop for a well-known trademark had obtained independent public recognition. To do so, it sent a questionnaire to one thousand potential purchasers which confronted them with the mark (without wording) and asked them to identify it. Of six-hundred-two respondents, four-hundred-seventy-six did. While applicant buttressed its survey with the usual evi-

---

[3] In re Water Gremlin Co., 204 USPQ 261 (TTAB 1970). See also infra fns 21 in Ch. 3 and 162 in Ch. 6.

[4] In re Raytheon Co., 202 USPQ 317 (TTAB 1979).

CCPA and PTO Interpretations / §3.02

dence of massive, long-term use and advertising, it evidently was the survey that tipped the scales. Indeed, with such a trite design, no other method would seem persuasive. The case is valuable in outlining the precautions and procedures utilized in administering such a survey relatively cheaply.

[3] **Miscellaneous**

Of interest to some foreign readers may be the Board's off-hand observation that there is nothing in United States law to preclude a single letter from functioning as a trademark, and indeed, as an arbitrary and strong one.[5] The mark in question, previously registered, was an X for tires.

**§3.02 Generic Names and "Merely Descriptive" Marks**

It has never been easy to distinguish generic names—called common descriptive names of articles or substances in the Act—from descriptive marks—called merely descriptive by the Act. While courts wrestle with the distinction with varying degrees of success, the Office often prefers to ignore it.

Thus, in refusing registration on the Principal Register of COASTER-CARDS as merely descriptive of beverage or container coasters suitable for direct mailing, the Board took the position that generic terms are prohibited from registration by Section 2(e)(i), because, as the CCPA has reasoned, "the name of a thing is the ultimate descriptiveness."[6] It would seem that, if anything, COASTER-CARDS is the name of the article, not simply descriptive of it. (The Board's test was whether the term forthwith conveyed an immediate idea of an ingredient, quality, characteristic, function or feature of the product. One could question that COASTER-

---

[5] Michelin Tire Corp. v. General Tire & Rubber Co., 202 USPQ 294, 298 (TTAB 1979). See also supra fn 34 in Ch. 2 and infra fns 70 in Ch. 5 and 165 in Ch. 6.

[6] In re Bright-Crest Ltd., 204 USPQ 591, 592 (TTAB 1979), quoting Weiss Noodle Co. v. Golden Cracknel & Specialty Co., 129 USPQ 411, 413 (CCPA 1961). See also infra fn 166 in Ch. 6.

23

§3.02 / Trademark Law

CARDS really conveys any clear idea of or about the product in a forthright, immediate manner.)

The problem with lumping generic and merely descriptive is that Section 2(f) of the Act is perfectly plain that merely descriptive marks can be registered if they have acquired distinctiveness in commerce, but Sections 14 and 15 of the Act provide for cancellation of any marks which become (or presumably always were) the common descriptive (generic) name of an article or substance. While there is Court of Customs and Patent Appeals support for the proposition that some terms are "too highly descriptive" to function as trademarks, that formulation is plainly unsatisfactory, since it is both too vague to understand and contrary to the statute.

The far better rationale is that the common descriptive (generic) name of an article or substance is not a trademark whereby the goods of one manufacturer may be distinguished in the first place, so is precluded for registration by the first sentence of Section 2, not by Section 2(e) which may be overcome under Section 2(f).

The Board opined that PROFESSIONAL ECONOMIC SERVICES was an "apt descriptive" and "readily understood" name for an applicant's services, and hence one of those "categories of terms in which no proprietary rights can exist" and in which no registration rights, even supplemental, could be acquired.[7] If the Board was correct as a matter of fact, there is no need to identify the services in issue—professional economic services is self-explanatory,[8] though it might seem to some that the words cover such a

[7] Professional Economics Inc. v. Professional Economic Services, Inc., 205 USPQ 368, 376 (TTAB 1979). See also supra fn 18 in Ch. 2 and infra fns 2 in Ch. 4, 38 in Ch. 5 and 8 in Ch. 6.

[8] Just in case others have trouble identifying what are professional economic services, according to the Board they are "services rendered to meet the professional economic needs or situations of . . . clients or economic services rendered to professionals." For those, like the author, who even without the "or" find that formulation vague, the canceled supplemental registration's recitation was "financial consulting services for professional men," particularly doctors. Id at 376.

wide variety of possible services that they only are suggestive. What the "category of terms in which no proprietary rights can exist" may be was not explained; in view of the confusion in this area it should have been. Presumably since a supplemental registration was canceled, this category is not, in the words of Section 23, "capable of distinguishing goods or services." That probably means that it is a generic or the "common descriptive name of an article or substance," which one can infer also covers services.[9] "Merely descriptive" terms, after all, are not precluded from the Supplemental Register. At least the Board so said.[10]

Two other cases, on the other hand, dealt directly with the question.

The Court of Customs and Patent Appeals held that for purposes of canceling a registered mark as a common descriptive name (TINKERTOY toy construction sets), the presumptions of validity afforded by Section 7(b) cannot be overcome by mere rhetoric.[11] Conceding the fame of TINKERTOY, the cancellation petitioner apparently argued that there was no evidence to suggest that it was not famous as a common descriptive name. That would not do to overcome the statutory presumption. Whether a term is a common descriptive name was a factual matter as to which "(p)urchaser testimony, consumer surveys, and listings in dictionaries, trade journals, newspapers and other publications, are useful evidence."[12] Argument was considered not to be very helpful.

While the court seemed implicitly to equate common descriptive name with generic, it did not, in affirming the Board, indicate any view of the Board's suggestion that there is some difference between the two.[13]

The Board held UPC to be unregistrable because it was

[9] See Section 3 of the Act.
[10] Supra fn 7 at 375.
[11] Dan Robbins & Associates, Inc. v. Questor Corp., 202 USPQ 100, 105–06 (CCPA 1979), affg 199 USPQ 358 (TTAB 1978), discussed in 69 TMR 551 fn 92. See also infra fns 12 in Ch. 5, 53 and 152 in Ch. 6.
[12] Id at 105.
[13] See 69 TMR 571 fn 143.

## §3.02 / Trademark Law

the abbreviation for "Universal Product Code," which in turn was the common descriptive name for bar and numeric symbols printed on packages.[14] Registration was sought for development and assignment of product codes to items produced and sold by applicant's membership. The Examiner rejected the application on grounds that it was merely descriptive under Section 2(e)(1) and was not used as a service mark. The latter determination was not reviewed.

The record seems reasonably clear that "Universal Product Code" was used as the identifying name for those bar and numeric symbols which lately have appeared on so many items of packaging. It also seems reasonably clear that the applicant used UPC as an abbreviation for that term. Indeed, it perhaps used UPC so pervasively that the abbreviation itself took on generic coloration. The result seems open to question, however. "Product code" seems pretty plainly to be generic; but UNIVERSAL seems to function as a mark for some products, though not others. UNIVERSAL presumably is protectible for motion pictures, but perhaps is not for certain types of hardware. Might it be that PC that is generic, and U that is arbitrary? One of the problems, of course, is that at present there is apparently only one system of product codes.

Assuming that the bar and number symbols applicant developed and assigned are UPCs (upcs?), there is still an unbuilt bridge to the conclusion that UPC is the common descriptive name of the service of developing and assigning such codes. It may be correct that the generic name of a business product cannot serve to identify the business that sells it, but this seems to be a more difficult question than the decision indicates.

Can a design mark dominated by a disclaimed generic word be registered if the generic term is confusingly similar to a previously registered mark for similar goods? The

---

[14] In re Uniform Product Code Council, Inc., 202 USPQ 618 (TTAB 1979).

Board may have said no without ever considering the question.[15] Applicant sought to register a seemingly distinctive display of the words THE CHIPPER for a grinder attachment for removing paint, rust, scale, etc. "Chipper" was disclaimed, but if unregistrable at all, and therefore subject to disclaimer, it may well, as used, have been generic rather than descriptive. CHIPPER was held to be confusingly similar to CLIPPER for similar goods, and registration was refused.

If CHIPPER is generic for the goods, this raises an interesting question. While it is true that one cannot escape confusing similarity with an earlier registered mark simply by disclaiming the similar part, and is also true that the disclaimed portion must be considered in determining likelihood of confusion with an earlier mark, here the only similarity lay in the disclaimed portion. The Board did not consider why "Chipper" was disclaimed. However if it was generic, which seems possible, the applicant had an absolute right to call his goods what they were, and it seems difficult to conceive of any reason why, if he had a distinctive display of that generic term, he could not register it. The mark would be weak, and only its design elements protectible, but it should be registrable within these limits. It is almost given that generic terms, per se, cannot infringe anything. If CHIPPER simply described the function of the grinder attachment, then the result is correct. Applicant has a right to describe that function, but not in a trademark manner. If CHIPPER was only suggestive, the disclaimer should not have been permitted, and, of course, the same result would have followed.

Four other cases holding marks merely descriptive are of more than routine interest.

1. QUIK-PRINT was held to be merely descriptive of print shop services that included printing, binding and

---

[15] Norton Co. v. Talbert, 202 USPQ 542 (TTAB 1979). See also infra fns 82 in Ch. 5, 43 and 47 in Ch. 6.

§3.02 / Trademark Law

other related services.[16] That other, non-printing, services were offered was considered to be irrelevant. Since QUIK-PRINT conveyed a simple idea directly, the Board considered it descriptive rather than suggestive. The CCPA affirmed, emphasizing that a term descriptive of any goods or services sold under it is merely descriptive.[17]

What makes the case curious is that applicant attempted to rely upon another's Section 2(f) registration of QUICK-PRINT for similar services to show that the mark was not descriptive. (The lurking Section 2(d) problem was more or less solved by applicant's claim of use in separate geographic areas.) The Board pointed out that Section 7(b) registration presumptions accrue only to registrants and some privies, not to strangers; that the Section 2(f) registration demonstrated that the term was descriptive; and that if there was use in geographically separate areas, no secondary meaning of registrant's mark would have rubbed off on applicant.

2. JOBBER AND WAREHOUSE EXECUTIVE was held merely descriptive of a periodical because it described the intended audience, albeit not the contents, of the magazine.[18] The Board said that while magazine marks are judged by the same criteria for descriptiveness as other marks, under Section 2(e)(1) it has been recognized (contrary to practice under Section 5(b) of the 1905 Act and authority following it under the new Act) that terms directly descriptive of qualities or contents, or of a class of intended users, of goods are merely descriptive. Board Chairman Lefkowitz' opinion provides a helpful review of this development. A prior registration of the same mark by the same applicant (canceled under Section 8) could not be ignored, but since its Section 7(b) presumptions had lapsed, the case had to be decided under current principles of interpretation.

3. PANTY TOP was held merely descriptive of panty hose

[16] In re Quik-Print Copy Shop, Inc., 203 USPQ 624 (TTAB 1979).
[17] 205 USPQ 505 (CCPA 1980).
[18] In re Hunter Publishing Co., 204 USPQ 957 (TTAB 1979). See also infra fn 167 in Ch. 6.

### CCPA and PTO Interpretations / §3.02

with panties sewn to the top of the hose.[19] The record seemed clear that the development of such panty hose was relatively new (prior panty hose had required separate undergarments) and that several manufacturers referred to panty hose with this feature as "panty top" or "pantie top" panty hose. Since either was considered an "apt descriptive appellation" of this particular type of panty hose, which several used, the registration was refused on the ground that the mark was merely descriptive. Opposer alleged that PANTY TOP was a "common descriptive term," but the Board did not decide that issue.

4. HOT WAX, with the word HOT in flaming letters, was refused registration on the Principal Register as merely descriptive.[20] Since applicant had disclaimed "hot wax" per se, the issue was whether acquired distinctiveness in commerce had been shown. The Board conceded that the display of hot was capable of functioning as a trademark, and thus eligible for the Supplemental Register. For Principal Register registration, the issue is whether the mark does function as a trademark, and as to this the Board was unconvinced. Sales persuaded the Board of the success of the product, but not that HOT WAX identified its origin. Substantial advertising was not persuasive because no examples were furnished so the Board could assess whether the advertising created a trademark impression. The lesson is that he who would show secondary meaning must show how his would-be mark is used in sales and advertising, as well as sales and advertising data.

In other cases, SINKER SELECTOR was held to be the (generic) common descriptive name of a container for fisherman's sinkers, which container included a clear movable top and aperture permitting inspection and selection of the sinkers displayed inside;[21] INTERNATIONAL TRAVEL-

[19] Virginia Maid Hosiery Mills, Inc. v. Collins & Aikman Corp., 203 USPQ 795 (TTAB 1979). See also infra fn 35 in Ch. 6.

[20] In re Behre Industries, Inc., 203 USPQ 1030 (TTAB 1979). See also supra fn 15 in Ch. 2. and infra fn 156 in Ch. 6.

[21] In re Water Gremlin Co., 204 USPQ 261 (TTAB 1979). See also supra fn 3 this chapter and infra fn 162 in Ch. 6.

§3.02 / Trademark Law

ERS CHEQUE for financial consulting services concerning travelers checks and bank drafts was held to be merely descriptive (since applicant disclaimed "travelers cheque," which precluded the probably hopeless argument that the words were not descriptive, the Board had little difficulty in concluding that INTERNATIONAL simply described services international in scope).[22]

In another case, though the registrant initially registered FLOSSAID for dental floss holders under Section 2(f), the Board noted that a viable argument could be made that the term was only suggestive.[23]

Not all marks alleged to be merely descriptive were held to be so. IT'S A REAL "TAIL WAGGER" and TAIL WAGGER were held not merely descriptive of dog food; at worst, they merely suggested one desirable result of use—the dog would show pleasure by wagging its tail.[24]

NEUROPAC was not merely descriptive of a neuropacer (a type of medical machine).[25] The PAC portion was intended to suggest "pack" or "package" and the double entendre or possible suggestiveness was sufficient to remove the mark from the realm of the merely descriptive. CRAZY was held not to be descriptive of ice cream cones.[26] The term seems more descriptive of the argument than of the goods.

Holdings reported without decision established the following marks to be merely descriptive: FRESHWATER for

[22] BankAmerica Corp. v. International Travelers Cheque Co., 205 USPQ 1233 (TTAB 1979). See also infra fns 19, 36, 41, 93 and 117 in Ch. 6.

[23] Floss Aid Corp. v. John O. Butler Co., 205 USPQ 274, 284 (TTAB 1979). See also supra fn 26 in Ch. 2 and infra fns 66 in Ch. 5, 54, 102 and 170 in Ch. 6.

[24] Allied Mills, Inc. v. Kal Kan Foods, Inc., 203 USPQ 390, 396 (TTAB 1979). See also infra fns 56 in Ch. 5 and 62 in Ch. 6.

[25] Medtronic, Inc. v. Medical Devices, Inc., 204 USPQ 317, 324 (TTAB 1979). See also infra fns 2 and 36 in Ch. 5 and 122 and 137 in Ch. 6.

[26] Safe-T Pacific Co. v. Nabisco, Inc., 204 USPQ 307, 313 (TTAB 1979). See also supra fn 27 in Ch. 2 and infra fns 60 in Ch. 5, 51 and 124 in Ch. 6.

activated charcoal filters;[27] FIBERICH for prepared baking mixes;[28] DESIGN ENGINEERING SHOW for industrial trade shows;[29] MOISTURE SUPPLEMENT for hair conditioning gel;[30] FOUR-WAY for shock absorbers;[31] DIET CENTER for weight control consulting services and diet programs employing nutritional control;[32] MOISTURE CONTROL for hair setting lotion;[33] TANDEM for sets for carding machines;[34] and CERTIFIED HOME INSPECTION SERVICES for building examination and evaluation services.[35] Digest decisions held TOPICAL NUTRITION for hair shampoo[36] and BANANA CRISP for breakfast cereal[37] not merely descriptive.

## §3.03 Geographic Marks

MONTE CARLO was held to be primarily geographically descriptive (or misdescriptive) of electronic digital watches, but not of electronic digital watches with game playing functions. The test, said the Board, is "whether the term conveys to customers primarily or immediately a geographical connotation."[38] MONTE CARLO was thought to do so for electronic digital watches simpliciter, but because Monte Carlo is known for its gambling casino, the Board felt that the mark would take on other connotations for such watchers with game playing functions. Accordingly, it permitted amendment of the description of goods and passed

[27] In re Lever Brothers Co., 205 USPQ 794 (TTAB 1979).
[28] In re Morrison Milling Co., 205 USPQ 835 (TTAB 1979).
[29] In re Industrial Expositions, Inc., 205 USPQ 840 (TTAB 1979).
[30] In re Helene Curtis Industries, Inc., 205 USPQ 1064 (TTAB 1979).
[31] In re Papousek, 203 USPQ 799 (TTAB 1979).
[32] In re Diet Center, Inc., 203 USPQ 800 (TTAB 1979).
[33] In re Helene Curtis Industries, Inc., 203 USPQ 400 (TTAB 1979).
[34] In re Crosrol, Ltd., 205 USPQ 968 (TTAB 1979). See also infra fn 116 in Ch. 5.
[35] In re Schenck, 205 USPQ 968 (TTAB 1979).
[36] In re Diagnostics & Designs, Inc., 205 USPQ 932 (TTAB 1979).
[37] In re Organic Milling Co., Inc., 205 USPQ 1090 (TTAB 1979).
[38] In re Datatime Corp., 203 USPQ 878, 879 (TTAB 1979).

§3.03 / Trademark Law

the mark to publication, as amended, without a showing of acquired distinctiveness.

The reasoning is fine as far as it goes. It does not, however, address the consequences of the result. Primarily geographic (or geographically misdescriptive) marks are unregistrable because it is believed that such terms should remain free for all until someone has preempted them by imbuing them with secondary meaning. Registration of MONTE CARLO for electronic digital watches with gaming functions presumably will preempt the mark for all watches, electronic or not, with or without gaming functions. If MONTE CARLO is primarily geographically descriptive or misdescriptive for non-specialized watches (which seems doubtful), then it seems odd that the Board should allow it to be preempted for such goods without a showing of secondary meaning. This appears to allow in the back door that which is barred from entering the front.

LOCH-A-MOOR was held not to be primarily geographically misdescriptive of a Scotch whisky based liqueur produced in the United States.[39] Conceding that LOCH-A-MOOR had, as applicant intended, a Scottish "feel" to it, the Board held that it did not identify a known location:

> The mere fact that a mark may consist of a word or words having a foreign suggestiveness, or more particularly a suggestiveness peculiar to a country, does not in and of itself render the mark primarily geographically descriptive or deceptively misdescriptive within the meaning of Section 2(e)(2) of the Statute.[40]

Such marks, said the Board, are common for vodka, pastas and other foods, and consumers presumably are not misled.

---

[39] Scotch Whiskey Assn. v. Consolidated Distilled Products, Inc., 204 USPQ 57 (TTAB 1979). See also infra fns 7 in Ch. 5, 6, 33, 37 and 103 in Ch. 6.

[40] Id at 63.

For a recitation of the standards to be applied to the mark under Section 2(a), see infra §5.01.

HULA was not considered to be primarily geographically descriptive in either HULA TAN suntan preparation or HULA HAND skin cream, though it was recognized to be geographically suggestive.[41]

## §3.04 Surnames

The Board rejected "drummonds," as primarily merely a surname when it was sought to be registered for retail specialty store and mail order services.[42] Earlier CCPA cases had established that six listings as a surname in a Manhattan telephone book were not enough to establish that DUCHARME was primarily merely a surname,[43] but that nineteen hundred listings in Cleveland and Maryland suburban (D.C.) directories sufficed to do so for HARRIS.[44] Here there were fifty-three listings in the Dallas-Fort Worth and Houston directories, which covered applicant's markets. The question, of course, was one of public perception. Practically, all an Examiner could do was to skim telephone books to see if the mark was a surname. It then was up to applicant to establish, if only by argument, either that the surname was so obscure as to be virtually unknown or that the word had other meanings. Here, applicant could do neither. Failure to capitalize, or use an apostrophe to make a proper possessive, was held not to change the predominantly surnominal impression of the mark.

BRANIFF for cigars, cigarillos and stogies, was refused

---

[41] Royal Hawaiian Perfumes, Ltd. v. Diamond Head Products of Hawaii, Inc., 204 USPQ 144, 147 (TTAB 1979). See also infra fns 39 in Ch. 5, 44, 48, 84 and 89 in Ch. 6.

[42] In re Directional Marketing Corp., 204 USPQ 675 (TTAB 1979).

[43] In re Kahan & Weisz Jewelry Mfg. Corp., 508 F2d 831, 184 USPQ 421 (CCPA 1975), discussed in 65 TMR 393 fn 78.

[44] In re Harris-Intertype Corp., 518 F2d 629, 186 USPQ 238 (CCPA 1975), discussed in 66 TMR 354 fn 68.

§3.05 / Trademark Law

registration as primarily merely a surname.[45] While there were comparatively few telephone directory listings, the word had no other "known" meaning, and appeared in the specimens under a portrait. Under these circumstances, the Board concluded that the significance of BRANIFF to purchasers would be surnominal.

### §3.05 Foreign Equivalents

While the doctrine of foreign equivalents may be employed to determine whether a mark is descriptive or generic, it has little, if any, potential for avoiding likelihood of confusion. In attempting to argue that its mark CHULA was not confusingly similar to KAHLUA for the same goods, applicant argued that CHULA was the feminine form of the Spanish word "chulo" which meant, inter alia, "pretty." Board Chairman Lefkowitz was unimpressed. "But, who would be aware of this meaning? . . . However, the concept or understanding of the general or ordinary purchaser . . . not that of linguistic experts or specialists or those few . . . familiar with a foreign language . . . is the controlling factor in determining the question of likelihood of confusion."[46]

### §3.06 Mutilation of Marks

A maker of several specialized photographic papers and films packaged each under a design that contained a vertical SG to the left, a twenty-five square grid to the right, and a horizontal rectangle beneath. On different products it drew different mathematical curves on the grid, somehow related to the technical characteristics of the product, and inserted in the rectangle such (presumably descriptive) words as "repro-proof" and "positive." It applied to register just the SG

---

[45] In re Villiger Sohne GmbH, 205 USPQ 462 (TTAB 1979). See also infra fn 155 in Ch. 6.

[46] Jules Berman & Associates, Inc. v. Consolidated Distilled Products, Inc., 202 USPQ 67, 70 (TTAB 1979). See also supra fn 28 in Ch. 2 and infra fns 16 in Ch. 5 and 102 in Ch. 6.

### CCPA and PTO Interpretations / §3.07

and blank grid, and in an opposition, was charged with attempting to register a mutilation of its mark(s).[47] The Board held that since the commercial impression rested in SG and the empty grid, it would be a pointless waste of everyone's time and money to require multiple registrations. (That one would seem to suffice for purposes of protection seems to reinforce the Board's view, if not its precise articulation of its reason.) While the Board also noted that it would be appropriate to recite the significance of the curve, the mark as applied for was bereft of any such curve.

### §3.07 Service Marks

A "no lemon" symbol was held unregistrable by the Court of Customs and Patent Appeals because it had not been used for cognizable services.[48] Applicant made and sold electrical meters. Previously, it had been refused registration of the mark for the service of "guaranteeing instrument replacement" on the ground that guaranteeing one's own goods is not a service cognizable by the Act.[49] It reapplied for the same mark for "repair or immediate replacement of" meters. It lost again because the activity remained "an inducement to the sale of Orion's own goods."

Exactly what the principle is seems unclear. While guaranteeing one's own goods probably is not an independent service (guaranteeing someone else's presumably is), and the mark, if any, probably is a trademark for the goods, the repair (or temporary) replacement of defective goods does not seem to be a service. VOLKSWAGEN probably is a service mark for repairing VOLKSWAGEN vehicles. Certainly independent service stations have infringed that mark several times. Such authorized service presumably is an inducement to the purchase of VOLKSWAGEN vehicles.

[47] Sheller-Globe Corp. v. Scott Paper Co., 204 USPQ 329, 336–37 (TTAB 1979). See also supra fn 3 in Ch. 2 and infra fns 78 in Ch. 5 and 87 in Ch. 6.
[48] In re Orion Research Inc., 205 USPQ 688 (CCPA 1980); affg 70 TMR 490 (TTAB 1979).
[49] 187 USPQ 485 (CCPA 1975), discussed in 66 TMR 353 fn 60.

## §3.08 / Trademark Law

For one of Orion's competitors to offer the same service under the same mark would seem also to be a wrong. What is the harm in permitting registration of such marks? One rationale for the result is suggested by the next case.

When a newspaper publisher sought to register the name of one of its sections, THE DAILY BREAK, as a service mark for distributing cultural and leisure information, the Board had occasion to consider the nature of a service mark.[50] Its conclusion was that one first identifies the principal activity under the mark—sale of an intangible service or tangible product—and then ascertains whether the described service is a qualitatively different economic activity. Here, obviously, the principal activity was selling newspapers—tangible goods—and the purported service was a necessary and expected part of the manufacture of the product. Registration was refused. *In re Great Gorge*,[51] which perhaps was distinguishable, was expressly overruled.

## §3.08 Collateral References

### [1] Generic Names and "Merely Descriptive" Marks

On generic names generally, see Ralph H. Folsom and Larry L. Teply, "Trademarked Generic Words," 70 TMR 206 (1980) and the spirited reply in Jerre B. Swann, "The Economic Approach to Genericism: A Reply to Folsom and Teply," 70 TMR 243 (1980). Also: Carol A. Melton, "Generic Term or Trademark? Confusing Legal Standards and Inadequate Protection," 29 Am U L Rev 109 (1979). Further discussion on the FTC and its powers vis-a-vis generic terms is found in Michael F. Kuzow, "The FTC and the Generic Doctrine: A New Rx for Pharmaceutical Trademarks," 15 Tulsa LJ 327 (1979); Alfred F. Dougherty, Jr., Paul C. Daw and John H. Evans, "Federal Trace Commission v. Formica: The Generic Trademark Issue," 2 Com and the Law 1

---

[50] In re Landmark Communications, Inc., 204 USPQ 692 (TTAB 1979). See also infra fn 383.

[51] 185 USPQ 572 (TTAB 1975), discussed in 65 TMR 392 fn 73.

(1980); John M. Fietkiewicz, "Section 14 of the Lanham Act—FTC Authority to Challenge Generic Trademarks," 48 Fordham L Rev 437 (1980).

## [2] Geographic Marks

For a discussion of collective and certification marks to avoid the geographically descriptive problem, see C. Bruce Hamburg, "Registering a Trademark Indicating Regional Origin of Goods," 79 Pat & TM Rev 210 (1980).

## [3] Surnames

See: Charles R. Fowler, Tips from the TTAB: When Are Surnames Registrable?, 70 TMR 66 (1980).

CHAPTER 4

# Supplemental Registration

Supplemental Register marks may be canceled, if, after hearing, it is found that at the time of application, the registrant was not entitled to register the mark.[1] Section 24 of the Act so provides. Section 23 states that Section 2(d), which prohibits registrations of marks confusingly similar to those previously used or registered, applies to the Supplemental Register as well as the Principal. Thus use or registration by one of a mark confusingly similar to that of another, prior to that other's use (in the case of prior use) or registration (in the case of prior registration) is ground for canceling the resulting supplemental registration (which, of course, cannot be opposed).

This happened to a registration of PROFESSIONAL ECONOMIC SERVICES when there was prior use of PROFESSIONAL ECONOMICS INCORPORATED for the same services.[2] The Board also held that cancellation was appropriate because such marks, to be registered, must be used in commerce, which means "lawful use," and that for use of such a merely descriptive term to be "lawful" it must be "exclusive" since merely descriptive terms should be free to be used by others in the field (descriptively) absent the acquisition of secondary meaning. This reasoning seems both strained and suspect. If there were secondary meaning, the mark would seem eligible for the Principal Register

[1] Medical Modalities Associates, Inc. v. ARA Corp., 203 USPQ 295, 300–01 (TTAB 1979). See also supra fn 19 in Ch. 2 and infra fns 30 in Ch. 5, 56, 66, 103 and 127 in Ch. 6.

[2] Professional Economics Inc. v. Professional Economic Services, Inc., 205 USPQ 368 (TTAB 1979). See also supra fns 18 in Ch. 2 and 7 in Ch. 3 and infra fns 38 this chapter and 8 in Ch. 6.

39

## Trademark Law

(unless generic? see supra §3.02). Moreover, there seems to be nothing unlawful about non-exclusive use of a descriptive term that has not acquired distinctiveness.

It was held that deceptive misdescriptiveness of marks on the Supplemental Register can be attacked only under Section 2(a)'s prohibition of deceptive marks, since Section 2(e) does not apply to such registration.[3]

[3] Tanners' Council of America, Inc. v. Samsonite Corp., 204 USPQ 150, 152 fn 2 (TTAB 1979). See also infra fns 6 this chapter, 13 and 67 in Ch. 6.

CHAPTER 5

# Confusing Similarity

## §5.01 False Suggestion of Connection with Persons or Institutions—Section 2(a)

Section 14 provides that after registration for five years, a mark can only be canceled on certain grounds. Likelihood of confusion with a previously registered or used mark, prohibited by Section 2(d), is not among those grounds; falsely suggesting a connection with persons or institutions, proscribed by Section 2(a), is among those grounds. It is not uncommon for cancellation petitioners faced with a typical Section 2(d) situation, but precluded from arguing that ground by Section 14, to charge a breach of Section 2(a). The overall legal problem is that if Section 2(a) is no more than an alternative to Section 2(d), then the five year "statute of limitations" of Section 2(d) claims embodied in Section 14 bars only the unimaginative. Section 2(a), then, must require something more than Section 2(d). The question is what.

One case simply noted that an opposer cannot prevail under Section 2(a) without establishing the likelihood of confusion required by Section 2(d).[1] That seems plain enough. Another case, however, ruled that for a mark to falsely suggest a connection, within the proscription of Section 2(a), there must exist the same likelihood of confusion required by Section 2(d), plus something more. That something more was defined as "an intent, implied or actual, on the part of [the accused] to trade on the goodwill possessed by [the

[1] R. C. Bigelow, Inc. v. Celestial Seasonings, Inc., 203 USPQ 542 (TTAB 1979). See also infra fns 57 in this chapter and 95 in Ch. 6.

§5.01 / Trademark Law

accuser] in the mark" in issue.[2]

Another held that to establish a false suggestion of connection with a person or institution, under Section 2(a), the proponent must establish "at the very least" the same likelihood of confusion required by Section 2(d).[3] The standard, whatever it is, was held to be met when a petition was brought to cancel registration of LLOYD'S OF LONDON for men's after-shave cologne and perfume. Since LLOYD'S OF LONDON is an arbitrary, world famous mark for insurance services, the Board had some difficulty finding a connection between the respective parties' products. It did so by "necessarily" and, no doubt, correctly, inferring registrant's familiarity with LLOYD'S OF LONDON, and that registrant therefore "adopted the mark with the intent to benefit from the celebrity of the mark and the reputation thereof."[4] Since LLOYD'S OF LONDON engaged in products liability insurance and was world famous for insuring unusual risks, the Board felt purchasers of LLOYD'S OF LONDON after-shave or cologne would assume falsely, but reasonably, that the toiletry was "licensed, sponsored, recommended, insured or otherwise guaranteed" as to quality by the famous insurer. Holding that even if the standards of Section 2(a) were not met, those of Section 2(d) were, the Board concluded its opinion with Learned Hand's famous Yale v. Robertson quote.[5]

There are, of course, other prohibitions in Section 2(a).

For a mark to be deceptive within the proscription of Section 2(a), "it must at the very least have a tendency to deceive or have the effect of deceiving the average purchaser of the goods" for which the mark is used. SOFTHIDE for

---

[2] Medtronic, Inc. v. Medical Devices, Inc., 204 U8PQ 317, 325 (TTAB 1979). See also supra fn 25 in Ch. 3 and infra fns 33 in this chapter, 122 and 137 in Ch. 6.

[3] Corp. of Lloyd's v. Louis D'Or of France, Inc., 202 USPQ 313, 316 (TTAB 1979). See also infra fns 67 this chapter and 128 in Ch. 6.

[4] Id at 316.

[5] Id at 317, quoting Yale Electric Corp. v. Robertson, 26 F2d 972 (CA 2 1928).

## CCPA and PTO Interpretations / §5.02[1]

imitation leather did, the Board concluded,[6] in a case discussed under Summary Judgment infra.

In the Scotch whisky/liqueurs case,[7] the Board stated that geographically misdescriptive marks may fall within the proscriptions of Section 2(a), covering deceptive matter, if three conditons are present: (1) the term must convey a geographic connotation primarily or immediately; (2) the goods must not come from the area named; (3) such use must be calculated to deceive the public as to geographic origin of the goods so as to bestow on the goods characteristics of increased saleability. Having stated the tests, the Board did not return to them because it found that the mark—LOCH-A-MOOR—did not violate the somewhat less rigid standards imposed by Section 2(e). The principle could, however, be applied in petitions to cancel marks registered more than five years.

## §5.02 Confusing Similarity with Previously Used or Registered Marks—Section 2(d)

The issue most frequently decided by the Board is likelihood of confusion, mistake or deception, but the Court of Customs and Patent Appeals dealt with the subject only three times.

### [1] CCPA Decisions

First, it upheld the Board's dismissal of an opposition to registration of SANDWICH CHEF and chef design by the registrant of BURGER CHEF and a different chef design, both for identical services.[8] The Board, said the Court, con-

---

[6] Tanners' Council of America, Inc. v. Samsonite Corp., 204 USPQ 150, 153 (TTAB 1979). See also supra fn 3 in Ch. 4 and infra fns 13 and 65 in Ch. 6.

[7] Scotch Whiskey Ass'n v. Consolidated Distilled Products, Inc., 204 USPQ 57, 62 (TTAB 1979). See also supra fn 39 in Ch. 3 and infra fns 6, 33, 37 and 103 in Ch. 6.

[8] Burger Chef Systems, Inc. v. Sandwich Chef, Inc., 608 F2d 875, 203 USPQ 733 (CCPA 1979), affg 201 USPQ 611 (TTAB 1978), discussed in 69 TMR 558 fn 111.

§5.02[1] / Trademark Law

sidered the proper factors, and its decision had "ample basis in the record."[9] (An earlier decision[10] in which the owner of BURGER CHEF repulsed registration of BURGER MAN was not considered to be a valid precedent for this case.)

In another, the court reviewed the Board's determination more critically, deciding that a probability of confusion the Board had declared "likely" was "unlikely."[11] The marks were one GP logo and another, stylized GP logo, both used for paper bags. The latter, held the court, projected the image of a distinctive design mark rather than the letter GP. Aural identity was unimportant with respect to such goods ordered mainly by purchasing officers who are aware with whom they are dealing.

As these cases demonstrate, the court's decisions indicate that its powers of review are more circumscribed in cases in which it decides to affirm than those in which it decides to reverse.

Finally, the Tinkertoy case[12] involved an agent who solicited non-toy licenses of the mark TINKERTOY for the owner of the mark. As licensing agent, he had acknowledged the owner's rights in the TINKERTOY mark. He developed a LI'L TINKER design mark (which included a depiction of some fanciful TINKERTOY construction set parts) to aid a potential licensing program for children's books which he claimed would "further strengthen the TINKERTOY image" and "open up a whole new dimension in our TINKERTOY licensing program." The owner of TINKERTOY never granted him permission to use the mark, so the agent applied to register it in his company's own name. The owner opposed.

[9] 203 USPQ at 735.
[10] Burger Chef Systems, Inc. v. Burger Man, Inc., 492 F2d 1398, 181 USPQ 168 (CCPA 1974), discussed in 64 TMR 403 fn 297.
[11] Georgia-Pacific Corp. v. Great Plains Bag Co., 204 USPQ 697 (CCPA 1980), affg 200 USPQ 601 (TTAB 1978), discussed in 69 TMR 573 fn 148. See also infra fns 30 and 126 in Ch. 6.
[12] Dan Robbins & Associates, Inc. v. Questor Corp., 202 USPQ 100 (CCPA 1979). See also supra fn 11 in Ch. 3 and infra fns 53 and 152 in Ch. 6.

## CCPA and PTO Interpretations / §5.02[2][a]

The court had little trouble affirming the Board's sustaining of the opposition. While there were mark and product differences, the Court felt free to examine "all the circumstances bearing on the marketing environment," which was the death knell for the agent-applicant:

> . . . Incorporation of a design depicting another's product, in a mark including a term similar to that other's word mark, must in this case be viewed as contributing to the likelihood of confusion.
>
> . . . A mark designed to maximize association between entities, as here, is likely to lead to confusion in the absence of a proper license relationship between those entities.[13]

### [2] TTAB Decisions—Reported

The Trademark Trial and Appeal Board, as always, determined whether there was likelihood of confusion in dozens of cases. While they stand as a large body of largely unconnected, not entirely consistent holdings, certain themes recur frequently, as will be seen.

#### [a] Alcoholic Beverages

Probably signifying nothing other than random chance, the Board began the year by upholding oppositions by the owners of two of our better known alcoholic refreshments, hopefully sparing inbibers the consequences of confusion.

In a Blue Nun case,[14] an application to register a BLUE ANGEL label for bottled wine was refused. While both wine labels featured depictions of females (which depictions few humans could confuse), the Board considered the words to

---

[13] Id at 104–05.

[14] H. Sichel Sohne, GmbH v. Michel Monzain Selected Wines, Inc., 202 USPQ 62 (TTAB 1979). See also supra fn 25 in Ch. 2 and infra fns 164 and 168 in Ch. 6.

§5.02[2][a] / Trademark Law

dominate the marks. Both marks comprised two words, the first of which was the arbitrary BLUE, and the second of which had religious connotations. Thus the Board felt that they had common general ideas and stimulated similar mental impressions. (The BLUE ANGEL label, in its entirety including the depiction of a young adult female, has about the same religious connotation as CHARLIE'S ANGELS.) Numerous third party registrations of BLUE marks for alcoholic beverages were dismissed as irrelevant because they did not have overall religious connotations, and marks had to be judged in their entireties.

Later in the year, BLUE CHAPEL for wine was held to be confusingly similar to BLUE NUN, because nuns pray or meditate in chapels.[15] The Board found greater connotational similarity than in the Blue Angel case, and resolved doubts against the newcomer. While BLUE was often registered for liquors, such registrations did not demonstrate use or consumer familiarity with BLUE marks.

The Board also found confusing similarity between KAHLUA and CHULA for fifty-three proof coffee liqueurs, the latter of which was advertised by a retailer, who pictured both products, as "Another Tasteful Choice at a Most Pleasing Price."[16] Identity of products, and aural similarity of marks for products frequently ordered orally in package stores and in crowded taverns and restaurants, convinced the Board that confusion was likely. KAHLUA liqueur, like BLUE NUN wine, was quite successful and well-known. Lack of evidence of actual confusion was considered unimportant because such evidence is difficult to obtain, particularly where there was no evidence of disparity of quality giving rise to likely complaints, and because there was no evidence of substantial enough market interface to create a climate in which confusion or mistake was likely to occur.

[15] H. Sichel Sohne, GmbH v. John Gross & Co., 204 USPQ 257 (TTAB 1979). See also infra fn 11 in Ch. 6.

[16] John Berman & Associates, Inc. v. Consolidated Distilled Products, Inc., 202 USPQ 67 (TTAB 1979). See also supra fns 28 in Ch. 2 and 46 in Ch. 3 and infra fn 102 in Ch. 6.

## CCPA and PTO Interpretations / §5.02[2][b]

The Board had three other occasions to ponder alcoholic beverages. (1) BUITONI for wines was held to be confusingly similar to the previously used BUTON for vermouth (a wine) and such related goods as brandy and liqueur.[17] (2) Extensive use and advertising (and a well-conceived survey) persuaded it that EL BRUJO and TORTILLA sangria labels with bull and matador designs would be likely to create confusion with YAGO SANT' GRIA, whose registered labels and advertising also employed bull and matador designs.[18] Applicant evidently argued the not unreasonable proposition that bull and matador designs were hardly distinctive of goods originating in Spain, but failed to "offer any evidence whatsoever in support" of that position.[19] (3) A digest decision reached a similar result with respect to LAURO and bullfighter and bull design for sangria.[20]

### [b] Design Marks

Four cases compared graphic marks, which cases can be hard to describe in words. (1) In a snow ski case,[21] both marks contained equilateral triangles, apex up. One had removed from its center a similar, small inverted triangle, so it could be viewed as a triangle of three triangles; the other had removed a small hexagon, with white lines extending from it to each of the triangle's points. Both were used for snow skis, and the previously used and registered one was quite widely used, extensively promoted and well-regarded in its field. The Board distinguished several other, similar marks on various grounds (different goods, not the best evidence,

---

[17] Gio. Buton & C. S.p.A. v. Buitoni Foods Corp., 205 USPQ 477 (TTAB 1979). See also supra fns 6 and 10 in Ch. 2 and infra fns 52 and 91 in Ch. 6.

[18] Monsieur Henri Wines Ltd. v. Duran, 204 USPQ 601 (TTAB 1979). See also infra fn 138 in Ch. 6.

[19] Id at 606.

[20] Monsieur Henri Wines Ltd. v. La Tarraco Vinicolo S.L., 204 USPQ 976 (TTAB 1979).

[21] Fischer Gesellschaft m.b.H. v. Molnar and Co., Inc., 203 USPQ 861 (TTAB 1979). See also infra fns 96, 99 and 112 in Ch. 6.

§5.02[2][b] / Trademark Law

only registered but barely used) to conclude that the first was quite distinct in its field. Relying on the vagaries of recall of trademarks, the Board found the two marks confusingly similar. (2) Two distinctly different graphic treatments of a soldier were held confusingly similar for retail food services, since the Board felt that each created a similar commercial impression.[22] (3) When the makers of PUMA sport shoes opposed registration of a stripe pattern on such shoes somewhat similar to the previously registered, used and promoted PUMA "Formstrip" for such shoes, they lost.[23] Evidence of a plethora of stripe and bar designs registered for and used on such shoes persuaded the Board that despite its considerable advertising and use the PUMA stripe was a weak mark. (4) A design of a dragon (and Chinese characters meaning GOLDEN DRAGON) for judo and karate uniforms was held not likely to be confused with various registered and used marks comprising alligator designs, ALLIGATOR and GOLD ALLIGATOR for various types of clothing.[24] While there were differences in goods, it was the difference in marks that led Board Member Kera to observe:

> St. George did not become the patron saint of England because he slew an alligator. . . .
> Mythological heroes made their reputations fighting dragons, not alligators. Dragons have horns, breathe fire and fly; alligators do not. Next to dragons, alligators are pussycats.[25]

The differences between the marks are apparent; they do not much look alike. The dragon obviously is that, and the Board noted that opposer's extensive sales and advertising

[22] In re Schmuck Markets, Inc., 202 USPQ 154 (TTAB 1979).

[23] Puma-Sportschuhfabriken Rudolf Dassler, K.G. v. Superga S.p.A., 204 USPQ 688 (TTAB 1979). See also infra fn 10 in Ch. 6.

[24] Lacoste Alligator S.A. v. Everlast World's Boxing Headquarters Corp., 204 USPQ 945 (TTAB 1979). See also infra fn 158 in Ch. 6.

[25] Id at 948.

## CCPA and PTO Interpretations / §5.02[2][b]

must have conditioned the public to identify its beast as an alligator.

Two other cases involved possible confusing similarity of words and pictures. (1) Having successfully opposed registration of HILLBILLY RESTAURANT,[26] the owners and registrants of a HILLBILLY (and hillbilly character design) bread trademark petitioned to cancel the restaurant's registration of the caricature it used in conjunction with HILLBILLY RESTAURANT.[27] Exacerbating whatever likelihood of confusion there may have been was the fact that the restaurant sold bread to go in plain plastic bags. The Board had earlier felt that HILLBILLY RESTAURANT bread and the well-known HILLBILLY bread were a bit difficult to distinguish (particularly for hillbillies?). This time, however, the Board felt that the restaurant's character did not much look like a hillbilly, and that even if it did, the hillbilly motif was so common for restaurants and foods (as shown by third party registrations, which usually do not prove use) that there could be no exclusive right to it for all foods and restaurants. The Board did concede that the pictorial equivalent of a word mark would be confusingly similar to the word mark because both would create the same impression. (2) STAG for golf clubs was held confusingly similar to the previously used and registered WHITE STAG and design of a leaping stag for a wide variety of sporting clothes, including golf clothes.[28] Opposer also had used the same or other STAG marks on sporting goods other than golf clubs, but little seemed to turn on that. WHITE STAG, by virtue of long use and extensive advertising, was held to be a strong, arbitrary mark. The Board considered STAG to dominate the mark, since WHITE simply modified the word. It also noted that STAG and a pictorial design of a stag are equivalent marks for purposes of Section 2(d). Three

[26] Roush Bakery Products Co., Inc. v. Ridlen, 190 USPQ 445 (TTAB 1976), discussed in 67 TMR 506 fn 113.

[27] Roush Bakery Products Co., Inc. v. Ridlen, 203 USPQ 1086 (TTAB 1979).

[28] Warnaco, Inc. V. Holiday Golf Products, 204 USPQ 69 (TTAB 1979). See also infra fns 141 and 157 in Ch. 6.

§5.02[2][c] / Trademark Law

factors persuaded the Board that the goods were closely related: (a) golf pro shops that carried STAG golf clubs also carried golf clothing; (b) other manufacturers sold coordinated lines of golf clothing and equipment under the same mark; (c) WHITE STAG had been extensively advertised and promoted in conjunction with several sports, including golf. Purchasers could encounter either or both marks in a commercial environment likely to give rise to confusion. While lack of demonstrated confusion was held always to be a factor, to be a vaild one there had to be contemporaneous use for an appreciable time so there was ample opportunity for confusion to arise if it was going to, and there would have been opportunity for the confused to be heard. Neither was the case here.

### [c] The Tuxedo Monopoly Case

In what may be the year's most controversial decision, MONOPOLY for wearing apparel was held confusingly similar to the previously used and registered MONOPOLY for a real estate trading game.[29] MONOPOLY unquestionably is a famous game mark, as was demonstrated. Registration for clothing presumably would preempt the game-maker's right (if any) to license the mark for such goods. The game-maker had done some licensing, and had refused requests to license MONOPOLY for clothing. The Board had sufficient doubts about likelihood of confusion to resolve them against the newcomer. As Board Member Kera pointed out in a vigorous dissent, the decision came uncomfortably close to granting a monopoly, or right in gross, in the trademark MONOPOLY. The precedent seems to be that "newcomers" in such areas as clothing, or in the other fields in which the Board might decide to judicially notice that famous marks often are licensed, must avoid choosing words that are famous marks in some other field. That seems

---

[29] General Mills Fun Group, Inc. v. Tuxedo Monopoly, Inc., 204 USPQ 396 (TTAB 1979). See also infra fns 98, 129 and 157 in Ch. 6. [EDITOR'S NOTE: The Board decision affirmed 209 USPQ 986 (CCPA 1981).]

a harsh rule. Arguably, there already are adequate bases for preventing clothing makers from trading on the good will of MONOPOLY, by using other indicia of the game, without foreclosing the use of (or refusing to register) the word simpliciter in a totally different manner.

### [d] Vitamin and Mineral Marks Including PLUS

In another seemingly close case, the prior user (and in some cases, supplemental registrant) of FE-PLUS, MG-PLUS, CA-PLUS, ZN-PLUS and MN-PLUS for mineral supplement pills, canceled a supplemental registration of K-PLUS for the same goods.[30] FE, MG, CA, ZN, MN and K are, respectively, the chemical symbols for iron, magnesium, calcium, zinc, manganese and potassium, each of which was the principal mineral supplement contained in the product bearing its symbol. The earlier user had plans to adopt K-PLUS also, but was beaten to the market.

The Board began with "skepticism and doubt" that one could form a family of marks consisting of generic chemical formulae and the highly suggestive word PLUS. Taking into consideration the prior user's intent to adopt such a series of marks to take advantage of the recognition of each mark, advertisement of the products together, long use, and no other readily recognizable source identification except the user's trade name, the Board concluded that it was "difficult to take a negative approach" to the claim of a family of marks. Even if a family of marks could not be established in such weak marks, the Board held that each mark individually was deserving of protection, and that K-PLUS was prohibited "not necessarily because it has used the [generic] chemical formula for potassium, per se, or the word 'PLUS,' per se, but because it has combined them in the same man-

[30] Medical Modalities Associates, Inc. v. ARA Corp., 203 USPQ 295 (TTAB 1979). See also supra fns 19 in Ch. 2 and 1 in Ch. 4 and infra fns 56, 66, 103 and 127 in Ch. 6.

§5.02[2][d] / Trademark Law

ner as petitioner has."[31] It is somewhat difficult to see how else they could be combined to convey the same message (PLUS K seems substantially different) except by addition of a house mark of some sort. Quite properly, the Board did not attempt to circumscribe the protection afforded petitioner's PLUS marks. Nevertheless, the question is interesting. Purported third party use or registration of other PLUS marks was held irrelevant because those parties were not in privity with registrant, and petitioner's only duty was to establish superior rights against the registrant, not the world.

The owner of another PLUS mark fared less well. The reasons for holding NATURE'S PLUS for vitamins not confusingly similar to the previously used PLUS, also for vitamins, were: (1) PLUS by its nature was a very weak, laudatory mark that had been registered as part of a mark eight times before, and seven times after, opposer's registration; and (2) NATURE'S was not mere surplusage in terms of commercial impression, but instead conveyed the meaning of something added from nature, while PLUS simply conveyed an impression of high quality.[32] Opposer had previously lost oppositions to PROTEIN PLUS for cereal and to NATURE PLUS for bread and cereal, and a declaratory judgment action against ACEROLA PLUS. It had prevailed against EARTH PLUS vitamins when the Board resolved doubts against the newcomer, but this time the Board eschewed any doubt. Most interesting was the Board's observation that the existing third party registrations justified three inferences: (1) opposer was satisfied to register PLUS alongside such existing marks as VITAMINS PLUS; (2) the PTO had long registered PLUS marks if there was some difference, even such non-distinctive differences at VITAMIN; and (3) a number of owners believed that such different PLUS marks could coexist without likelihood of confusion.

[31] Id at 302.
[32] Plus Products v. Natural Organics, Inc., 204 USPQ 773 (TTAB 1979). See also infra fns 47, 90, 98, 101, 109 and 123 in Ch. 6.

## [e] Health Care Marks

In still another interesting, health-related case, the Board held NEUROPAC confusingly similar to the previously used and registered NEUROMOD. Both were used for biomedical devices known as neurological stimulating appliances, or, sometimes, neuropacers.[33] The goods were similar, albeit not identical, moved through the same trade channels and were marketed in the same way to the same class of customers for the same purpose. The basis for the decision seemed to be a marriage of the doctrine of greater care with respect to medicines and medical products with the principle of resolving doubts about likelihood of confusion against newcomers. The marks seemed to be sufficiently different so that if used for other products, the Board might have tolerated coexistence. Acknowledging that purchasers were sophisticated medically, the Board pointed out that such people are not immune from trademark confusion. NEURO was a common formative in the field, and third party registrations were competent to show that the PTO did not regard the common presence of NEURO per se to generate likelihood of confusion. The suffixes, however, PAC suggesting package and MOD suggesting module, gave the marks sufficient connotational similarity so the Board had "serious misgivings" as to whether the marks differed sufficiently to avoid confusion.

In its simplest form, the justification for the rule of greater care is that with medicines and the like, mistakes can maim or kill. The statute, however, does not distinguish. Likelihood of confusion between medicines and fly swatters is equally forbidden. While there can be no quarrel with the humanitarian motive underlying the doctrine of greater care for such products, the negative implication—that since confusion is less harmful for other products, some can be permitted and more lax standards applied in judging likeli-

[33] Medtronic, Inc. v. Medical Devices, Inc., 204 USPQ 317 (TTAB 1979). See also supra fns 25 in Ch. 3 and 2 in this chapter and infra fns 122 and 137 in Ch. 6.

§5.02[2][f] / Trademark Law

hood of confusion—seems contrary to the statute and inimical to the commercial purposes of the Act.

Without reference to the doctrine of greater care, the Board held that ADD-A-LINE for parental solution administration sets was confusingly similar to the previously used and registered ADD-A-FLOW for control valve and extension tube for directing the flow of parenteral fluids.[34] The goods were closely related, used in conjunction with each other in hospitals, and moved through similar marketing channels to common potential purchasers. Similarity of meaning and overall commercial impression struck the Board. It noted: (1) no matter how weak a mark, if registered, it still must be protected from registration of other marks that would result in likelihood of confusion; (2) doubts should be resolved against applicant, who failed to introduce testimony to support its pleading of no likelihood of confusion; and (3) in the absence of evidence of the extent of applicant's use, absence of evidence of confusion was particularly immaterial, because there was no way of assessing the opportunities for confusion.

[f] The Barber Pole Case

THE BARBER POLE for teaching, instructing and consulting with reference to hair care services was held confusingly similar to a series of previously used and registered marks comprising THE BARBERS and a very stylized barber pole design for essentially similar services and hair care products.[35] Both parties appeared to be in the business of operating (fancy) barber shops and instructing others how to do so. The prior user undoubtedly had built a reputation, though its mark perhaps was less than a household word, even in the barbering business. While the decision resolved doubts against the newcomer, and stressed that it viewed

[34] American Hospital Supply Corp. v. Baxter Travenol Laboratories, Inc., 202 USPQ 226 (TTAB 1979).

[35] Barbers, Hairstyling for Men & Women, Inc. v. Barber Pole, Inc., 204 USPQ 403 (TTAB 1979). See also infra fns 157 and 164 in Ch. 6.

## CCPA and PTO Interpretations / §5.02[2][g]

the marks in their entireties, it avoided one provocative issue—whether or not anyone can appropriate BARBER or a barber pole for such services. BARBER obviously is generic for barber shop services, and is extraordinarily highly descriptive for a closely related instructional service, if not generic. So is a barber pole. Absent an overwhelming showing of secondary meaning, both seemingly should be publici juris. It is difficult to see how one could venture much further from THE BARBERS and a barber pole design than THE BARBER POLE without avoiding what seems to be in the public domain—BARBER and the pole.

### [g] Actual Confusion Not Determinative

AMICA for perfume and eye makeup removal pads was held not to be confusingly similar to the previously registered mark AMICA for insurance services and for various promotional goods for those services including publications, lighters and matches, key chains, ball point pens, pocket knives, folders and clipboards.[36] With the identity of marks, the reason was difference of products. The main obstacle to the holding was the existence of ten letters over five years apparently evidencing actual confusion. In light of receipt of a million or so letters a year (presumably most relating to insurance), the Board chose to regard this quantum as de minimus and of no legal significance. Opposer's use and promotion of AMICA undoubtedly gave it an "umbrella" of protection, but third party registrations and use, and the fact that cosmetics were not normal promotional goods for insurance services, persuaded the Board that cosmetics were not covered by that "umbrella." The actual confusion seemed still to bother the Board, for it returned to the topic:

> ... some few people, on occasion, appear to be confused. This is somewhat inevitable in many situations for, while the average consumer exercises due care in

[36] Amica Mutual Insurance Co. v. R. H. Cosmetics Corp., 204 USPQ 155 (TTAB 1979). See also supra fn 5 in Ch. 2 and infra fn 28 in Ch. 6.

§5.02[2][h] / Trademark Law

> making purchases, there are no doubt careless or inattentive buyers who must face the consequence of their acts and not have them control or dictate a decision in a proceeding of this character.[37]

However, one would not expect the average "careless or inattentive buyer" to pen a letter of complaint. That ten did so, even over a period of five years, suggests that the amount of confusion may not have been limited to the "careless or inattentive."

Another case also noted that some actual confusion, if properly proven (which it was not in that case) could be dismissed as de minimus in the context of the total operations of the parties.[38] Despite this, PROFESSIONAL ECONOMIC SERVICES was held confusingly similar to the previously used PROFESSIONAL ECONOMICS INCORPORATED when both were used for rendering various consulting economic services to such professionals as doctors.

[h] The "Reaction Factor" Test

HULA HAND for cosmetic skin cream was held confusingly similar to the previously registered HULA TAN ("tan" disclaimed) for suntan preparation.[39] With no record other than opposer's registration to work from, the Board viewed the products as related toiletries moving through the same outlets to the same class of purchasers. It concluded, given the descriptive or suggestive nature of HAND and TAN, that HULA constituted the "reaction factor" of both marks —that is, it served as "the essential recognition element

---

[37] Id at 166.

[38] Professional Economics Inc. v. Professional Economics Services, Inc., 205 USPQ 368, 371–72 (TTAB 1979). See also supra fns 18 in Ch. 2, 7 in Ch. 3 and 2 in Ch. 4 and infra fn 8 in Ch. 6.

[39] Royal Hawaiian Perfumes, Ltd. v. Diamond Head Products of Hawaii, Inc., 204 USPQ 144 (TTAB 1979). See also supra fn 41 in Ch. 3 and infra fns 44, 48, 84 and 89 in Ch. 6.

triggered" by both marks.[40] Because of their descriptive or suggestive connotations for their respective goods, TAN and HAND did not diminish any substantial similarity attributable to HULA; indeed, the marks in their entireties suggested a tanning lotion and hand cream from a common source. The mode of analysis of the similarities and differences of the two marks is interesting, perhaps more for its unusual phraseology than intellectual content.

### [i] Refusal to Register Marks that Can Be Used

Two cases reflect the Board's refusal to sully the purity of the Register by reflecting actual rights to use. In one, RICHARD BERTRAM & CO./YACHTS and eagle design for yacht repair, maintenance, docking and brokerage services was held confusingly similar to the previously registered BERTRAM and eagle design for boats and ships.[41] Contributing to this obvious conclusion were: (1) the marks had a common origin, (2) the applicant had been the builder's dealer, and (3) other of the builder's dealers were authorized to use BERTRAM for their boatyard activities. While there was evidently no doubt that both had rights to use as a result of past agreements, the Board refused to permit separately-owned registrations of two confusingly similar marks merely to reflect rights to use.

In the other, ARBY'S roast beef restaurants and ABBY'S pizza restaurants had begun about the same time and coexisted since the mid sixties, two outlets within a few hundred yards of each other since 1975, with no known confusion.[42] Nevertheless, when registration was sought of ABBY'S, it was opposed by the owner of ARBY'S. The Board acknowledged that confusion did not appear to be occurring in the real world, apparently due to use of distinctively different

[40] Id at 148.
[41] In re Richard Bertram & Co., 203 USPQ 286 (TTAB 1979). See also infra fns 119 this chapter and 9 in Ch. 6.
[42] Arby's, Inc. v. Abby's Pizza Inns, 205 USPQ 762 (TTAB 1980). See also supra fn 17 in Ch. 2 and infra fns 47, 63, 157 and 164 in Ch. 6.

§5.02[2][j] / Trademark Law

signs and the different types of restaurant, but that the word marks ARBY'S and ABBY'S simpliciter were too similar to register for identical (restaurant) services.

[j]   Magazine Trademarks

Three cases dealt with trademarks for magazines. In the first, the Board found confusing similarity "doubtful" between MAN'S DAY and WOMAN'S DAY, and for applicant prevailed on grounds of acquiescence.[43] One factor giving rise to doubt was proven coexistence on newsstands of such titles as PLAYBOY/PLAYGIRL, APARTMENT LIVING/ APARTMENT LIFE and WOMAN'S DAY/WOMAN TO-DAY. Magazine readers, one surmises, must be a wary bunch. Another factor was the WOMAN'S DAY publisher's knowledge and encouragement of the development of MAN'S DAY. As Board Member Fowler put it:

> If Fawcett Publications, over such a long period of time did not regard its mark "WOMAN'S DAY" and applicant's mark MAN'S DAY to be confusingly similar . . . who are we to say that [they are?].[44]

In another, OUTDOOR SPORT for magazines was held to be confusingly similar to the previously registered and widely used OUTDOOR LIFE.[45] The reasoning, which is interesting is: (a) since OUTDOOR was highly suggestive, if not descriptive, its presence in both marks could not, per se, create confusion; (b) the marks, however, had to be considered in their entireties, so OUTDOOR could not be ignored; (c) while SPORT and LIFE presented no conflict, prefacing each with OUTDOOR gave each a new dimension, and brought "the marks as a whole into the same 'ballpark.' "[46]

[43] CBS Inc. v. Man's Day Publishing Co., Inc., 205 USPQ 470 (TTAB 1980). See also supra fn 22 in Ch. 2 and infra fns 20 and 47 in Ch. 6.
[44] Id at 476.
[45] Times Mirror Magazines, Inc. v. Sutcliffe, 205 USPQ 656 (TTAB 1979). See also supra fn 7 in Ch. 2 and infra fns 92 and 157 in Ch. 6.

Finally, the owners of VOGUE magazine, which customarily featured material and advertising on travel, had a travel editor and distributed travel information and brochures, successfully opposed registration of VOGUE for travel agency services.[47] The decision is notable for its compendium of authorities in which magazine titles have been protected against activity in other areas.

### [k] Carpet Cleaning Products

Somewhat improbably, two cases were decided involving marks for various carpet cleaning products. In the first, the registrant, and prior user, of SPIN KLEAN for carpet scrubbing pads successfully petitioned to cancel SPEED CLEAN for carpet cleaning pads and SPEED-CLEAN for carpet cleaning chemical and conditioning solution.[48] Since the goods and trade channels were the same or closely related, the issue was similarity of the marks. Registrant, predictably, argued that in view of the weakness of SPIN KLEAN, the marks were distinguishable. Board Member Fowler dealt with the argument in textbook fashion for such situations (at least where the result is a holding of likelihood of confusion):

> Of paramount importance in considering the marks before me is not the fact that they both possess the descriptive word "CLEAN" or its phonetic equivalent "KLEAN," and also the suggestive and/or descriptive terms "SPEED" or "SPIN," but the effect of the overall commercial impression derived by viewing the marks as a whole.
>
> In comparing the respondent's marks "SPEED CLEAN" and "SPEED-CLEAN" with petitioner's mark "SPIN KLEAN," not only do we find the marks

---

[46] Id at 662.

[47] Conde Nast Publications, Inc. v. Vogue Travel, Inc., 205 USPQ 579 (TTAB 1979). See also infra fn 114 in Ch. 6.

[48] South Eastern Cordage Co. v. Tu-Way Products Co., 203 USPQ 221 (TTAB 1979). See also infra fns 27 and 105 in Ch. 6.

§5.02[2][k] / Trademark Law

as a whole to be similar in sound and appearance, but we note that they also possess a somewhat similar connotation in that the words "SPEED" and "SPIN" both denote the action of "moving swiftly."[49]

Even weak marks were held entitled to protection against confusingly similar marks. Absence of evidence of confusion was discounted because there was insufficient evidence of "what opportunity has existed for confusion to arise if it was going to," because "evidence of actual confusion is notoriously hard to come by,"[50] and because Section 2(d) requires only a likelihood of confusion.

One can question that in such cases connotational similarity is sufficient. Weak marks seem deserving of some protection, but what makes them weak usually is that they connote attributes which all should be free to connote. Here, SPEED CLEAN, with or without hyphen, and SPIN KLEAN are hard to differentiate and it would seem that they easily could be confused by those with everyday recollections of trademarks. WHIRL KLEAN, RAPID KLEAN or TURBO KLEAN, however, probably should escape due to visual and auditory differences despite connotational similarity.

In the second, RINSENVAC for carpet rinsing machines and chemicals was held not to be confusingly similar to the earlier registered and used SPRAY 'N VAC for aerosol carpet cleaners.[51] The case, a consolidated opposition and cancellation proceeding, involved two successful merchants of two obviously similar products that moved through similar, and sometimes the same, trade channels. Conceding that because the goods were not precisely described in the respective registrations and applications they had to be considered legally identical, the Board "opted" for the "practical" approach of considering market place realities.

[49] Id at 224.
[50] Ibid.
[51] Glamorene Products Corp. v. Earl Grissmer Co., Inc., 203 USPQ 1090 (TTAB 1979). See also infra fns 94, 98, 102, 116, and 140 in Ch. 6.

These, the Board decided, were that SPRAY 'N VAC was a light spray carpet cleaner that the user vacuumed up, while RINSENVAC was a heavy chemical carpet cleaner system that consumers rented. There was almost no likelihood either would use its mark on the other's product. VAC too was commonly used as an abbreviation for vacuum. Both marks were so strongly suggestive for their respective products, and composed of such readily recognizable and remembered words, that the Board concluded that customers would distinguish them. The Board seemed particularly impressed by the fact that with over twenty-five million cans of SPRAY 'N VAC sold and nearly a million RINSENVAC rentals—often through the same stores—there was no evidence of confusion known to either party.

The result seems most supportable on the basis of the weakness of the marks (and, perhaps, on the failure of the owners of SPRAY 'N VAC to act sooner). If one assumes SPRAY 'N VAC to be a valid mark for the aerosol spray and vacuum carpet cleaner, it seems not unlikely that consumers would suppose that RINSENVAC would be a complementary rinsing and vacuuming process for cleaning carpets. As the Board often says, confusion is awfully difficult to discern; particularly is this so in cases such as this where the products are indirectly, not directly, competitive. These marks look very much like companion marks for complementary products. The public probably will distinguish the products, but it will not necessarily attribute them to different producers.

### [l] Food Products

The Board faced arguments of likelihood of confusion in six cases involving products found on supermarket shelves:

1. SWEET & SLIM for an artificial sweetening compound was held confusingly similar to SWEET'N LOW for low calorie sugar substitute.[52] SWEET'N LOW was an enormously

[52] Cumberland Packing Corp. v. American Sweetener Corp., 203 USPQ 292 (TTAB 1979). See also infra fn 83 in Ch. 6.

§5.02[2][l] / Trademark Law

successful trademark, enjoying annual sales of fifty million dollars and having multimillion dollar advertising support. Complicating opposer's case was that it had previously lost oppositions to SWEET & KIRK[53] and SWEET 'N LEGAL (for dieting frozen desserts).[54] Helping it was the fact that the stylized "S" used by applicant bore a suspiciously close resemblance to the musical clef invariably used on SWEET'N LOW packaging. Opposer had also sometimes used the word "slimming" to describe the effect of its product.

Board Chairman Lefkowitz rationalized the result in language that expresses the Board's thinking in such cases with uncommon clarity:

> ... In this regard, the Board must make a subjective opinion as to the reaction of purchasers and prospective purchasers to applicant's "SWEET & SLIM" product after many years of exposure to opposer's "SWEET'N LOW" artificial sweetener and the extensive promotional effort behind the product. In making this determination there are a number of basic factors or principles that must be cranked into this adjudication process, namely the recognition that the average purchaser's recognition of the marks that he or she encounters in the marketplace and advertising media is often imprecise as to details retaining but a vague and general or overall recognition of the marks with the result that there is a tendency for individuals to equate a new mark or experience with one that they long have experienced without making an effort to ascertain whether or not they are the same marks and the recognition that it is generally the initial impact of a mark that projects the commercial impression.[55]

[53] Cumberland Packing Corp. v. Alberto-Culver Company, 172 USPQ 414 (TTAB 1971), discussed in 62 TMR 441 fn 223.
[54] Cumberland Packing Corp. v. McMahani Products, Inc., 189 USPQ 428 (TTAB 1976).
[55] Supra fn 52 this chapter at 294–95.

It seemed clear to the Board that this was a case of sufficient pointers of similarity to SWEET'N LOW to confuse customers combined with enough differences to attempt (in vain) to confuse the trier of fact.

2. Registration of KAL KAN MEALTIME WITH TAIL-WAGGIN' TASTE FOR DOGS for dog food was successfully opposed by the registrant and user of IT'S A REAL "TAIL WAGGER" and TAIL WAGGER for dog food.[56] Applicant disclaimed "for dogs" and evidently owned separate registrations of KAL KAN and MEALTIME.

The Board initially focussed upon the WITH TAIL WAGGIN' TASTE portion of the applied-for mark to find that both parties' marks communicated to buyers the same critical sales message. Arguing the TAIL-WAGGER or its ilk were merely descriptive was unavailing for two reasons: applicant had not disclaimed TAIL-WAGGIN', and the Board did not think that it was descriptive. Applicant then advanced the not implausible argument that inclusion of its registered marks KAL KAN and MEALTIME in the entire mark obviated likelihood of confusion. Not so, said the Board, because the well-known tendency of consumers to shorten or abbreviate names could result in purchase of either for the other. A number of third party registrations were rejected as distinguishable and not pertinent anyway, since registration was not evidence of use or of impression made on the public by the mark.

3. LEMON MIST ("lemon" disclaimed) was found not to be confusingly similar to the previously registered and extensively used LEMON LIFT ("lemon" also disclaimed) for tea.[57] The differences of goods were immaterial; both parties had considerable use as a part of a line of teas, each variety of which apparently was sold under a common house mark. A number of market place purchases, made of record, convinced the Board that consumers were accustomed to

---

[56] Allied Mills, Inc. v. Kal Kan Foods, Inc., 203 USPQ 390, 396 (TTAB 1979). See also supra fn 24 in Ch. 3 and infra fn 62 in Ch. 6.

[57] R. C. Bigelow, Inc. v. Celestial Seasonings, Inc., 203 USPQ 542 (TTAB 1979). See also supra fn 1 this chapter and infra fn 95 in Ch. 6.

§5.02[2][l] / Trademark Law

prominent descriptive uses of LEMON. These uses, plus third party registrations, justified the inference that the commercial judgment of business people was that inclusion of LEMON, on products and in trademarks, was possible without creating likelihood of confusion.

The Board held LIFT and MIST readily distinguishable, but conceded that it must consider the marks in their entireties. So doing, the Board found "no connotative resemblance between LEMON LIFT and LEMON MIST." Because each sold its tea largely in self-service outlets and from displays, the Board considered visual similarity more important than auditory. (That neither application nor registration limited the goods to those sold through such channels was ignored.) Because LEMON was so widely used in the market place, the Board felt consumers would focus, at least subconsciously, on the LIFT and MIST features of each mark. Similarly, it felt that in normal speech, the accent fell on the last word of each mark.

4. Registration of CAPTN'S PICK for fish and seafood mail order services was successfully opposed by the long time user and registrant of CAPTAIN'S CHOICE ("choice" disclaimed in one registration) for frozen fish and shellfish.[58] There were third party registrations of CAPT'N BENNY, CAPT'N BOB, CAPT'N PRIDE, CAPT'N FAVORITE and CAPT'S BEST. The two marks in issue, however, considered in their entireties, were believed to project identical commercial impression of a captain's selection, which would be likely to confuse consumers with fallible memories. That CAPTAIN (or its equivalents) and CHOICE could not be the exclusive property of opposer did not matter; the whole mark was, and disclaimed or other weak portions could not be ignored, because the public saw the marks as they were without disclaimers. The Board noted that even applicant's services (selling fish by mail) were closely enough related to frozen seafood for confusion to be likely. Lack of actual

---

[58] Safeway Stores, Inc. v. Captn's Pick, Inc., 203 USPQ 1025 (TTAB 1979). See also infra fns 103 and 157 in Ch. 6.

confusion was irrelevant in the absence of a "track record" of contemporaneous use of both marks.

5. When the owner and prior registrant of VISTA and VISTA-PAK for cookies and crackers opposed registration of VISTA for fresh strawberries, avocados and vegetables, the Board faced the stark question whether or not the goods were so related that confusion was likely.[59] It decided that they were. Acknowledging that no rule of case law dictated that when different foods are sold under the same or similar marks confusion is likely, the Board pointed out that this was the frequent result in such cases. Here, it rested on similarity of goods, (foods), channels of trade and classes of purchasers. In addition, it considered produce and cookies or crackers to be complementary, since they could be eaten together.

6. KRAZY GLAZY ("glazy" disclaimed), registered for toaster pasties, was held not to be confusingly similar to the previously used and registered CRAZY, CRAZY CONES, -CUPS and -PACKS for ice cream cones.[60] What persuaded the Board was the difference in the goods (and perhaps the sheer artificiality of petitioner's argument that the goods were so similar), the alternative, distinguishing character of KRAZY GLAZY, and a number of third party registrations showing CRAZY to be a popular component of food marks. That both would be sold in supermarkets impressed the Board not at all, because modern grocers sell so many different products.

[m] **Health and Beauty Aids**

AMOROUS for cologne was held to be confusingly similar to the previously registered and used AMOUR AMOUR for a line of toiletries including eau de cologne.[61] Holding that

[59] Midwest Biscuit Co. v. John Livacich Produce, Inc., 203 USPQ 628 (TTAB 1979). See also infra fns 85 and 98 in Ch. 6.

[60] Safe-T Pacific Co. v. Nabisco, Inc., 204 USPQ 307 (TTAB 1979). See also supra fns 27 in Ch. 2 and 26 in Ch. 3 and infra fns 51 and 124 in Ch. 6.

[61] Jean Patou, Inc. v. Aristocrat Products Corp., 202 USPQ 130 (TTAB 1979). See also supra fn 29 in Ch. 2 and infra fns 7, 100 and 157 in Ch. 6.

§5.02[2][m] / Trademark Law

the marks differed visually but were "substantially similar in sound," the Board relied on the common general connotation—love—of the two marks. This was said to be particularly significant when "the fallibility of memory over a period of time" of the average purchasers was considered, since he (or she) normally retained a general rather than specific recollection of trademarks. Lack of evidence of actual confusion was dismissed not only as irrelevant because the test is likelihood of confusion, but also as perhaps explicable by differences in types of cologne and channels of trade which "may have helped to prevent confusion." Since these differences previously had been dismissed as factors in judging likelihood of confusion, the Board quickly added that if registration were granted for colognes, registrant would be free to change its product to eliminate the differences at any time.

Use of MENNEN since 1878 as a trademark and trade name for a wide variety of toiletries including toilet soap, over $360 million in advertising and promotion since 1930, and over a billion dollars of sales in that period, persuaded the Board that the original surname MENNEN had become a "celebrated trademark."[62] That conclusion seems reasonable. Because the average consumer's recollection of trademarks is not infallible, the Board was persuaded that MINON for toilet soap would be confusingly similar to MENNEN.

WELLCOME was used as part of the trade name BURROUGHS-WELLCOME and as part of the trademark for, or the mark for, several drugs and pharmaceuticals. One was WELLCOME brand lanoline sold over the counter. Use was long standing, extensive and well-supported by advertising. Such use was sufficient to result in cancellation of WELCOME TOUCH and WELCOME FEELING for hand lotion,[63] and in a successful opposition to registration of

---

[62] Mennen Co. v. Yamanouchi Pharmaceutical Co., Ltd., 203 USPQ 302 (TTAB 1979). See also infra fns 83, 135 and 137 in Ch. 6.

[63] Burroughs Wellcome Co. v. Warner-Lambert Co., 203 USPQ 191 (TTAB 1979). See also supra fn 35 in Ch. 2 and infra fns 21 and 102 in Ch. 6.

WELCOME RELIEF for medicated lotion for dry, chapped skin.[64]

Registration of a design mark dominated by HEAD START above the smaller COSVETIC for hair conditioning vitamins, hair conditioner and shampoo was refused in light of an existing registration for HEAD START, originally for men's hair lotion and after shave but renewed only for after shaving lotion.[65] The goods were all toiletries (except applicant's hair vitamins) moving through similar trade channels, and the marks were considered not to be different enough to avoid confusion.

FLOSSAID and FLOSSMATE for dental floss holders were considered not to be confusingly similar, since even in their entireties, the marks were distinguishable from each other, the only common element being the generic term "floss."[66]

LLOYD'S OF LONDON after shave or perfume was held likely to be mistakenly associated with the world-famous insurers.[67] The holding was made only as a back-up to a finding of false suggestion or connection under Section 2(a).

[n] The Automotive After-Market

CW within a circle for vehicle wheels was held not to be confusingly similar to the famous VOLKSWAGEN "VW" within a circle.[68] While Volkswagen did offer the same goods under its mark, its inability to claim rights in the common circle made its cause difficult. Its argument that if

---

[64] Burroughs Wellcome Co. v. Warner-Lambert Co., 203 USPQ 201 (TTAB 1979). See also supra fn 35 in Ch. 2 and infra fns 21, 45 and 102 in Ch. 6

[65] In re Cosvetic Laboratories, Inc., 202 USPQ 842 (TTAB 1979). See also infra fns 121 this chapter, 12 and 153 in Ch. 6.

[66] Floss Aid Corp. v. John O. Butler Co., 205 USPQ 274 (TTAB 1979). See also supra fns 26 in Ch. 2 and 23 in Ch. 3 and infra fns 54, 102 and 170 in Ch. 6

[67] Corp. of Lloyd's v. Louis D'Or of France, Inc., 202 USPQ 313 (TTAB 1979). See also supra fn 3 this chapter and infra fn 128 in Ch. 6.

[68] Volkswagenwerk Ag v. Clement Wheel Co., Inc., 204 USPQ 76 (TTAB 1979). See also infra fns 69 and 157 in Ch. 6.

§5.02[2][n] / Trademark Law

VOLKSWAGEN dealers dealt in opposer's goods there would be confusion was met by the Board's observation that the confusion would arise from the dealer's display of the VW marks, not from use of the opposed mark on the goods. Such confusion the Board was powerless to prevent. Volkswagen's argument that on the goods the CW logo could be illegible was found unsupported by proof that the mark was illegible and rejected even if proven. "If a viewer could not make out what applicant's mark is, how could that viewer confuse it with opposer's mark? The answer is self-evident."[69] Actually, the Board's answer may be unfair; the risk is that applicant's mark would be unclear enough to be mistaken, but not totally obliterated. The mistake, though, would seem to have to arise from the circle, which is unprotectable per se. Phonetic similarity was considered unimportant for these goods, since they must be carefully inspected before purchase. Since neither mark had any intrinsic meaning, there was no connotational similarity.

In a case involving steel belted radial tires, the Board canceled registrations of STEELEX LUG RADIAL and STEELEX LPT RADIAL, and sustained opposition to STEELEX RADIAL.[70] Everything but STEELEX was disclaimed. Petitioner-opposer in this consolidated proceeding had made long and extensive use of the registered trademark X, in recent years exclusively for steel belted radials. The Board stated that the general rule that marks must be considered in their entireties "is not inviolate." One or more parts of a mark could become dominant either in presentation or because the remainder was merely descriptive or otherwise so lacking in appeal as to make little impact. What dominated the STEELEX marks was STEELEX. The Board felt customers asking for, or familiar with, the famous X steel tires might believe STEELEX tires were the same ones,

[69] Id at 86.
[70] Michelin Tire Corp. v. General Tire & Rubber Co., 202 USPQ 294 (TTAB 1979). See also supra fns 34 in Ch. 2 and 5 in Ch. 3 and infra fn 165 in Ch. 6.

since the two marks evoked the same commerical impression.

DIAMOND, registered for tires, barred registration of RED DIAMOND for storage batteries.[71] The opinion belabored the obvious—both products were automotive vehicle replacement parts, moving through the same trade channels to the same potential purchasers.

[o] **Store Names**

WIN-WAY DOLLAR STORE, with "dollar store" disclaimed, were held confusingly similar to the previously registered and used WINN'S, both for retail variety store services.[72] Deciding that because the advertising of both variety store chains played on the word "win," WIN was dominant in applicant's mark, the Board resolved doubts against the newcomer to sustain the opposition.

PLAQUE VILLAGE and PLAK-SHACK were held not confusingly similar for stores selling, and instructing customers how to decorate, plaster lamps and wall plaques.[73] Plaque was undoubtedly the common descriptive name of the plaques each business sold, so PLAQUE and PLAK would be given little weight in analyzing the marks; consumers would give such terms little or no significance as an indication of origin. Since SHACK and VILLAGE lacked visual, aural or connotational similarity, the Board believed confusion unlikely.

[p] **Discriminating Consumers**

In another dispute involving service marks, LOGISTI-

[71] In re Red Diamond Battery Co., 203 USPQ 472 (TTAB 1979). See also infra fn 154 in Ch. 6.
[72] Winn's Stores, Inc. v. Hi-Lo, Inc., 203 USPQ 140 (TTAB 1979). See also infra fns 38 and 97 in Ch. 6.
[73] Plak-Shack, Inc. v. Continental Studios of Georgia, Inc., 204 USPQ 242 (TTAB 1979). See also supra fn 21 in Ch. 2 and infra fns 40, 47, 136 and 169 in Ch. 6. The Board adhered to this conclusion on reconsideration, 204 USPQ 1059 (TTAB 1979). See also infra fn 134 in Ch. 6.

§5.02[2][q] / Trademark Law

CON and LOGICON were held not to be confusingly similar for services in the computerized materials handling systems business.[74] Both systems were costly—costing up to millions of dollars per installation—and obviously would be bought carefully by highly sophisticated customers who would have ample opportunity to discover the differences between the two marks. Given the difference in sound, appearance and meaning—LOGICON obviously was derived from "logic"; LOGISTICON from "logistics"—the complexity of the services persuaded the Board that confusion was unlikely.

[q] Miscellaneous

VITTORIO RICCI for sweaters, belts, neckties, shoes and women's blouses was held confusingly similar to the registered mark NINA RICCI (for perfumes, toiletries and women's hosiery, lingerie, brassieres, girdles, shoes, hats, scarves and ties). Also registered by opposer were MADEMOISELLE RICCI (for women's hats, coats, dresses, hosiery, lingerie, brassieres, girdles, scarves and ties), SIGNORICCI (for perfumes, toilet waters, ties, neckware and handkerchiefs) and CAPRICCI (for perfumes and toilet waters).[75] NINA RICCI and the unregistered RICCI had been used and advertised for some time. Some use of the other RICCI marks appeared. All of opposer's registrations had coexisted with a third party registration of ROBERT RICCI (which was not renewed) for women's and misses' cloaks, dresses, gowns, slacks, suits, vests and two-piece suits.

Persuaded that NINA RICCI had acquired "fame, prestige and reputation" in the ladies' apparel field, the Board held that RICCI had become a valuable property of opposer. Any weakness that had initially attached to the surname RICCI was overcome by statutory presumptions, incontesta-

[74] Logicon, Inc. v. Logisticon, Inc., 205 USPQ 767 (TTAB 1980). See also infra fns 113, 115 and 119 in Ch. 6.
[75] Nina Ricci, S.A.R.L. v. ETF Enterprises, Inc., 203 USPQ 947 (TTAB 1979). See also infra fn 47 in Ch. 6.

## CCPA and PTO Interpretations / §5.02[2][q]

bility of the registrations and long use. Since the goods were obviously related, if not identical, the Board held that any other RICCI mark would risk consumer confusion.

In a cancellation proceeding, CRYSTAL-AQUA for swimming pool water treatment chlorine and chlorine stabilizer, which was an algaecide product, was held confusingly similar to the previously used CRYSTAL ALGAECIDE for swimming pool water treatment.[76] Because ALGAECIDE was descriptive, the Board concluded that CRYSTAL dominated the prior mark, and concluded that the marks for the products conveyed essentially the same meaning and created substantially similar commercial impressions. Third party registrations and directory listings were irrelevant because they did not establish use (and were off target where the two products were for use in swimming pools), and absence of actual confusion was irrelevant in view of the difficulty in obtaining such evidence and evidently few sales in the same geographic area.

A TT logo mark for tubular metal products was held confusingly similar to the previously registered and extensively used "tt" for a wide range of metal products including tubular ones.[77] The record showed that some of the same or comparable goods were sold to the same general class of, and in some cases the same, customers. Fallibility of memory of design marks furnished the basis for the holding of likelihood of confusion. The fact that purchasers were discriminating was of no avail. Lack of actual confusion was held pertinent only where there is substantial contemporaneous use for some time and an opportunity for the purchasing public to be heard, neither of which was the case here.

In a case that turned on priority because opposer failed to prove its registrations, the record established opposer's first use of SG on office filing and related supplies, applicant's

---

[76] Malter International Corp. v. Bison Laboratories, Inc., 202 USPQ 188 (TTAB 1979). See also infra fns 29 and 50 in Ch. 6.

[77] Chemetron Corp. v. Morris Coupling and Clamp Co., 203 USPQ 537 (TTAB 1979). See also infra fn 108 in Ch. 6.

§5.02[2][q] / Trademark Law

intervening use of SG on photographic film and paper for use for blueprints and certain copying or stencil processes, and opposer's subsequent use of SG on copying and duplicating machines and supplies.[78] The Board held that filing supplies were not closely enough related to photographic film and paper to give opposer priority by the doctrine of natural expansion, and, in any event largely differing trade channels and characters of the goods avoided conflict between the marks.

The owner and long time user of NORDICA for ski boots succeeded in preventing registration of NS/NORIDIC SPORT design, with "nordic sport" disclaimed, for javelins, cross-bows, skis, ski poles, bindings and boots, and for ski wear clothing.[79] The fact "nordic sport" was disclaimed was of no help to applicant, since it was the dominant feature of the overall mark, and hence most likely to create an impression upon prospective purchases. Lack of evidence of actual confusion was dismissed as insignificant in view of applicant's relatively few sales for a brief period and the difficulty of obtaining evidence of actual confusion.

Because SUPER is obviously weak and was shown to be widely registered and used in the field of trade, SUPER-SAUNA for reducing undergarments was held not confusingly similar to SUPER LOOK or SUPER LOOK PLUS (or "+") for bras or panties.[80]

In a decision more interesting for the issues it ignored than for those it resolved,[81] the Board held CHIPPER for grinder attachments for removing paint, rust, scale, etc., to be confusingly similar to the previously registered CLIPPER for a number of tools, some of which could perform the

[78] Sheller-Globe Corp. v. Scott Paper Co., 204 USPQ 329 (TTAB 1979). See also supra fns 3 in Ch. 2 and 47 in Ch. 3 and infra fn 87 in Ch. 6.

[79] Nordica di Franco e Giovanni Vaccari & C. s.a.s. v. Nordic Sport Ltd., 202 USPQ 860 (TTAB 1979). See also infra fn 157 in Ch. 6.

[80] Menzies v. International Playtex, Inc., 204 USPQ 297 (TTAB 1979). See also infra fns 24, 34, 88, 118 and 133 in Ch. 6.

[81] See §3.02 at supra fn 15.

same task or be used to treat the same work surface.[82] The goods being so related, the aural similarity alone was sufficient to establish likelihood of confusion.

FINANCEAMERICA, actually used in the form "FinanceAmerica," for consumer and commercial loan and installment financing services at the wholesale and retail level was held confusingly similar to the long previously-used trade name THE FINANCE COMPANY OF AMERICA for commercial loan financing.[83] Buttressing opposer's case was considerable evidence of actual confusion reflected by misdirected mail and telephone calls. Applicant argued many things, including different services and association of this mark with its better known "BankAmerica" mark. The Board, however, passed judgment on the mark and description of services shown in the application.

### [3] TTAB Decisions—Reported in Digest

In decisions reported only in digest form, the Board held the following marks to be confusingly similar: FARMAX and FARMALL for farm tractors;[84] SHEEVA and SHEVELVA for fabrics and garments;[85] RANGER recreational vehicles and highway motor trucks;[86] LUXXTRA and LUXTROL for lighting fixtures;[87] DRY 'N FIRM and DRI-GRIP for material facilitating gripping of sports equipment;[88] SCOTT for Christmas trees and SCOTTS for lawn and garden products;[89] FAST FILL for gasoline station services and

[82] Norton Co. v. Talbert, 202 USPQ 542 (TTAB 1979). See also supra fn 15 in Ch. 3 and infra fns 43 and 47 in Ch. 6.
[83] Finance Co. of America v. BankAmerica Corp., 205 USPQ 1016 (TTAB 1980). See also infra fns 49, 121, 157 and 165 in Ch. 6.
[84] International Harvester Co. v. Oppenheimer-Farmax, Inc., 205 USPQ 679 (TTAB 1979).
[85] V.F. Corp. v. Collins & Aikman Corp., 205 USPQ 680 (TTAB 1979).
[86] In re Ranger Plastics Corp., 205 USPQ 680 (TTAB 1979).
[87] Superior Electric Co. v. LAM, Inc., 205 USPQ 680 (TTAB 1979).
[88] Salamon v. Claro Laboratories, Inc., 205 USPQ 968 (TTAB 1979).
[89] O. M. Scott & Sons Co. v. Scott Paper Co., 205 USPQ 968 (TTAB 1979).

§5.02[3] / Trademark Law

FILL-EM-FAST for petroleum products;[90] SSD or SSD-55 and SS-25 for degreasers;[91] LB with golf ball and tee design for girls' clothing and LB and dog's head design for girls' shoes;[92] BAJA for after shave and MAJA for perfume, cologne and face powders;[93] EASY RIDER for lawn mowers and E-Z RIDER for motor driven power scooters;[94] S. MARTINHO for wines and MARTINI or MARTINI & ROSSI for wines, vermouth, etc.;[95] MISS INTERNATIONALE TEEN-USA PAGEANT and MISS U.S.A. for beauty contests;[96] CODE FOUR for flashlights for police use and CODE 3 for police and emergency vehicle lighting equipment;[97] TECH STEREO for hi-fi and stereo retail store services and STEREOTECH for AM-FM radios;[98] MAPLECREST and design for lunch meats and MAPLECREST and MAPLECREST FARMS for fresh eggs, chickens and turkeys;[99] WINTER TAMER or SNOW TAMER and ROAD TAMER for tires;[100] THE MANNY SLACK and MANN for slacks;[101] BAREFOOT for retail clothing and sporting goods service and BAREFOOT ORIGINALS for women's shoes, slippers, boots, and insoles;[102] M/T CHALLENGER for shock ab-

---

[90] In re Standard Oil Co., 205 USPQ 949 (TTAB 1979).
[91] National Chemsearch Corp. v. State Chemical Mfg. Co., 205 USPQ 920 (TTAB 1979).
[92] The Juvenile Shoe Corp. of America v. General Mills, Inc., 205 USPQ 914 (TTAB 1979).
[93] Selected Creations Inc. v. Armour-Dial, Inc., 205 USPQ 696 (TTAB 1979).
[94] Alexander-Reynolds Corp. v. MTD Products, Inc., 205 USPQ 720 (TTAB 1979).
[95] Martini & Rossi Corp. v. Jose Agostinho Filhos & Ca., 205 USPQ 722 (TTAB 1979).
[96] Miss Universe, Inc. v. Miss Internationale Teen-USA Pageant & Scholarship Foundation, 205 USPQ 722 (TTAB 1979).
[97] Public Safety Equipment, Inc. v. L. A. Seven Products, Inc., 205 USPQ 827 (TTAB 1979).
[98] In re Rowe, 205 USPQ 872 (TTAB 1979).
[99] In re Maplecrest Sausage Co., Inc., 205 USPQ 1150 (TTAB 1979).
[100] In re J. C. Penney Co., Inc., 205 USPQ 1248 (TTAB 1979).
[101] Hortex, Inc. v. Manny Apparel Corp., 205 USPQ 1248 (TTAB 1979).
[102] In re Barefoot Sports, Inc., 205 USPQ 1248 (TTAB 1979).

## CCPA and PTO Interpretations / §5.02[3]

sorbers and CHALLENGER for exhaust system parts;[103] LOV and design for sugar-free confectionary and LOVE'S for bread;[104] HOT BUG for bait traps and pesticide holders and HOT SHOT for insecticides;[105] ESPRIT NOUVEAU and BRIE NOUVEAU for brie cheese;[106] GAS UR FAST and FAST GAS for gasoline services;[107] JOY and design for women's clothing and lingerie and JOY for hosiery;[108] PONY SHOP for retail toy stores and PONY TOYS for miniature playthings;[109] PAK-A-PAN for foil lined paper trays and PAN-PAK for paperboard cartons;[110] PLUS ULTRA and design for blouses, pants, suits, slacks, and pull-overs and ULTRA PRESS for shirts, pants, and jeans;[111] DOUBLE PLAY and design for boys' shirts and sweaters on the one hand and DOUBLE PLAY for such allegedly related goods as girdles and brassieres on the other;[112] and SAFARI INN for motorists' and campers' service facility and SAFARI for a resort hotel.[113]

Other decisions reported in digest form only held the following not to be confusingly similar: LAWN CARE magazine and TURF CARE herbicide;[114] ANTIPOL for designing services for plants and equipment for treating noxious effluents on the one hand and water system corrosion and fouling

---

[103] In re Mickey Thompson Products, Inc., 204 USPQ 906 (TTAB 1979).

[104] ITT Continental Baking Company v. Aktiebolaget Sunoco, 204 USPQ 938 (TTAB 1979).

[105] Conwood Corporation v. Lutes, 204 USPQ 941 (TTAB 1979).

[106] Lankor International, Inc. v. Otto Roth & Co., Inc., 204 USPQ 941 (TTAB 1979).

[107] In re Town and Country Food Markets, Inc., 204 USPQ 976 (TTAB 1979).

[108] In re Joy Shops, Inc., 205 USPQ 96 (TTAB 1979).

[109] In re F.A.O. Schwarz, 205 USPQ 290 (TTAB 1979).

[110] American Can Co. v. Hoerner Waldorf Corp., 203 USPQ 800 (TTAB 1979).

[111] Ely & Walker, Inc. v. Plus Ultra Corp., 203 USPQ 80 (TTAB 1979).

[112] In re Coral Industries, Inc., 204 USPQ 520 (TTAB 1979).

[113] Ramada Inns Inc. v. United Safari International, Inc., 202 USPQ 127 (TTAB 1978).

[114] O. M. Scott & Sons Co. v. Diamond Shamrock Corp., 205 USPQ 1086 (TTAB 1979).

§5.03 / Trademark Law

inhibitors on the other;[115] TANDEM for sets of carding machines and TANDEMATIC for units for controlling material processing through a closed loop;[116] SPORTS ELBOW and TENNIS ELBOW for jackets and sweaters on the one hand and ELBEO for knitted hosiery on the other;[117] and PONTET LATOUR for regional wines and GRAND VIN DE CHATEAU LATOUR or LES FORTS DE LATOUR for chateau wines.[118]

## §5.03 Letters of Consent

Richard Bertram started a yacht building, selling and servicing business. He transferred rights to build and sell yachts under the Bertram name to another, who registered BERTRAM and an eagle design for boats and ships. The original servicing business then applied to register RICHARD BERTRAM & CO./YACHTS and an eagle design for yacht maintenance and repair, yacht docking and yacht brokerage services. Registration, predictably, was refused under Section 2(d).[119]

Applicant petitioned to cancel the registration, lost, appealed and settled, apparently on a "live and let live" basis. Registrant furnished a consent stating that there was no conflict or confusion between the businesses, and consenting to registration. That was unavailing because it was considered to be a naked consent. Applicant had also licensed the boat building registrant, royalty free and in perpetuity, to authorize its dealers in BERTRAM yachts also to use BER-

---

[115] In re Institut Francais Du Petrole, Des Carburants et Lubrifiants, 205 USPQ 1150 (TTAB 1979).

[116] In re Crosrol Ltd., 205 USPQ 968 (TTAB 1979). See also supra fn 34 in Ch. 3.

[117] Elbeo G.m.b.H. v. McQuade Bloomhorst, Inc., 204 USPQ 520 (TTAB 1979).

[118] Societe Civile du Vignoble de Chateau Latour v. Societe Civile Agricole du Chateau Grant Pontet Domaine Baron et Guestier, 204 USPQ 520 (TTAB 1979), req for reconsid and mod 70 TMR 491 (September-October, 1980).

[119] In re Richard Bertram & Co., 203 USPQ 286 (TTAB 1979). See also supra fn 41 this chapter and infra fn 9 in Ch. 6.

## CCPA and PTO Interpretations / §5.03

TRAM for their boatyard services similar to those for which registration was sought. That, in the opinion of the Board, highlighted the likelihood of confusion.

The 1973 DuPont case[120] established that when an applied-for-mark appears to conflict with a previously registered one, a carefully drafted, detailed consent by registrant to applicant's registration and use will carry considerable weight. Conversely, it has now been held that a naked consent carries little weight.[121]

---

[120] In re E. I. du Pont de Nemours & Co., 476 F2d 1357, 177 USPQ 563 (CCPA 1973), discussed in 64 TMR 343 fn 44.

[121] In re Cosvetic Laboratories, Inc., 202 USPQ 842, 844 (TTAB 1979). See also supra fn 65 this chapter and infra fns 12 and 153 in Ch. 6.

CHAPTER 6

# Procedure

## §6.01 Inter Partes Proceedings

### [1] Res Judicata

The Court of Customs and Patent Appeals considered a case that began on Halloween, 1955 when an applicant sought to register WELLS CARGO for semi-trailers. The application was opposed by a party claiming prior use of WELLS CARGO for freight transportation services. The opposition was dismissed when applicant withdrew its application " 'with prejudice to its right to file a similar application . . . at a later date,' " opposer consenting. Twenty years later (less four months), applicant's successor reapplied and opposer reopposed. Both parties moved for summary judgment. Opposer won.[1]

The court disagreed with the Board's conclusion that the parties were bound by res judicata because there was no prior determination on the merits or judgment of any kind, both of which are prerequisites for res judicata. The talismanic phrase in situations where there is no judgment is "equitable estoppel." The heart of the doctrine is that "a party is estopped from asserting a right by an act causing his opponent to rely on a reasonable belief that the right has been abandoned."[2]

On appeal, applicant first argued that opposer should have litigated the earlier opposition to final judgment; but

[1] Wells Cargo, Inc. v. Wells Cargo, Inc., 606 F2d 961, 203 USPQ 564, 566 (CCPA 1979), affg 197 USPQ 569 (TTAB 1977), discussed in 68 TMR 742 fn 140.
[2] 203 USPQ at 567.

§6.01[1] / Trademark Law

"[c]ommon sense and considerations of judicial economy dictate that parties be not only permitted but encouraged to avoid needless litigation."[3] Next, applicant argued that promises not to register are inimical to a Principal Register of marks used in commerce. The Court pointed out that there is a "competing policy favoring voluntary settlement of actual disputes" and the latter policy prevailed. Finally, applicant urged that its continued use and advertising constituted a change of circumstances. Not sufficient to overcome its promise, said the court.

One can wonder if opposer's apparent acquiescence to twenty years' infringing use by applicant might not raise some sort of equitable estoppel to protest applicant's use. It should not, though, estop opposer from objecting to applicant's registration, which would give applicant prima facie rights of exclusivity.

In another previous opposition, General Electric, prior owner and registrant of FLAMENOL for electrical wires, cables, conductors and insulating or jacketing material, had barred registration of FLAMTROL for insulated wire. Applicant filed a new application for FLAMTROL for insulated wire designed solely for nuclear reactors and sold only to engineers for use on nuclear reactors.[4] GE opposed again, then moved for summary judgment on grounds of res judicata. The only difference between the first application and the second was the more limited description of goods in the second (and a different claimed date of use, which was of no moment). In fact, the applicant's goods had not changed, and before the first proceeding it had sold them to the limited market of nuclear engineers, among others.

The Board held that res judicata applied. In its view, the doctrine applied not only to the goods described in the first application, but to all goods encompassed within that description of goods. Since applicant could have sought to amend its description of goods in the earlier proceeding, the

---

[3] Id at 568.
[4] General Electric Co. v. Raychem Corp., 204 USPQ 148 (TTAB 1979). See also infra fns 18 and 160 this chapter.

present issue was considered to be one that could have been litigated earlier:

> To allow an applicant to avoid res judicata under these circumstances would be to put an opposer to the intolerable burden of facing a never-ending series of proceedings against an applicant who loses an opposition on a broad identification of goods and then proceeds to file successive applications for the same mark on narrow identifications of goods or on goods directed solely to one trade channel or another despite the fact that the mark was so used at the time of the first proceeding.[5]

The choice is less easy than the Board makes it seem. Applicant presumably had reasonable grounds for believing FLAMTROL and FLAMENOL sufficiently different to coexist. Had it given up the broad description, it might have surrendered that to which it was entitled. Had it conditionally amended to a narrower description then, assuming such a procedure would have been permitted, it would, practically, have confessed an uncertainty many lawyers are loath to acknowledge in litigation.

The decision confronts future applicants in similar situations with a difficult choice. While such applicants ought not to be allowed endless bites of the same apple, perhaps they should be allowed a second. Possibly the answer is that after losing the first opposition, applicant should have moved to amend its description of goods and moved for reconsideration. Such a procedure would have preserved applicant's right to contest the initial issue and to exercise his option to amend and contest that issue, while imposing minimal added burdens on opposer and the Board. Of course, that procedure would have put an applicant who sought to appeal the Board decision in an unusual—some would say compromising—posture on appeal.

Regulations of the Bureau of Alcohol, Tobacco and Fire-

[5] Id at 150.

§6.01[1] / Trademark Law

arms proscribe labeling that is misleading of origin. Does BATF approval bind the Board in a case involving alleged geographic misdescriptiveness of a liquor mark? The Board held that while normally it looks to the entire marketing environment, BATF approval of the labeling is "persuasive" that the label apart from the mark was not geographically misdescriptive, but that the Board would apply the statutory test and its own standards to determine the question.[6] The basis for this dichotomy was that only the brand name, not the entire label, was before the Board in the opposition, and it would not unnecessarily rule in apparent conflict with another agency. As a matter of comity, that seems reasonable. Possibly by "persuasive" the Board only meant that it was inclined to agree; precedent, even ex parte administrative precedent, can be "persuasive." If the Board meant that it was bound by the BATF determination, it would appear to be incorrect. At least absent verbatim identity of statutory standards of proscription, and perhaps even then, the Board would seem obligated to apply its own statute and principles to matters before it, whether or not a different agency purporting to apply similar standards reaches a different result.

In another case, when applicant's parent had previously registered a mark despite opposer's registration, then allowed the registration to expire, the previous coexistence was of no help to the applicant.[7] Even assuming privity, which was in some doubt, the Board held that the previous coexistence on the Register was irrelevant because opposition was predicated upon opposer's registration rights, not on any rights it may formerly have had (or not had) against applicant's predecessor. This is facile, but unsatisfactory. A better reason is that mistakes by Examiners, or registrants in policing, are not good precedent for repeating the mistakes (assuming no intervening equities resulting from

[6] Scotch Whiskey Ass'n v. Consolidated Distilled Products, Inc., 204 USPQ 57, 63 (TTAB 1979). See also supra fns 39 in Ch. 3 and 7 in Ch. 5 and infra fns 33, 37 and 103 this chapter.

[7] Jean Patou, Inc. v. Aristocrat Products Corp., 202 USPQ 130, 133 (TTAB 1979). See also supra fns 29 in Ch. 2 and 61 in Ch. 5 and infra fns 100 and 157 this chapter.

## CCPA and PTO Interpretations / §6.01[1]

laches or the like). Quite correctly, if obviously, the Board held that it was not bound by the examining branches' passage of a mark to publication. In ex parte matters, doubts should be resolved in favor of applicant. Mistaken denials are uncorrectable, but mistaken passage can be cured by opposition. In oppositions, doubts are more commonly resolved against the newcomer.

A state court decision holding one party's use of a mark "an unfair practice" in disregard of unfair competition law because the use was undertaken to dilute the value of the other's name and to mislead and cause confusion, was held to be persuasive but "not binding" on the Board in a cancellation proceeding between the same parties.[8] There was no indication why it was not binding (though it appeared the decision might be appealed).

Settlement of a civil action that stipulated that there was no likelihood of confusion between two parties was not held binding in an ex parte appeal of refusal of registration of one party's mark due to confusing similarity with the registered mark of the other party.[9]

Other cases established obvious principles. In an opposition proceeding, evidence of the outcome of a German opposition involving the same marks, goods and parties was rejected since it had "no probative value" in a proceeding to be determined under United States law.[10]

A trademark Examiner's implicit finding of no confusing similarity between a previously registered and applied-for mark was held not binding on the Board in a subsequent opposition or cancellation.[11]

Obviously, the fact that the applicant in an opposition

---

[8] Professional Economics Inc. v. Professional Economic Services Inc., 205 USPQ 368 (TTAB 1979). See also supra fns 18 in Ch. 2, 7 in Ch. 3, 2 in Ch. 4 and 38 in Ch. 5.

[9] In re Richard Bertram & Co., 203 USPQ 286 (TTAB 1979). See also supra fns 41 and 119 in Ch. 5.

[10] Puma Sportschuhfabriken Rudolf Dassler, K.G. v. Superga, S.p.A., 204 USPQ 688, 689–90 fn 3 (TTAB 1979). See also supra fn 23 in Ch. 5.

[11] H. Sichel Sohne, GmbH. v. John Gross & Co., 204 USPQ 257, 261 (TTAB 1979). See also supra fn 15 in Ch. 5.

§6.01[2] / Trademark Law

proceeding had established rights to its mark in a previous court action against a third party unrelated to opposer, had no bearing on its rights against the opposer.[12]

The related doctrine of stare decisis is discussed in the first case in the next section.

[2] Summary Judgment

When Samsonite obtained a supplemental registration of SOFTHIDE for imitation leather, the Tanners' Council petitioned to cancel on grounds that the mark was deceptive.[13] It also moved for summary judgment. In granting the matter, the Board held that CCPA cases refusing registration to VYNAHYDE and DURAHYDE in 1964 established, presumably as a rule of law, that use of HIDE for imitation leather is deceptive and proscribed by Section 2(a). It noted that a 1967 CCPA decision denying cancellation of TUFIDE turned on essentially equitable considerations and distinguished two other cases.[14]

The decision seems wrong. If, as the Board stated, the test under Section 2(a) is tendency to deceive an average purchaser, that is essentially one of fact. Fifteen-year-old decisions of what will deceive average purchasers are not necessarily still valid. Lots of things—including average purchasers' perceptions—can change significantly in fifteen years. Narrow rules of law dictating the outcome of basically factual issues—What sort of marks deceive? What sort of goods are related?—are inherently suspect, and grow more

---

[12] In re Cosvetic Laboratories Inc., 202 USPQ 842, 844 (TTAB 1979). See also supra fns 65 and 121 in Ch. 5 and infra fn 153 this chapter.

[13] Tanners' Council of America, Inc. v. Samsonite Corp., 204 USPQ 150 (TTAB 1979). See also supra fns 3 in Ch. 4 and 6 in Ch. 5 and infra fn 287.

[14] See R. Neumann & Co. v. Bon-Ton Auto Upholstery, Inc., 326 F2d 799, 140 USPQ 245 (CCPA 1964) (VYNAHYDE), discussed in 54 TMR 698 fn 178; R. Neumann & Co. v. Overseas Shipments, Inc., 326 F2d 786, 140 USPQ 276 (CCPA 1964) (DURAHYDE), discussed in 54 TMR 698 fn 179; and W. D. Byron & Sons, Inc. v. Stein Bros. Mfg. Co., 153 USPQ 749 (CCPA 1967) (TUFIDE), discussed in 57 TMR 699 fn 297.

## CCPA and PTO Interpretations / §6.01[3]

so over time. That is not to say that the ultimate conclusion here was wrong, only that it should have been open to reexamination. The opinion is not clear whether the Tanners' Council moved for summary judgment as a matter of law or on the basis of undisputed facts. To the extent it was the latter, Samsonite may have been remiss in not persuasively showing that facts were in dispute.[15] The opinion was clear, however, that the Board reached its conclusion that SOFTHIDE was deceptive "as a matter of law."[16]

It is elementary that summary judgment should be granted when there is no issue of material fact, in order to dispose of cases and to avoid trial. The Board held that admissions of no sales, manufacture or advertising of products under a mark were not overcome by four shipments each month under the mark to four different locations.[17] Accordingly, summary judgment was granted canceling registration of the mark.

Res judicata is a question of law; therefore, where there was res judicata (and, presumably this also would apply to, collateral estoppel) summary judgment was held appropriate.[18]

Two other cases were decided by summary judgment.[19]

### [3] Equitable Defenses

Acquiescence and other equitable defenses are only applicable when there is doubt as to likelihood of confusion. Acquiescence may constitute a type of estoppel arising out

---

[15] There is at least a suggestion of this in supra fn 13 at 153 fn 3.
[16] Id at 155.
[17] Block Drug Co., Inc. v. Morton-Norwich Products, Inc., 202 USPQ 157 (TTAB 1979). See also supra fn 11 in Ch. 2.
[18] General Electric Co. v. Raychem Corp., 204 USPQ 148, 149 (TTAB 1979). See also supra fn 4 this chapter and infra fn 160 this chapter.
[19] BankAmerica Corp. v. International Travelers Cheque Co., 205 USPQ 1233 (TTAB 1979) (see also supra fn 22 in Ch. 3 and infra fns 36, 41, 93 and 117 this chapter); Home Federal Savings & Loan Ass'n v. Home Federal Savings & Loan Ass'n of Chicago, 205 USPQ 467 (TTAB 1979) (see also supra fn 24 in Ch. 2 and infra fns 86 and 171 this chapter).

§6.01[3] / Trademark Law

of conduct by one amounting to an express or implied assurance relied upon by another that the one will not assert trademark rights against the other. Indicating acceptability of the other's known acts falls within this definition. The Woman's Day/Man's Day opposition was held to constitute "a classic example of acquiescence."[20] While he was a vice president of Fawcett (publisher of WOMAN'S DAY and various other magazines), the eventual founder of MAN'S DAY had recommended development of a magazine under the title, secured permission to do so independently, been given counsel and encouragement in his venture, and, when he had resigned to oversee his new venture, been given a farewell party and a scroll wishing him well with MAN'S DAY. Since confusing similarity between the titles was doubtful, applicant prevailed on acquiescence.

The Burroughs Wellcome litigations involved flurries of charges of inequitable conduct. Out of them came several rulings.

First, it was held not inequitable for a cancellation petitioner (or an opposer) to charge abandonment of registered trademarks when there was fair ground for such a charge (indeed, one of the two marks was held abandoned).[21]

Second was the losing argument that a petitioner who had waited three years after registration of marks allegedly confusingly similar to its own to petition to cancel them was guilty of laches. Assuming the delay to protest had been inexcusable, all that the registrant had ever done under the mark was to sell six units, print some labels, do some consumer testing of the product (at a cost of $16,600) and undertake to further develop plans to market hand lotion under the mark. This was insufficient to show the sort of prejudicial

[20] CBS Inc. v. Man's Day Publishing Co., Inc., 205 USPQ 470 (TTAB 1980). See also supra fns 22 in Ch. 2 and 43 in Ch. 5 and infra fn 47 this chapter.

[21] Burroughs Wellcome Co. v. Warner-Lambert Co., 203 USPQ 191, 199 (TTAB 1979) (see also supra fns 31 in Ch. 2 and 63 in Ch. 5 and infra fn 102 this chapter); Burroughs Wellcome Co. v. Warner-Lambert Co., 203 USPQ 201, 207 (TTAB 1979) (see also supra fns 31 in Ch. 2 and 64 in Ch. 5 and infra fns 45 and 102 this chapter).

## CCPA and PTO Interpretations / §6.01[3]

change of position in reliance on delay necessary to sustain the laches defense.

Third, in a related opposition to registration of WELCOME RELIEF, applicant charged that the delay to petition to cancel two registrations it owned of WELCOME TOUCH and WELCOME FEELING constituted laches to oppose the new mark. Since the charge of confusion was based on opposer's ownership of WELLCOME, the Board entertained, but rejected, the charge of laches. The applicant's sole use being one $3.60 shipment, the prejudice necessary to sustain the laches defense was found wanting.[22]

Finally, during prosecution of its application for WELCOME RELIEF, the applicant relied on its prior ownership of registrations of WELCOME TOUCH and WELCOME FEELING. Since applicant knew of the facts that led opposer to challenge both registrations on grounds of abandonment, opposer argued that such reliance on registrations of marks known to be abandoned was inequitable. Opposer's argument obviously lost considerable force when only one of the two earlier registered marks was held to be abandoned. The Board, however, took the position that, in view of the presumptions afforded the existing registrations and that all applicant claimed was the true fact of these registrations, there was no inequity.[23] If this is an endorsement of reliance on registrations of marks known to be abandoned, one may wonder if it is appropriate.

The Board reiterated that fraud on the PTO involves a willful withholding of material facts or information which, if made known, would result in refusal of registration.[24] Sworn statements of applicant's exclusive right to use are fraudulent only where there is known to be a substantially identical mark for substantially identical goods or services. A belief,

---

[22] Burroughs Wellcome Co. v. Warner-Lambert Co., 203 USPQ at 209–10.

[23] Id at 209.

[24] Menzies v. International Playtex, Inc., 204 USPQ 297, 305 (TTAB 1979). See also supra fn 80 in Ch. 5 and infra fns 34, 88, 118 and 133 this chapter.

even a false belief, that the differences are material avoids fraud.

FRCP 9(b) requires fraud to be pleaded with particularity. A cancellation petitioner alleged that: (a) the registration was obtained fraudulently because the mark was not first used on the date claimed in the application, and "other statements" in the application were false; and (b) the Office, relying upon such misrepresentations, allowed the mark and registered it. This was considered by the Board to be insufficient particularity.[25] The reasons were that: (1) a misstatement of date of first use does not necessarily constitute fraud; and (2) the alleged "other statements" were not specified. As to (1), the reasoning seems incorrect. Whatever the defect of the claim, it is not lack of particularity; rather it is failure to state a claim. As to (2), the ruling seems correct.

> A misstatement of the date of first use does not, per se, constitute fraud because any use prior to the filing date is sufficient for purposes of registration.[26]

So said the Board in a case in which it held that fraud had not been pleaded with sufficient particularity. While one may agree that a misstatement of first use date need not necessarily constitute fraud—indeed it hardly could be since it is not always clear what constitutes "use"—there would appear to be cases where a deliberate misstatement, made to publicize a false claim of earlier priority than truth could support should constitute fraud. Perhaps that explains the words "per se."

Several other cases dealt with the defense of laches.

Grounds for asserting laches should be set forth with some particularity in pleadings; a fortiori, a conclusory pleading of laches, never supported by evidence or argument, was ig-

[25] General Mills, Inc. v. Nature's Way Products, Inc., 202 USPQ 840, 841 (TTAB 1979). See also infra fns 46 and 64 this chapter.
[26] Id at 841.

## CCPA and PTO Interpretations / §6.01[3]

nored by the Board.[27] Laches was held to be an affirmative defense which had to be pleaded, or at least litigated so the pleadings could be deemed amended under FRCP 15(b); raising it in a brief just would not do.[28] Curiously, the Board went on to decide that no case for laches seemed to have been made, because (1) more than mere delay was needed to sustain laches, and (2) where continued use rested on the belief that the use was not in conflict with any other use, the necessary reliance on inaction was absent. The latter view seems suspiciously close to stating that to raise the equitable defense of laches, one must first have (at least semi-) unclean hands.

The elements of laches were said to be (1) actual or constructive notice of the adverse party's use, (2) inexcusable delay in enforcement for an undue period of time, and (3) consequent prejudice.[29] Eighteen months was held not to be an undue period of delay, nor was promptly petitioning to cancel, rather than opposing, the registration laches.

To prove laches, one must show that he who would be lached had actual knowledge of the trademark use by the claimant of the defense, or that it is inconceivable that he would be unaware of the mark.[30] Continual observation of the mark in corporate use by salesmen aware that the respective parties made similar products sufficed. According to the court, knowledge of adverse mark usage gained by clerks and dock workers will not be imputed to their employer because their duties do not require sensitivity to the value of their employer's marks. Knowledge by salespeople, who should be familiar with their employer's good will in his

---

[27] South Eastern Cordage Co. v. Tu-Way Products Co., 203 USPQ 221, 222 fn 7 (TTAB 1979). See also supra fn 48 in Ch. 5 and infra fn 105 this chapter.

[28] Amica Mutual Insurance Co. v. R. H. Cosmetics Corp., 204 USPQ 155, 163 (TTAB 1979). See also supra fns 5 in Ch. 2 and 36 in Ch. 5.

[29] Malter International Corp. v. Bison Laboratories, Inc., 202 USPQ 188, 190–91 (TTAB 1979). See also supra fn 76 in Ch. 5 and infra fn 50 this chapter.

[30] Georgia-Pacific Corp. v. Great Plains Bag Co., 204 USPQ 697 (CCPA 1980). See also supra fn 11 in Ch. 5 and infra fn 126 this chapter.

## §6.01[4] / Trademark Law

marks, will be imputed to the employer. Increasing sales volume several dozen times during the period of delay created sufficient prejudice to the party asserting laches, in event of a disturbance of the trademark status quo, to permit the raising of the defense.

### [4] Oppositions

BOZO TEXINOS—A MEXICANA CAFE is almost as bizarre a mark for restaurant services as the case it spawned.[31] The owner of BOZO THE CLOWN for television shows and spin-off products opposed on grounds of likelihood of confusion and also alleged that applicant had never used the mark in intra- or interstate commerce. Bozo restaurant denied confusing similarity but admitted never having used the mark. Bozo the Clown moved for judgment on the pleadings.

Since opposer had proved no damage from confusing similarity, the Board denied judgment, which would have had res judicata effect (at least in the PTO). Nonuse is a classic "ex parte" issue, and it seemed appropriate to revive the doctrine recently put to rest.[32] The distinction is that after a factual hearing, all issues are decided (and have res judicata effect), whereas here the confusing similarity issue had simply been alleged and denied. At the same time, the application obviously was void ab initio, but Trademark Rule 2.131 permits remand to the Examiner only after "termination of the inter partes case," which in this case would not be terminated by denying the motion for judgment. The Board solved the dilemma by allowing applicant to elect whether to take a dismissal as moot, without prejudice, or to continue and obtain an adjudication of likelihood of confusion.

Strange situations beget strange results.

---

[31] Larry Harmon Pictures Corp. v. Bozo Texinos-A Mexican Cafe, Inc., 204 USPQ 430 (TTAB 1979).

[32] Norac Company Inc. v. Occidental Petroleum Corp., 197 USPQ 306 (TTAB 1977), discussed in 68 TMR 760 fn 176.

## CCPA and PTO Interpretations / §6.01[4]

Other cases established a grab-bag of principles. In one, the Board indicated that the only statutory basis upon which it could consider whether a mark is primarily geographically deceptively misdescriptive is Section 2(e) of the Act.[33] It noted, however, that a term violative of Section 2(e) also would violate Section 43(a) and Paris Convention Articles 10 and 10 bis. The interesting question is what would happen in the event a mark were contrary to the geographically descriptive provisions of Section 43(a) or the Convention, but not of Section 2(e). Evidently the answer is that the remedy, if any, would lie in the court, not before the Board.

The Board considered itself to be without jurisdiction to hear or determine charges of unfair competition.[34]

When the issue was whether a mark was descriptive, evidence of facts occurring up to the close of the trial period could be considered; the record did not close as of applicant's filing date.[35] One who opposes on such ground need only show the descriptiveness of the mark and that he would be in a position to use the term descriptively; he need not have used it prior to applicant, or, indeed, at all.[36]

An association of Scotch whisky producers had standing to oppose registration of a mark for liqueurs that was alleged to be geographically deceptively misdescriptive of such liqueurs in that it indicated Scottish origin.[37] It is reasonable to assume that if this were so and consumers were misled, the sales of opposer's members would be likely to suffer.

---

[33] Scotch Whiskey Ass'n v. Consolidated Distilled Products, Inc., 204 USPQ 57, 60 fn 2 (TTAB 1979). See also supra fns 39 in Ch. 3 and 7 in Ch. 5 and infra fns 6 this chapter.

[34] Menzies v. International Playtex, Inc., 204 USPQ 297, 306 fn 11 (TTAB 1979). See also supra fns 80 in Ch. 5 and 24 this chapter and infra fns 88, 118 and 133 this chapter.

[35] Virginia Maid Hosiery Mills, Inc. v. Collins & Aikman Corp., 203 USPQ 795, 797 (TTAB 1979). See also supra fn 19 in Ch. 3.

[36] Id at 796. See also BankAmerica Corp. v. International Travelers Cheque Co., 205 USPQ 1233, 1236 (TTAB 1979). See also supra fns 22 in Ch. 3 and 19 this chapter and infra fns 41, 93 and 117 this chapter.

[37] Scotch Whiskey Ass'n v. Consolidated Distilled Products, Inc., 204 USPQ 57, 60 (TTAB 1979). See also supra fns 39 in Ch. 3, in Ch. 5, 7 and infra fn 6 and 33 this chapter/ 103 this chapter.

§6.01[4] / Trademark Law

Arguing that confusion in trade was unlikely because there was geographic separation of the two users was unavailing in the absence of some geographic limitation in opposer's registration and the opposed application.[38] Since virtually all registrations and applications are geographically unrestricted, such arguments seem to be a dead issue.

Amending a notice of opposition to allege that the applied-for mark was merely descriptive and incapable of distinguishing the applicant's goods in commerce was permitted, despite considerable passage of time, prior to opening of testimony periods, in view of the liberal policy of FRCP 15(a).[39] In such situations, a reopening of discovery might be appropriate, if requested. It was not here.

One can suggest that if, during an opposition, an application of opposer matures into registration, the proper procedure is to seek to amend the notice of opposition.[40] Since both parties in this particular case acknowledged the fact, the notice was deemed to be amended.

Board rules neither provide for nor prohibit filing reply briefs on motions. Generally, the Board does not favor reply briefs unless necessary to clarify matters newly raised by the brief in opposition.[41] In one proceeding, the Board considered an opposer's brief that was filed a few days late, apparently because objection was "somewhat belated" and because the Board was "desirous" of obtaining applicant's views on the issues.[42] Opposer did, however, lose the opposi-

---

[38] Winn's Stores, Inc. v. Hi-Lo, Inc., 203 USPQ 140, 144 (TTAB 1979). See also supra fn 72 in Ch. 5 and infra fn 97 this chapter.

[39] Dynachem Corp. v. Dexter Corp., 203 USPQ 218, 220 (TTAB 1979). See also infra fn 61 this chapter.

[40] Plak-Shack, Inc. v. Continental Studios of Georgia, Inc., 204 USPQ 242, 243 (TTAB 1979). See also supra fns 21 in Ch. 2 and 73 in Ch. 5 and infra fns 47, 136 and 169 this chapter.

[41] BankAmerica Corp. v. International Travelers Cheque Co., 205 USPQ 1233, 1235 (TTAB 1979). See also supra fns 22 in Ch. 3, 19 and 36 this chapter and infra fns 193 and 117 this chapter.

[42] Liqwacon Corp. v. Browning-Ferris Industries, Inc., 203 USPQ 305 (TTAB 1979). See also supra fn 1 in Ch. 2 and infra fn 145 this chapter.

## CCPA and PTO Interpretations / §6.01[4]

tion. Had opposer prevailed, there could have been an interesting question for appeal.

The Board had occasion to repeat, and elaborate upon, at least three long, firmly established doctrines: (1) An applicant failing to submit evidence is limited to the filing date of his application for his date of first use.[43] (2) The validity of an opposer's registration cannot be attacked except by counterclaim for cancellation.[44] (That petition need not be by counterclaim; it may be by separate proceeding.[45] If one has counterclaimed to cancel the registration, it is not improper to deny its validity in the answer to the notice of opposition.)[46] (3) Priority of use is not an issue when opposer relies on an existing registration, since the Act forbids registration of marks confusingly similar to previously registered marks.[47]

It was not necessary in order to win an opposition to submit any evidence other than to prove opposer's prior

[43] Norton Co. v. Talbert, 202 USPQ 542 (TTAB 1979). See also supra fns 15 in Ch. 3 and 82 in Ch. 5 and infra fn 47 this chapter.

[44] Royal Hawaiian Perfumes, Ltd. v. Diamond Head Products of Hawaii, Inc., 204 USPQ 144, 147 (TTAB 1979). See also supra fns 41 in Ch. 3 and 39 in Ch. 5 and infra fns 48, 84 and 89 this chapter.

[45] Burroughs Wellcome Co. v. Warner-Lambert Co., 203 USPQ 201, 208 fn 7 (TTAB 1979). See also supra fns 31 in Ch. 2, 64 in Ch. 5 and 21 this chapter and infra fn 102 this chapter.

[46] General Mills. Inc. v. Nature's Way Products, Inc., 202 USPQ 840, 842 (TTAB 1979). See also supra fn 25 this chapter and infra fn 64 this chapter.

[47] Norton Co. v. Talbert, 202 USPQ 542, 543 (TTAB 1979) (see also supra fns 15 in Ch. 3, 82 in Ch. 5 and 43 this chapter). See also Nina Ricci, S.A.R.L. v. ETF Enterprises, Inc., 203 USPQ 947, 949 (TTAB 1979) (see also supra fn 75 in Ch. 5); Arby's Inc. v. Abby's Pizza Inns, 205 USPQ 762, 765 (TTAB 1980) (see also supra fns 17 in Ch. 2 and 42 in Ch. 5 and infra fns 63, 157 and 164 this chapter); CBS Inc. v. Man's Day Publishing Co., Inc., 205 USPQ 470, 473 (TTAB 1980) (see also supra fns 22 in Ch. 2, 43 in Ch. 5 and 20 this chapter); Plus Products v. Natural Organics, Inc., 204 USPQ 773, 778 (TTAB 1979) (see also supra fn 32 in Ch. 5 and infra fns 90, 98, 101, 109 and 123 this chapter; Plak-Shack, Inc. v. Continental Studios of Georgia, Inc., 204 USPQ 242, 244 (TTAB 1979) (see also supra fns 21 in Ch. 2, 73 in Ch. 5 and 40 this chapter and infra fns 137 and 169 this chapter).

§6.01[5] / Trademark Law

registration.[48] Opposers should be forewarned, however, that the case should be very clear before that procedure can be relied upon safely.

The Board also held that oppositions may be based upon previously used, but unregistered marks (which seems obvious from Section 2(d), and that applicant's prior knowledge of such use would not, absent an intent to trade on opposer's reputation, be critical. If doubt should develop as to the outcome, such doubt would be resolved by requiring the applicant to have selected a mark free of any likelihood of confusion with the mark of an established prior user.[49]

[5] Cancellations

A question that continually intrigues is whether the burden of proof on a cancellation petitioner is heavier than that on an opposer. After three discussions of the subject by the Board, we can report that the question remains intriguing. There is "no hard and fast rule" said the Board, in one, because each case must be considered on its own facts.[50] This is true, of course, but not very pertinent to the issue of burden of proof. The question is whether there is, in any set of circumstances, a point at which certain proof would sustain an opposition but not a cancellation. There would seem to be, since as the Board pointed out, a registrant does enjoy the benefits of the prima facie presumptions afforded by the registration, and the longer the delay in petitioning to cancel, the more likely equities are to develop. On the other hand, said the Board, the pivotal question (usually) is likeli-

[48] Royal Hawaiian Perfumes, Ltd. v. Diamond Head Products of Hawaii, Inc., 204 USPQ 144 (TTAB 1979). See also supra fns 41 in Ch. 3, 39 in Ch. 5 and 44 this chapter and infra fns 84 and 89 this chapter.

[49] Finance Co. of America v. BankAmerica Corp., 205 USPQ 1016, 1026 (TTAB 1980). See also supra fn 83 in Ch. 5 and infra fns 121, 142, 157 and 165 this chapter.

[50] Malter International Corp. v. Bison Laboratories, Inc., 202 USPQ 188, 191–92 (TTAB 1979). See also supra fns 76 in Ch. 5 and 29 this chapter.

### CCPA and PTO Interpretations / §6.01[5]

hood of confusion in either proceeding; that issue seems unrelated either to prima facie presumptions or to equities.

What the Board seemed to say in the second decision was that basically the burden is flexible in each case, depending upon the equities disclosed by the record as to the duration and extent of each party's use. However, "the balancing of the equities in a cancellation proceeding may be tilted in behalf of the registrant where established and valuable rights have accrued over the years in the registered mark."[51] Of course, at least with respect to certain possible grounds for cancellation, the presumptions afforded the registration may raise an obstacle that an opposer need not overcome.

The third case concluded that there was no real difference in burdens of proof in oppositions and cancellations based on likelihood of confusion.[52]

In other cases, it was held that a registration sought to be canceled was presumed to be valid under Section 7(b). It was the petitioner's burden to rebut that presumption by a preponderance of the evidence.[53] The presumption could not be overcome with unsupported argument. In such proceedings, the Board was not bound by the trademark Examiner's determination of registrability.[54] Nevertheless, Section 7(b) invested the registration with certain presumptions of validity that only were rebuttable by establishing conclusively that there was earlier error in allowing the registration. All evidence to the close of the testimony periods was pertinent.

[51] Safe-T Pacific Co. v. Nabisco, Inc., 204 USPQ 307, 313 (TTAB 1979). See also supra fns 27 in Ch. 2, 26 in Ch. 3 and 60 in Ch. 5 and infra fn 124 this chapter.

[52] Gio. Buton & C. S.p.A. v. Buitoni Foods Corp., 205 USPQ 477, 480 (TTAB 1979). See also supra fns 6 and 10 in Ch. 2 and 17 in Ch. 5 and infra fn 91 this chapter.

[53] Dan Robbins & Associates, Inc. v. Questor Corp., 202 USPQ 100, 105 (CCPA 1979). See also supra fns 11 in Ch. 3 and 12 in Ch. 5 and infra fn 152 this chapter.

[54] Floss Aid Corp. v. John O. Butler Co., 205 USPQ 274, 283 (TTAB 1979). See also supra fns 26 in Ch. 2, 23 in Ch. 3 and 66 in Ch. 5 and infra fns 102 and 170 this chapter.

§6.01[5] / Trademark Law

The Court of Customs and Patent Appeals has established that in opposition proceedings based on likelihood of confusion with a previously registered mark, priority of the parties' use is not an issue.[55] In analogous cancellation proceedings, however, priority was said to be an issue, because the presumptions of Section 7(b) extended to both registrations.[56] (Actually, the petitioner's registrations and the registrant's registration both were Supplemental Register registrations, which carried no presumptions of validity, so priority was an issue anyway.)

Since the presumptions of Section 7(b) are validity of the registration, registrant's ownership of the mark, and registrant's exclusive right to use the mark in commerce, this rationale is difficult to fathom. The Board had originally held that priority of use by the applicant/registrant negated the necessary damage to opposer/petitioner. The court rejected that on the ground that Section 2(d) does not permit adjudication of priority. The Board seems to have attempted here to revive the doctrine in cancellation proceedings by resort to the presumptions afforded by Section 7(b). While the presumption of validity may have some bearing on likelihood of confusion, it is difficult to see how any of the Section 7(b) presumptions affect the question of priority. Section 2(d) still seems to dictate that a mark confusingly similar to an earlier registered mark should not have been registered. This is true no matter what the lineup of principal or supplemental registrations.[57]

A petition to cancel ST. MICHAEL raised a novel, albeit not particularly difficult, question of statutory interpreta-

---

[55] King Candy Co. v. Eunice King's Kitchen, Inc., 496 F2d 1400, 182 USPQ 108 (CCPA 1974), discussed in 64 TMR 404 fn 300.

[56] Medical Modalities Associates, Inc. v. ARA Corp., 203 USPQ 295, 301 fn 7 (TTAB 1979). See also supra fns 19 in Ch. 2, 1 in Ch. 4 and 30 in Ch. 5 and infra fns 66, 103 and 127 this chapter.

[57] However, since a supplemental registration carries no presumptions, he relying on it must show facts entitling him to the registration—adoption and use. Priority vis-a-vis the petitioner, however, seems not to be such a fact; it can be attacked by cross-petition, but not otherwise.

## CCPA and PTO Interpretations / §6.01[5]

tion.[58] Petitioner alleged that the mark was geographically descriptive or deceptively misdescriptive. Since the registration was more than five years old, those claims were stricken because Section 14(c) precluded cancellation on such grounds. Petitioner then amended its petition to claim that because the mark was geographically descriptive or deceptively misdescriptive, the mark was being used to misrepresent the source of the goods. Such use to misrepresent is a ground for cancellation of any registration.

The Board concluded that "misrepresentation of source" in Section 14(c)

> ... refers to situations where it is deliberately misrepresented by or with the consent of the registrant that goods and/or services originate from a manufacturer or other entity when in fact those goods and/or services originate from another party.[59]

As the Board pointed out, the clear exclusion by Section 14(c) of Section 2(e)(2) as a basis for cancellation compelled this interpretation:

> ... to allow a claim of misrepresentation of source based on a mark's alleged geographical descriptiveness or deceptive misdescriptiveness would be, in effect, to allow through the back door what is essentially an allegation under Section 2(e)(2) which is prohibited from coming in through the front door.[60]

Section 2(a), which is ground for cancellation under Section 14(c), has been held to require allegations of "at least" the likelihood of confusion required by Section 2(d), which under Section 14(c), is not a permissible ground for cancellation of registrations more than five years old. An applicant

---

[58] Osterreichischer Molkerei-und Kaseweband Registriete GmbH v. Marks and Spencer Ltd., 203 USPQ 793 (TTAB 1979).
[59] Id at 794.
[60] Ibid.

§6.01[5] / Trademark Law

counterclaimed to cancel opposer's five-year old registration by alleging that likelihood of confusion between the two marks disparaged or falsely suggested a trade connection or brought applicant into contempt or disrepute.

Quite correctly, the Board held that this just would not do. If Section 2(d) confusion per se were translated into Section 2(a) false suggestion of trade connection, etc., the Section 14(c)'s elimination of likelihood of confusion as a ground for canceling over five-year old marks would be pointless. What the Board held was necessary to state a Section 2(a) claim was "an intent, implied or actual, on the part of respondent to trade in on the goodwill and reputation, if any, of the mark on which [petitioner] relies." While the statute does compel "something more," and such intent would seem to be sufficient, it may not be the only example of the necessary "something more."[61] For cases involving more substantive aspects of this rule see supra §5.01.

Canceling registrations more than five years old on the ground that the mark was merely descriptive was not permitted under Section 14.[62] Such allegations can be stricken from cancellation petitions. The case involved a petition to cancel registrations of IT'S A REAL "TAIL WAGGER" and TAIL WAGGER for dog food. Since the former was more than five years old and could not be attacked on grounds of descriptiveness, the petition to cancel the latter was dismissed. While the latter could be attacked on grounds of descriptiveness, the Board felt that since the first registration was invulnerable, the petitioner could not be damaged by the second.

It is a familiar Board rule that one cannot be damaged by registration (or continued registration) of a mark that the applicant/registrant previously had registered. The invulnerable, or unattacked, registration that triggers the rule must, however, be essentially the same as the one under

---

[61] Dynachem Corp. v. Dexter Corp., 203 USPQ 218, 220 (TTAB 1979). See also supra fn 39 this chapter.

[62] Allied Mills, Inc. v. Kal Kan Foods, Inc., 203 USPQ 390, 391–92 (TTAB 1979). See also supra fns 24 in Ch. 3 and 56 in Ch. 5.

## CCPA and PTO Interpretations / §6.01[5]

attack. (Presumably this sameness must be determined from the point of view of the would-be opposer or cancellation petitioner.) IT'S A REAL "TAIL WAGGER" and TAIL WAGGER appear to be different enough so that perhaps the rule should not have been applied automatically. It is possible that registration of either mark could do damage not done by the other (though, of course, the petitioner or opposer should have had to show that such a case existed).

In another case, the Board noted that an "incontestable" registration could not be attacked on grounds of prior use by the attacker.[63]

Two cases involved standing to cancel. (1) A cancellation petitioner normally must allege facts showing damage resulting from continued registration of the mark sought to be canceled; likelihood of confusion is one such sort of damage. That requirement was excused, however, when the cancellation petitioner was an applicant counterclaiming to cancel his opposer's registrations.[64] The rationale of requiring allegations of damage is to establish petitioner's standing; the other party's opposition already had adequately established the petitioner-applicant's stake in the controversy. (2) A trade association of tanners, alleging that SOFTHIDE for imitation leather was deceptive, and would deceive customers into purchasing such material instead of products of its members, was afforded standing to petition to cancel the registration.[65] Indeed, it seems not to have been even a disputed issue.

Though one might have thought there was no doubt, the Board did find occasion to affirm that the words of Section 2(d) "a mark registered in the Patent and Trademark Office or a mark or trade name previously used in the United States

---

[63] Arby's Inc. v. Abby's Pizza Inns, 205 USPQ 762, 765 (TTAB 1980). See also supra fns 17 in Ch. 2, 42 in Ch. 5 and 47 this chapter and infra fns 157 and 164 this chapter.

[64] General Mills, Inc. v. Nature's Way Products, Inc., 202 USPQ 840, 841 (TTAB 1979). See also supra fns 25 and 46 this chapter.

[65] Tanners' Council of America, Inc. v. Samsonite Corp., 204 USPQ 150, 152 (TTAB 1979). See also supra fns 3 in Ch. 4, 6 in Ch. 5 and 13 this chapter.

§6.01[6] / Trademark Law

and not abandoned" referred to unregistered, previously-used marks.[66]

When a cancellation petitioner, after many adjournments to answer a motion for summary judgment, requested still more time and petitioned to suspend pending the outcome of court litigation, the Board apparently became fed up. It denied both the request and petition and awarded summary judgment by default. The court found no abuse of discretion.[67]

[6] Concurrent Use

To determine conditions and limitations of concurrent registration, all facts extant up to the close of the testimony period were considered.[68]

[7] Evidence

A Volkswagen opposition contained a veritable feast of evidentiary rulings, some routine, some not.[69] (1) Ownership of a registration could be proven by introducing certified PTO copies showing status and title. This was the "full equivalent" of a notice of reliance, and is also valid under Section 7(e) of the Act and Federal Rules of Evidence 803(8) and 902(1).[70] (2) However, certified status copies without title did not prove a party's ownership of the registration.[71] (3) Objections (to exhibits) not argued in a brief were

---

[66] Medical Modalities Associates, Inc. v. ARA Corp., 203 USPQ 295, 301 (TTAB 1979). See also supra fns 19 in Ch. 2, 1 in Ch. 4, 30 in Ch. 5 and 56 this chapter and infra fns 103 and 127 this chapter.

[67] Chesebrough-Pond's, Inc. v. Faberge, Inc., 205 USPQ 888 (CCPA 1980). See also infra fn 150 this chapter.

[68] Weiner King, Inc. v. Wiener King Corp., 204 USPQ 820, 832 fn 11 (CCPA 1980). See also supra fns 23 and 33 in Ch. 2 and infra fns 143 this chapter and 5 in Ch. 7.

[69] Volkswagenwerk Ag v. Clement Wheel Co., Inc., 204 USPQ 76 (TTAB 1979). See also supra fn 68 in Ch. 5 and infra fn 157 this chapter.

[70] Id at 80–81.

[71] Id at 81.

deemed waived.[72] (4) That an exhibit was detached from other, unidentified papers was not good ground for objection when the proffered exhibit was self sufficient and supported by testimony.[73] (5) Objections that an exhibit was not produced in response to a request for production of documents were overruled; the requester had moved to compel, but after the motion was denied as premature, allowed the matter to drop. One can preclude evidence for failure to make discovery under FRCP 37(6) (2) (b), but only after filing a motion to compel.[74] (6) Handwritten summaries of data, prepared by someone other than the witness and not within the witness' knowledge were not ordinary business records, and were not competent to prove the data shown thereby.[75] (7) To be excluded, however, such exhibits had to be objected to on proper grounds.[76] (8) Excerpts from agreements as to which the witness had no knowledge were excluded.[77] (9) Objections to evidence briefed by one party and not answered by the other were deemed to be conceded by the offering party.[78] (10) Objections to exhibits adduced during testimony had to be raised during the taking of the testimony; objections made in a brief deprived the offeror of the opportunity to correct the defect.[79] (11) The fact certain evidence that was properly objectionable had been accepted in earlier proceedings was of no help to the offeror when properly objected to in a later proceeding in the absence of collateral estoppel.[80] (12) Third party catalogs, when properly objected to as hearsay, were admissible only for the limited purpose of showing the display of the third party's mark on their covers.[81] (13) Finally, the Board

[72] Id at 82.
[73] Ibid.
[74] Id at 82 fn 4.
[75] Id at 82.
[76] Ibid.
[77] Ibid.
[78] Id at 82–83.
[79] Id at 83.
[80] Id at 83 fn 5.
[81] Id at 83.

§6.01[8] / Trademark Law

felt that an exhibit showing hundreds of millions of advertising expenditures over nearly two decades should have been supported by more than isolated examples of such advertising and reliable circulation or broadcast audience data. It was, however, willing to concede that an automotive manufacturer who had sold over six million vehicles and had over one thousand dealers "must have made an impression."[82]

Several of these themes were repeated in other cases.

[8] Proving Priority of Use

When priority of use was an issue, an applicant who offered no evidence of use received the filing date of its application as a priority date for use of its mark.[83] In another case, a prior registration owned by opposer established his priority.[84] So did a registration applied for before applicant applied.[85] An Affidavit that a bank was chartered in 1934 did not establish use as of that date; applicant (in an opposition) thus was limited to its 1975 filing date as a priority date (on motion for summary judgment).[86]

[9] Proving Registrations

There are three ways for proving registrations: (1) submitting two status and title copies with pleadings; (2) serving a notice of reliance during testimony period with a status and title copy; and (3) having a knowledgeable witness testify

[82] Id at 84 fn 6.
[83] Mennen Co. v. Yamanouchi Pharmaceutical Co., Ltd., 203 USPQ 302, 304 (TTAB 1979) (see also supra fn 62 in Ch. 5 and infra fns 135 and 137 this chapter); Cumberland Packing Corp. v. American Sweetener Corp., 203 USPQ 292, 293 (TTAB 1979) (see also supra fn 52 in Ch. 5).
[84] Royal Hawaiian Perfumes, Ltd. v. Diamond Head Products of Hawaii, Inc., 204 USPQ 144, 145–47 (TTAB 1979). See also supra fns 4 in Ch. 3, 39 in Ch. 5, 44 and 48 this chapter and infra fn 89 this chapter.
[85] Midwest Biscuit Co. v. John Livacich Produce, Inc., 203 USPQ 628, 629 (TTAB 1979). See also supra fn 59 in Ch. 5 and infra fn 98 this chapter.
[86] Home Federal Savings & Loan Ass'n v. Home Federal Savings & Loan Ass'n of Chicago, 205 USPQ 467, 468 (TTAB 1979). See also supra fns 24 in Ch. 3 and 19 this chapter and infra fn 171 this chapter.

## CCPA and PTO Interpretations / §6.01[9]

thereto and introduce them as exhibits. Offering certified copies, not showing title, during testimony of a witness not shown to have knowledge of the registrations, did not suffice.[87] A pro se litigant found a fourth way—have your opponent concede it.[88] The first of these methods rests upon Trademark Rule of Practice 2.122(b) which provides that an opposer's or petitioner's pleaded registration is received in evidence if two status and title copies (or an order therefore) accompany the notice or petition. It can happen that such a registration is pleaded after the Section 8 affidavit is submitted, but that the ordered status copies do not show such filing; PTO records are not updated instantaneously. That happened in one case, and applicant urged that, since six years had passed with no showing of a Section 8 affidavit, the registration had to be presumed canceled.[89] The Board held that there was no obligation to update such pleaded registrations, so it would investigate the PTO records itself. If those records showed that the Section 8 affidavit had been filed, the registration would be accepted as evidence.

Another way of getting a registration into evidence is to stipulate that the registration is owned, and somehow to get into the record a copy of the registration (here, by annexing a copy showing neither status nor ownership to the notice of opposition); when no copy of the registration was in the record, such stipulation was of no avail, because the Board did not take judicial notice of registration.[90] Submitting a 1973 licensing agreement incorporating two registrations did not suffice to prove the registrations, because there was

---

[87] Sheller-Globe Corp. v. Scott Paper Co., 204 USPQ 329, 331 fn 2 (TTAB 1979). See also supra fns 3 in Ch. 2, 47 in Ch. 3 and 78 in Ch. 5.

[88] Menzies v. International Playtex, Inc., 204 USPQ 297, 301 fn 7 (TTAB 1979). See also supra fns 80 in Ch. 5, 24 and 34 this chapter and infra fns 118 and 133 this chapter.

[89] Royal Hawaiian Perfumes, Ltd. v. Diamond Head Products of Hawaii, Inc., 204 USPQ 144, 146–47 (TTAB 1979). See also supra fns 41 in Ch. 3, 39 in Ch. 5, 44, 48 and 84 this chapter.

[90] Plus Products v. Natural Organics, Inc., 204 USPQ 773, 774 fn 2 (TTAB 1979). See also supra fns 32 in Ch. 5 and 47 this chapter and infra fns 98, 101, 109 and 123 this chapter.

§6.01[10] / Trademark Law

no proof that they were subsisting and still owned.[91] Third party registrations, in an opposition, had to be made of record in the same manner as any other registration; the Board would not take notice of them.[92] Even on motions, the Board would not take judicial notice of active registrations in the absence of submitted copies of them.[93] Filing a notice of reliance upon third party applications was futile because they constituted evidence of filing and of nothing else.[94] Presumably if such filings could somehow become an issue, the gesture would not be so futile.

[10] Third Party Registrations

Objections to third party registrations made of record went to probative value rather than admissibility, and therefore were considered at final hearing rather than on motion to strike.[95] While they would not be stricken as irrelevant, the weight to be accorded to them was for the Board to determine.[96] Usually, little or no weight is given such registrations.

In an opposition, third party use of marks with the same salient characteristic as the marks in issue was said to have "no direct bearing" on whether the marks were confusingly

---

[91] Gio. Buton & C. S.p.A. v. Buitoni Foods Corp., 205 USPQ 477, 480 fn 1 (TTAB 1979). See also supra fns 6 and 10 in Ch. 2, 17 in Ch. 5 and 52 this chapter.

[92] Times Mirror Magazines, Inc. v. Sutcliffe, 205 USPQ 656, 660 (TTAB 1979). See also supra fns 7 in Ch. 2 and 45 in Ch. 5 and infra fn 157 this chapter.

[93] BankAmerica Corp. v. International Travelers Cheque Co., 205 USPQ 1233, 1237 (TTAB 1979). See also supra fns 22 in Ch. 3, 19, 36 and 41 this chapter and infra fn 117 this chapter.

[94] Glamorene Products Corp. v. Earl Grissmer Co., Inc, 203 USPQ 1090, 1092 fn 5 (TTAB 1979). See also supra fn 51 in Ch. 5 and infra fns 98, 102, 116 and 140 this chapter.

[95] R. C. Bigelow, Inc. v. Celestial Seasonings, Inc., 203 USPQ 542, 542–43 fn 3 (TTAB 1979). See also supra fns 1 and 57 in Ch. 5.

[96] Fischer Gesellschaft m.b.H. v. Molnar and Co., Inc., 203 USPQ 861, 864 fn 4 (TTAB 1979). See also supra fn 21 in Ch. 5 and infra fns 99 and 112 this chapter.

similar, and rights of third parties to use such mark were of no help to an applicant not in privity with such third party users.[97] Since the uses were otherwise found distinguishable from the use in the case at bar, this stood mainly as a statement of principle. However, the principle, well-established though it may be, seems overly broad. If one starts with the presumption that confusion in the market place does not abound, a showing that other merchants actually share what is common to the marks in issue seems pertinent. Whether the bearing be "direct" or indirect, the inference seems plain that if two or more can share a characteristic without creating confusion, then one more can too. Indeed, such a state of affairs could give rise to a cross-petition to cancel for abandonment (loss of function as an indication of origin). It is well-settled, however, that an opposer's registration cannot be attacked except by cross-petition to cancel.

[11] **Affirmative Defenses Must Be Proven**

Four cases noted that affirmative defenses such as laches, acquiescence and estoppel will be ignored if no evidence is offered or the defense is neither briefed nor argued.[98]

---

[97] Winn's Stores, Inc., v. Hi-Lo, Inc., 203 USPQ 140, 144 (TTAB 1979). See also supra fns 72 in Ch. 5 and 38 this chapter.

But see the discussion in Diane G. Fitz-Gerald, "Third Party Registrations: An Evidentiary Problem in Trademark Opposition Proceedings," 28 Emory LJ 825 (1979).

[98] Midwest Biscuit Co. v. John Livacich Produce, Inc., 203 USPQ 628, 629 fn 4 (TTAB 1979) (see also supra fns 59 in Ch. 5 and 85 this chapter); Plus Products v. Natural Organics, Inc., 204 USPQ 773, 775 (TTAB 1979) (see also supra fns 32 in Ch. 5, 47 and 90 this chapter and infra fns 101, 109 and 123 this chapter); General Mills Fun Group, Inc. v. Tuxedo Monopoly, Inc., 204 USPQ 396, 397–98 (TTAB 1979) (see also supra fn 29 in Ch. 5 and infra fns 125, 129 and 157 this chapter); Glamorene Products Corp. v. Earl Grissmer Co., Inc., 203 USPQ 1090, 1091 (TTAB 1979) (see also supra fns 51 in Ch. 5 and 94 this chapter and infra fns 102, 116 and 140 this chapter).

§6.01[12] / Trademark Law

[12] Notices of Reliance

One of the more unusual aspects of PTO practice is the notice of reliance. Attempts to utilize it, and failures to do so, were noted in many cases.

In one of the most interesting, a cancellation respondent took a third party deposition by written questions during the discovery period. Petitioner failed to attend or propound questions. When registrant filed a notice of reliance on the deposition, petitioner objected. His objection was sustained, in a long opinion that relied heavily on policy behind and the intent of various of the Trademark Rules of Practice, Federal Rules of Civil Procedure, and Federal Rules of Evidence.[99] Stripped to its essentials, the Board's reasoning was that discovery is one sort of procedure—one for ascertaining facts—and testimony is another—one for making the record on which the case will be decided. Different rules apply to each, and different considerations govern attendance, participation and conduct by the other party. To allow evidence adduced under the discovery set of circumstances to be considered in the decision-making context could seriously prejudice the other party, who had no notice that the discovery could be used at trial. In the absence of compelling need to the contrary, the Board will uphold the dichotomy.

Timing of filing of the notice can be important. One case gives pause to even experienced practitioners.[100] The sequence: (i) On June 30, 1977, applicant's trial period was set to close October 28, 1977. On November 21, 1977, applicant filed a notice of reliance upon certain interrogatory answers, at the same time moving to reopen discovery and its own testimony period. On December 27, the Board reset the closing of applicant's testimony period for January 11, 1978, with the opening thirty days prior thereto (December 12,

[99] Fischer Gesellschaft m.b.H. v. Molnar and Co., Inc., 203 USPQ 861, 864-67 (TTAB 1979). See also supra fns 21 in Ch. 5 and 96 this chapter and infra fn 112 this chapter.

[100] Jean Patou, Inc. v. Aristocrat Products Corp., 202 USPQ 130, 131 fn 1 (TTAB 1979). See also supra fns 29 in Ch. 2, 61 in Ch. 5 and 7 this chapter and infra fn 157 this chapter.

## CCPA and PTO Interpretations / §6.01[12]

1977), which was, of course, after the filing of the notice of reliance. The Board noted that the interrogatory answers were not filed during any testimony period it had set, but since opposer did not object, and both parties dealt with the answers in briefs, considered them. Another case held that when the filing of the notice of reliance was prior to the testimony period, the error was not prejudicial and the opponent did not object, the evidence would not be excluded.[101]

Five cases established that failure to make interrogatory answers, trademark searches or other documents of record by filing a notice of reliance will result in their exclusion from the record.[102]

Some things were held not properly to be subject to notice of reliance:

One's own interrogatory answers were not properly the subject of a notice of reliance.[103] The same was true of dis-

---

[101] Plus Products v. Natural Organics, Inc., 204 USPQ 773, 775 fn 5 (TTAB 1979). See also supra fns 32 in Ch. 5, 47, 90 and 98 this chapter and infra fns 109 and 123 this chapter.

[102] Burroughs Wellcome Co. v. Warner-Lambert Co., 203 USPQ 191, 194 (TTAB 1979) (see also supra fns 31 in Ch. 2, 63 in Ch. 5 and 21 this chapter); Burroughs Wellcome Co. v. Warner-Lambert Co., 203 USPQ 201, 203–04 fn 1 (TTAB 1979) (see also supra fns 31 in Ch. 2, 64 in Ch. 5, 21 and 45 this chapter); Jules Berman & Associates, Inc. v. Consolidated Distilled Products, Inc., 202 USPQ 67, 68 fn 2 (TTAB 1979) (see also supra fns 28 in Ch. 2, 46 in Ch. 3 and 16 in Ch. 5); Glamorene Products Corp. v. Earl Grissmer Co., Inc., 203 USPQ 1090, 1092 fn 4 (TTAB 1979) (see also supra fns 51 in Ch. 5, 94 and 98 this chapter and infra fns 116 and 140 this chapter); Floss Aid Corp. v. John O. Butler Co., 205 USPQ 274, 278 (TTAB 1979) (see also supra fns 26 in Ch. 2, 23 in Ch. 3, 66 in Ch. 5 and 54 this chapter and infra fn 170 this chapter).

[103] Scotch Whiskey Ass'n v. Consolidated Distilled Products, Inc., 204 USPQ 57, 59 fn 1 (TTAB 1979) (see also supra fns 39 in Ch. 3, 7 in Ch. 5 and 6 and 37 this chapter); Oxford Pendaflex Corp. v. Rolodex Corp., 204 USPQ 249, 251 fn 2 (TTAB 1979) (see also supra fn 1 in Ch. 3 and infra fns 110 and 120 this chapter); Medical Modalities Associates, Inc. v. ARA Corp., 203 USPQ 295, 297 fn 2 (TTAB 1979) (see also supra fns 19 in Ch. 2, 1 in Ch. 4, 30 in Ch. 5, 56 and 66 this chapter and infra fn 127 this chapter); Safeway Stores, Inc. v. Captn's Pick, Inc., 203 USPQ 1025, 1027 fn 1 (TTAB 1979) (see also supra fn 58 in Ch. 5 and infra fn 157 this chapter).

§6.01[12] / Trademark Law

covery depositions of one's own witnesscs,[104] or one's responses to requests to admit.[105] If the opposing party relied upon such material (or some of it), the answerer could rely upon additional answers which ought, in fairness, to be considered.[106] If no objection was taken to such evidence, and the opponent dealt with it on the merits, it would be deemed "stipulated" and considered by the Board.[107]

One could not, by notice of reliance, introduce documents that were the subject of a request to produce[108] unless they were subsequently authenticated by interrogatory answer or admission.[109] However, when both parties noticed reliance on such documents, they were deemed stipulated into evidence.[110]

Discovery depositions of non-party witnesses could not be made of record, over objection, by notice of reliance, particularly by the party not taking them. But they could by stipulation, either express or implied when both parties treated them as evidence.[111]

A notice of reliance upon published materials that failed to indicate the relevance of such materials was defective and the materials were not considered.[112] And articles and

[104] Oxford Pendaflex Corp., supra fn 1 in Ch. 3.
[105] South Eastern Cordage Co. v. Tu-Way Products Co., 203 USPQ 221, 222 fn 8 (TTAB 1979). See also supra fns 48 in Ch. 5 and 27 this chapter.
[106] Medical Modalities, supra fn 19 in Ch. 2 and Oxford Pendaflex, supra fn 1 in Ch. 3.
[107] Medical Modalities, supra fn 19 in Ch. 2 and Safeway Stores, supra fn 58 in Ch. 5.
[108] Chemetron Corp. v. Morris Coupling and Clamp Co., 203 USPQ 537, 539 fn 5 (TTAB 1979). See also supra fn 77 in Ch. 5.
[109] Plus Products v. Natural Organics, Inc., 204 USPQ 773, 775 fn 4 (TTAB 1979). See also supra fns 32 in Ch. 5, 47, 90, 98, 101 this chapter and infra fn 123 this chapter.
[110] Oxford Pendaflex Corp. v. Rolodex Corp., 204 USPQ 249, 251 fn 2 (TTAB 1979). See also supra fns 1 in Ch. 3 and 103 this chapter and infra fn 120 this chapter.
[111] Electro-Coatings, Inc. v. Precision National Corp., 204 USPQ 410, 412 (TTAB 1979). See also supra fn 32 in Ch. 2 and infra fns 146 and 161 this chapter.
[112] Fischer Gesellschaft m.b.H. v. Molnar and Co., Inc., 203 USPQ 861, 864 fn 3 (TTAB 1979). See also supra fns 21 in Ch. 5, 96 and 99 this chapter.

## CCPA and PTO Interpretations / §6.01[13]

the like properly introduced by notice of reliance were evidence only of the fact that they were published, not the truth of what they said (which was hearsay).[113]

Trademark Rule 2.122(c) provides for the introduction by notice of reliance only of printed matter available to the general public in libraries of general circulation and of such "official records" as are prepared by a public officer and are self-authenticating. Contracts, agency agreements and the like with quasi-public agencies did not fall within the Rule (although if the opponent accepted such a notice of reliance, the documents would be deemed stipulated into the record).[114] Company annual reports, while perhaps available in some libraries, were not the sort of printed publication contemplated by Rule 2.122(c) to be introduced by notice of reliance.[115] Neither were third party product promotional brochures. The reason relied-upon material must be available to the general public in libraries of general circulation is to permit the other party readily to corroborate or refute what is offered. In cases of doubt as to general availability, the burden of persuasion was held to be the offerors'.[116]

### [13] Ignoring Requests to Admit

Failing to respond to requests for admission can be dangerous; they are deemed admitted. When one litigant moved to withdraw answers to such requests previously ruled admitted by default, the Board noted that the motion —in effect a request for reconsideration—was untimely, and

---

[113] Fischer, supra fn 21 in Ch. 5; Logicon, Inc. v. Logisticon, Inc., 205 USPQ 767, 768 fn 8 (TTAB 1980). See also supra fn 74 in Ch. 5 and infra fns 115 and 119 this chapter.

[114] Conde Nast Publications, Inc. v. Vogue Travel, Inc., 205 USPQ 579, 580 fn 5 (TTAB 1979). See also supra fn 47 in Ch. 5.

[115] Logicon, Inc. v. Logisticon, Inc., 205 USPQ 767, 768 fn 6 (TTAB 1980). See also supra fns 74 in Ch. 5 and 113 this chapter and infra fn 119 this chapter.

[116] Glamorene Products Corp. v. Earl Grissmer Co., Inc., 203 USPQ 1090, 1092 fn 5 (TTAB 1979). See also supra fns 54 in Ch. 5, 94, 98 and 102 this chapter and infra fn 140 this chapter.

§6.01[14] / Trademark Law

that no satisfactory explanation for the default had been shown.[117] Then, however, in a summary judgment proceeding, the Board agreed not to base summary judgment on those matters deemed admitted as to which subsequent evidence had raised an issue of fact. The ruling was stated to be "in the interests of justice." Certainly it was not in those of orderly procedure.

### [14] When to Submit Evidence

Other litigants had trouble with their timing of evidence. Exhibits relating to an opposer's activities could not be introduced during cross examination of applicant's witnesses because they related to opposer's case, not applicant's.[118] Evidence of an opposer's business, customers and the like was properly part of a case in chief and was improper rebuttal evidence; if opponent did not object, however, such evidence could be received.[119] Evidence discovered after the close of one's testimony period could not be introduced on cross examination of an opponent's witness unless it fell within the scope of that witness' direct testimony. Proper procedure would have been to move to reopen the testimony period, though to win such a motion one would have been to show that the evidence could not have been discovered earlier by the exercise of due diligence.[120]

Similarly, in an opposition, it was held that evidence of actual confusion is part of an opposer's case in chief, and may

---

[117] BankAmerica Corp. v. International Travelers Cheque Co., 205 USPQ 1233, 1235 (TTAB 1979). See also supra fns 22 in Ch. 3, 19, 36, 41 and 93 this chapter.

[118] Menzies v. International Playtex, Inc., 204 USPQ 297, 301 fn 8 (TTAB 1979). See also supra fns 80 in Ch. 5, 24, 34 and 88 this chapter and infra fn 133 this chapter.

[119] Logicon, Inc. v. Logisticon, Inc., 205 USPQ 767, 768 fn 7 (TTAB 1980). See also supra fns 74 in Ch. 5, 113 and 115 this chapter.

[120] Oxford Pendaflex Corp. v. Rolodex Corp., 204 USPQ 249, 255 fn 8 (TTAB 1979). See also supra fns 1 in Ch. 3, 103 and 110 this chapter.

not be introduced in rebuttal; proper procedure is to move to reopen.[121]

### [15] Objecting to Evidence

Objections to testimony, such as hearsay and competency, were waived when not repeated in a brief, especially when such testimony was relied upon in the objector's brief.[122] The Board, however, weighed such evidence for its "probative value."

### [16] Methods of Proof

It is customary, during discovery and later, to give sales data in terms of "in excess of" or "approximately," presumably to preserve confidential business information. One litigant disclosed sales "in excess of $10,000" and later offered evidence that sales equaled $25,000. "Such a discrepancy is too wide," said the Board, stating that such approximations should be "a maximum deviation" from reality of fifteen to twenty percent.[123] The litigant was bound by its earlier disclosed figure.

The common practice of summarizing sales and advertising figures in a specially prepared exhibit sponsored by a responsible officer was challenged under the best evidence rule in one case. The challenge failed. The document was accepted to the extent testimony, by officers in a position to know, supported the data.[124] But, in another case, when the offeror of the evidence did not know who prepared the

---

[121] Finance Co. of America v. BankAmerica Corp., 205 USPQ 1016, 1028 (TTAB 1980). See also supra fns 83 in Ch. 5 and 49 this chapter and infra fns 142, 157 and 165 this chapter.

[122] Medtronic, Inc. v. Medical Devices, Inc., 204 USPQ 317, 320 fn 11 (TTAB 1979). See also supra fns 25 in Ch. 3, 2 and 33 in Ch. 5 and infra fn 137 this chapter.

[123] Plus Products v. Natural Organics, Inc., 204 USPQ 773, 778 (TTAB 1979). See also supra fns 32 in Ch. 5, 47, 90, 98, 101 and 109 this chapter.

[124] Safe-T Pacific Co. v. Nabisco, Inc., 204 USPQ 307, 311 fn 5 (TTAB 1979). See also supra fns 27 in Ch. 2, 26 in Ch. 3, 60 in Ch. 5 and 51 this chapter.

§6.01[17] / Trademark Law

tabulation or verify its accuracy, such data were stricken as hearsay.[125]

Holding actual confusion was entitled to great weight "only if properly proven," the court rejected as such proof testimony of a jobber of one party's products that one customer had called him and that he, the jobber, had been confused by the similarity of marks reported to him by his customer.[126]

[17] **Sufficiency of Evidence to Establish Particular Points**

When a cancellation petitioner relied upon prior use of descriptive marks similar to the registered mark it attacked, the Board found it "noteworthy" that applications to register those marks had been accepted by the Examiner under Section 2(f). However the Board held that the customer letters relied upon in the ex parte application proceeding were of no worth in the inter partes cancellation proceeding:

> ... To accept these letters at their face value ... would do an injustice to our adversary practice as well as to the accepted rules of evidence which provide, in most instances, an opportunity for a party to a proceeding to confront and interrogate witnesses for the other party.[127]

Excerpts from books and articles dealing with the history and background of a venerable party (Lloyds of London) were held admissible for the truth of their contents. Such an

---

[125] General Mills Fun Group, Inc. v. Tuxedo Monopoly, Inc., 204 USPQ 396, 398 (TTAB 1979). See also supra fns 29 in Ch. 5 and 98 this chapter and infra fns 129 and 157 this chapter.

[126] Georgia-Pacific Corp. v. Great Plains Bag Co., 204 USPQ 697, 701 (CCPA 1980). See also supra fns 11 in Ch. 5 and 30 this chapter.

[127] Medical Modalities Associates, Inc. v. ARA Corp., 203 USPQ 295, 299 (TTAB 1979). See also supra fns 19 in Ch. 2, 1 in Ch. 4, 30 in Ch. 5, 56, 66 and 103 this chapter.

## CCPA and PTO Interpretations / §6.01[17]

historical account was considered the best evidence available under the circumstances, and this not barred by the hearsay rule. The impact of this ruling, however, may be mitigated by the Board's considering it "significant" that the opposing party did not object.[128]

Two unusual bits of evidence emerged in the Monopoly case.[129] Widespread public protest when the Atlantic City Commissioner of Public Works proposed to change the names of Baltic and Mediterranean Avenues "demonstrated the popularity of the 'MONOPOLY' game."[130] The Board also took judicial notice "that famous marks are frequently used on certain types of items, such as clothing, glassware, trash cans, pillows, etc., which are unrelated in nature to those goods on which the marks are normally used."[131] Dissenting Member Kera took vigorous exception to such judicial notice.[132]

Goods purchased on the open market were good evidence of third party use whether or not their labeling identified the manufacturer. Under the anonymous source rule, words on such packages could be regarded as trademarks.[133]

Claims that "infringements" have been suppressed should be supported by copies of decrees, settlements or correspondence so that the Board can see what was agreed or ordered and on what terms.[134] One case seemed to hold, for unexplained reasons, that dictionary excerpts (of unspecified nature) offered by notice of reliance during rebut-

[128] Corp. of Lloyd's v. Louis D'Or of France, Inc., 202 USPQ 313, 315 (TTAB 1979). See also supra fns 3 and 67 in Ch. 5.
[129] General Mills Fun Group Inc. v. Tuxedo Monopoly, Inc., 204 USPQ 396 (TTAB 1979). See also supra fns 29 in Ch. 2, 98 and 125 this chapter and infra fn 157 this chapter.
[130] Id at 398.
[131] Id at 400.
[132] Id at 402.
[133] Menzies v. International Playtex, Inc., 204 USPQ 297, 303 fn 16 (TTAB 1979). See also supra fns 80 in Ch. 5, 24, 34, 88 and 118 this chapter.
[134] Plak-Shack, Inc. v. Continental Studios of Georgia, Inc., 204 USPQ 1059 (TTAB 1979). See also supra fn 73 in Ch. 5.

§6.01[17] / Trademark Law

tal testimony period were not competent evidence.[135] State trademark registrations were not competent to establish use of a registered mark.[136]

In litigating the phonetic and visual similarities of and differences between MINON and MENNEN, both opposer and applicant took testimony of expert witnesses—professors of linguistics and of English—as to likely pronunciations and visual perceptions of the marks. The Board ruled that the testimony of each canceled that of the other, and adhered to its "long-held view that the opinions of witnesses, including those qualified as expert witnesses, on the question of likelihood of confusion are entitled to little, if any weight and should not be substituted for the opinion of the tribunal charged with the responsibility for the ultimate opinion on the question."[137] In the absence of a competently designed and executed survey, the tribunal felt compelled to make its own subjective evaluation of average consumer reactions.

This familiar theme in Board proceedings seems unduly cynical. While expert witnesses normally support their employers, that does not necessarily mean that the testimony of one cancels that of the other. Of course much expert testimony is nonsense, but some experts, by virtue of the inherent logic of their testimony, or even their credentials, are more credible and persuasive than others. Some expert testimony can provide insights, mode of analysis, or even factual data, not otherwise available to the trier of fact. True, the ultimate decision is for the trier, and it may often be

[135] Mennen Co. v. Yamanouchi Pharmaceutical Co., Ltd., 203 USPQ 302, 304 (TTAB 1979). See also supra fns 62 in Ch. 5 and 83 this chapter and infra fn 137 this chapter.

[136] Plak-Shack, Inc. v. Continental Studios of Georgia, Inc., 204 USPQ 242, 246 fn 5 (TTAB 1979). See also supra fns 21 in Ch. 2, 73 in Ch. 5, 40 and 47 this chapter and infra fn 169 this chapter.

[137] Mennen Co. v. Yamanouchi Pharmaceutical Co., Ltd., 203 USPQ 302, 305 (TTAB 1979). See also supra fns 62 in Ch. 5, 83 and 135 this chapter. Similarly see Medtronic, Inc. v. Medical Devices, Inc., 204 USPQ 317, 325–26 (TTAB 1979). See also supra fns 25 in Ch. 3, 2 and 33 in Ch. 5 and 122 in this chapter.

## CCPA and PTO Interpretations / §6.01[18]

subjective; but one would think it could better be made in light of, rather than in disregard of, expert testimony. Subjectively, the Board's position seems to smack of the ultimate cynicism: experts are a waste of money, but if your opponent uses one, all that is necessary to eliminate his impact is to present your own.

### [18] Surveys

The Yago sangria case[138] contained a textbook illustration of how to conduct a survey showing consumer awareness and identification of a pictorial label element. The Board seemed impressed, though it preserved its usual position that such a survey was "not controlling" but was "probative for the purpose of corroborating our conclusion" based on extensive use and advertising evidence.[139] With all due respect, the survey seems far more persuasive a demonstration of public opinion than the Board's expert conjecture of what public impression use and advertising would have produced.

The Spray 'N Vac/Rinsenvac case contained a detailed discussion of the conditions that had to be satisfied to admit company-commissioned surveys taken for ordinary business purposes rather than litigation.[140] Use of market research, taken for ordinary business purposes and not in contemplation of litigation, was approved in the White Stag case.[141]

The FinanceAmerica case illustrated a survey rejected on several bases, both methodological and substantive. The principal substantive defect was that the survey explored

---

[138] Monsieur Henri Wines Ltd. v. Duran, 204 USPQ 601 (TTAB 1979). See also supra fn 18 in Ch. 5.

[139] Id at 604.

[140] Glamorene Products Corp. v. Earl Grissmer Co., Inc., 203 USPQ 1090, 1093 (TTAB 1979). See also supra fns 51 in Ch. 5, 94, 98, 102 and 116 this chapter.

[141] Warnaco, Inc. v. Holiday Golf Products, 204 USPQ 69, 74–75 (TTAB 1979). See also supra fn 28 in Ch. 5 and infra fn 157 this chapter.

§6.01[19] / Trademark Law

only recognition of one mark, while the issue was likelihood of confusion between two marks.[142]

### [19] Miscellaneous Matters

One litigant objected to certain interrogatories on grounds of relevance and materiality. The objection later was held to be a representation that evidence not already of record on those subjects would not be introduced. When the litigant then attempted to introduce such evidence through testimony, the original interrogator objected. The CCPA held that the objection was well-taken and that the evidence could not be considered.[143] There was no need to test the validity of the objection by motion to compel. Although the Board had held that the benefit of the disputed evidence in resolving a complicated controversy outweighed the prejudice, the court held that use of the disputed evidence violated the original interrogator's procedural rights, and that the litigant had raised an "equitable estoppel" against reception of the evidence.

A purely procedural ruling set forth several rules applicable to discovery disputes, none very startling:[144] (1) To obtain a Board order directing response to discovery, a party must specifically move for such an order. (2) Dismissal for failure to make discovery is not appropriate until such a motion has been made and granted. (3) A party refusing to obey a Board order directing discovery forfeits his right to object to such discovery, absent excusable neglect. (4) A motion to compel will only be entertained when supported by a written statement that movant or his attorney has conferred with opposing party or his attorney in a good faith effort to resolve their differences. (5) The Board has no au-

[142] Finance Co. of America v. BankAmerica Corp., 205 USPQ 1016, 1030 et seq (TTAB 1980). See also supra fns 83 in Ch. 5, 49 and 121 this chapter and infra fns 157 and 165 this chapter.

[143] Weiner King, Inc. v. Wiener King Corp., 204 USPQ 820, 828–29 (CCPA 1980). See also supra fns 23 and 33 in Ch. 2 and 68 this chapter and infra fn 5 in Ch. 7.

[144] MacMillan Bloedel Ltd. v. Arrow-M Corp., 203 USPQ 952 (TTAB 1979).

## CCPA and PTO Interpretations / §6.01[20]

thority to award attorney's fees and expenses in discovery proceedings (or, one supposes, in any other proceeding).

Admission of evidence in the form of exhibits introduced during testimony was objected to as irrelevant and not supporting the witness' testimony.[145] The Board noted that such evidence "is not ordinarily stricken" but assured that it had been considered only if relevant and material for the purpose for which it was presented.

Parties are encouraged to list the matters of record in briefs in Board proceedings. Where one did and the other did not except or offer a counter-list, all listed matters were treated as of record.[146]

### [20] Rehearing and Reopening

Nearly two years before, the Board had ordered cancellation of a registration of LEE for belts and buckles. This had resulted after cross motions for summary judgment in which registrant did not deny petitioner's priority of use for the goods in question. Registrant appealed to a District Court, then "discovered" evidence of use of the mark long before petitioner's use. The court directed the parties to resubmit the issue to the Board, so the case arose on a motion to reopen under FRCP 60(b).[147]

The Board applied two tests for relief: (1) failure earlier to adduce the evidence must not have resulted from lack of due diligence. (2) The evidence must be admissible, credible and so material and controlling as probably to change the outcome. Neither test was met. The reason the evidence had not been found earlier seemed to be that nobody had bothered to look in old company records because it had not been thought that they would show what they did when

---

[145] Liqwacon Corp. v. Browning-Ferris Industries, Inc., 203 USPQ 305, 307 fn 1 (TTAB 1979). See also supra fns 1 in Ch. 2 and 42 this chapter.

[146] Electro-Coatings, Inc. v. Precision National Corp., 204 USPQ 410, 412 (TTAB 1979). See also supra fns 32 in Ch. 2 and 111 this chapter and infra fn 161 this chapter.

[147] Lee Byron Corp. v. H.D. Lee Co., Inc., 203 USPQ 1097 (TTAB 1979). See also supra fn 4 in Ch. 2.

finally they were examined. That struck the Board as less than due diligence. Moreover, the evidence, per se, only established earlier sale of belts and buckles, but did not establish that they bore the name LEE. Registrant's counsel speculated that perhaps a witness who remembered the period could be found to establish the fact. The Board required a stronger offer of proof than that.

### [21] Scope of Review

What TTAB action can be reviewed by the CCPA? The question arose in five cases this year.

In one, a tee-shirt manufacturer opposed a well-known university's application to register OHIO STATE and BUCKEYES on grounds of abandonment of the trademarks by acquiescence in use by others, estoppel by laches and acquiescence, and damages to opposer by virtue of applicant's attempts to enforce its trademark rights. All charges were stricken as irrelevant, and opposer attempted to appeal.[148] Charges that the marks were merely descriptive, geographically descriptive and had been otherwise abandoned remained.

The court dismissed the appeal, holding it could only review "decisions" of the Board, which normally means final decisions. Orders striking some, but not all, pleadings are only reviewable on an interlocutory basis when (1) the stricken issues are "separate and distinct" from those remaining, and (2) the goal of judicial economy would be served. Opposer flunked the latter test, whose factors are (1) whether inconvenience and cost of piecemeal review are outweighed by danger of denial of justice by delay (plainly not the case here), and (2) whether an appellate decision is fundamental to further conduct of the case (a reversal would seem to be). If opposer fails on its remaining claims (some of which seem to verge on the frivolous), and then appeals again and is sustained on appeal, it has a long road ahead.

---

[148] Champion Products, Inc. v. Ohio State University, 204 USPQ 833 (CCPA 1980).

## CCPA and PTO Interpretations / §6.01[21]

In another, application for MODUMATIC for hot water boilers and steam generators was opposed by the registrant and alleged user of MODULATIC for similar goods.[149] Applicant sought to amend its answer to petition for cancellation of opposer's registration. The motion was denied on the ground that the proposed counterclaim did not set forth a claim cognizable by law. Applicant tried to appeal and opposer moved to dismiss the appeal.

The court granted the motion to dismiss. It reasoned that exceptions to the finality rule exist only to correct rulings "fundamental to the further conduct of the case" or to avoid a danger of denying justice by delay. Neither was considered to be such a danger as to justify "interlocutory" appeal prior to review of the Board's ultimate decision. With all due respect, a decision to strike applicant's petition to cancel opposer's registration could be quite "fundamental to the future conduct of the case." If the cancellation remedy should be available and cancellation is applicant's only hope, it seems reasonably cumbersome and wasteful to force litigation and resolution of an opposition whose outcome is in no doubt, only to get the case in an appropriate posture to reverse and relitigate on the ground that applicant should have been allowed to attack opposer's registration.

The court reviewed a Board-granted summary judgment on default where the motion for summary judgment had not been opposed. In the cancellation proceeding, requests for extension of time and to suspend the proceeding had been pending at the time of default. While only "final" decisions are reviewed, this decision was held to have crossed the line of finality because it had finally dismissed the counterclaim, and the issues were separate and distinct. In effect, the ruling had been substantive, not procedural.[150] Denial of summary judgment was distinguished, for obvious reasons, in terms of finality.

---

[149] Aerco International, Inc. v. Vapor Corp., 608 F2d 518, 203 USPQ 882 (CCPA 1979). See also infra fn 176 this chapter.

[150] Chesebrough-Pond's, Inc. v. Faberge, Inc., 205 USPQ 888 (CCPA 1980). See also supra fn 67 this chapter.

§6.01[21] / Trademark Law

The Mushroom(s) case has been fought in federal courts, in state courts, and before the Trademark Trial and Appeal Board, where the owner and registrant of MUSHROOMS for women's shoes opposed registration of MUSHROOM and design for women's sportswear. Based on the outcome of the civil litigation, applicant moved for summary judgment. The Board denied the motion, but certified it to the CCPA as one that appeared to be appealable on the issue of res judicata. A seemingly flabbergasted court declined to hear the appeal. It is only empowered by the Act to review "decisions," which it has long read to mean "final decisions." In some circumstances, the granting of summary judgment might qualify, but denial could not.[151] Thus, the fascinating question of what happens when an opposer seems already to have established "likelihood of confusion" between two marks but nevertheless lost its claim of infringement in the courts remains for future determination.

Finally, the court held that decisions on interlocutory issues are appealable only if they are "logically related" to the basic substantive issues in the case.[152] Characterizing the Board's denial of a motion to strike discovery deposition testimony not served until after briefing as "purely procedural," the Court held that the question of untimeliness was "not sufficiently related to be reviewable here." The reasoning seemed to be that Section 21(a) of the Act permits only appeal of the Board's "decision."

On its face, this doctrine seems curious. Since Board decisions are based on such evidence as is in the record, admission or exclusion can be outcome, and thus "decision" determinative. If such "purely procedural," motions are never reviewable, then the correctness of the bases for the Board's "decision"—particularly in cases where evidence might be improperly excluded—seems unreviewable. If the

[151] R. G. Barry Corp. v. Mushroom Makers, Inc., 609 F2d 1002, 204 USPQ 195 (CCPA 1979).
[152] Dan Robbins & Associates, Inc. v. Questor Corp., 202 USPQ 100, 104 (CCPA 1979). See also supra fns 11 in Ch. 3, 12 in Ch. 5 and 53 this chapter.

## CCPA and PTO Interpretations / §6.02

court is only saying that it will decline to review procedural determinations that could have no bearing on the ultimate outcome, one can hardly quarrel. Those are harmless error, if error at all. One could, however, wish that the court had expressed itself in terms other than "reviewable," which implies appealability, and "purely procedural" which implies non-substantive. Procedural decisions that influence substantive outcome normally are, and should be, reviewable, and reviewed.

### §6.02 Ex Parte Appeals

Third party registrations are not very popular with the Board. One case said they were of little weight in determining likelihood of confusion because they did not establish use or public awareness of the registered marks, and the existence already of confusingly similar registered marks could not justify registration of another.[153] That third party registrations do not establish use is a proposition most often voiced in oppositions where it has some validity, particularly when the opposer has shown use. In ex parte appeals, where use is rarely at issue, it is hard to see why third party registrations are of no pertinence. While it is true that confusingly similar registrations already extant cannot justify another—past mistakes do not excuse more mistakes—third party registrations would seem to shed considerable light on what Examiners have, and have not, considered confusingly similar in the past. That does seem pertinent, albeit not necessarily conclusive.

Another case held that third party registrations are not of record in ex parte appeals, and would not be judicially noticed, unless copies were "made of record . . . during the prosecution of the application."[154] The procedure for doing

---

[153] In re Cosvetic Laboratories, Inc., 202 USPQ 842, 844 (TTAB 1979). See also supra fns 65 and 121 in Ch. 5 and 12 this chapter. See Fitz-Gerald article, supra fn 97 this chapter.

[154] In re Red Diamond Battery Co., 203 USPQ 472, 473 fn 4 (TTAB 1979). See also supra fn 71 in Ch. 5.

## §6.03 / Trademark Law

this during the prosecution stage is not clear, from either the opinion or the Trademark Rules of Practice.

An Examiner's introduction, during the course of an ex parte appeal, of added evidence as to the unregistrability of a mark ordinarily will not be considered, since such appeals normally are based upon the evidence already of record when the refusal to register was made. Ex parte appeals are not intended to be what is, in effect, a reopening of the examination procedure. In one case, though, such evidence was reviewed because the applicant expressly waived objection upon the condition that it too be allowed to "bolster" the record.[155]

In appealing a refusal to register a merely descriptive mark, the burden was on applicant to establish that the mark was recognized in the market place as identifying its goods to the exclusion of those of others.[156] Failure to meet that burden will result in refusal to register.

### §6.03  Applications

#### [1]  Description of Goods

How one chooses to describe goods (or services) can have subtle ramifications. Shoes, for example, can be sold through various trade channels and are of numerous types and styles. One describing his goods as "shoes" will be presumed to sell all types of shoes sold through all possible trade channels.[157] This is advantageous once registration is obtained, but in-

---

[155] In re Villiger Sohne GmbH, 205 USPQ 462, 465 (TTAB 1979). See also supra fn 45 in Ch. 3.

[156] In re Behre Industries, Inc., 203 USPQ 1030 (TTAB 1979). See also supra fns 15 in Ch. 2 and 20 in Ch. 3.

[157] See Jean Patou, Inc. v. Aristocrat Products Corp., 202 USPQ 130, 132 (TTAB 1979) (see also supra fns 29 in Ch. 2, 61 in Ch. 5, 7 and 100 this chapter); Nordica di Franco e Giovanni Vaccari & C. s.a.s. v. Nordic Sport Ltd., 202 USPQ 860, 862 (TTAB 1979) (see also supra fn 79 in Ch. 5); Safeway Stores, Inc. v. Captn's Pick, Inc., 203 USPQ 1025, 1028 (TTAB 1979) (see also supra fns 58 in Ch. 5 and 103 this chapter); Warnaco, Inc. v. Holiday Golf Products, 204 USPQ 69, 76 (TTAB 1979) (see also supra fns 28 in Ch. 5 and 141 this chapter); Volkswagenwerk Ag v. Clement

## CCPA and PTO Interpretations / §6.03[1]

creases chances of conflict with previously used or registered marks. On the other hand, "ballet slippers sold through dancing studios" is more readily registrable, but would be less likely to bar future registration of a similar mark for combat boots sold by mail (unless they are described as "shoes").

While description of goods, if unrestricted, will be read broadly as to types of product and trade channels, there are some limits. "Judo and Karate Uniforms and Belts" were not read to comprehend all possible belts, at least not where the record showed that they were limited to belts for martial arts uniforms.[158] Amendment of the description to "Judo and Karate Uniforms and Karate Belts" was, however, recommended.[159]

Another case reaffirmed that an application need not list, or even broadly cover, all items for which applicant uses the mark in question, even within the same class.[160] The applicant is free to select those goods for which he wishes to register the mark. In event of potential conflict as to some goods he is free to choose to register for less than all goods.

When multiple class applications are opposed, or, presumably, sought to be canceled, the Board will consider the

---

Wheel Co., Inc., 204 USPQ 76, 85 (TTAB 1979) (see also supra fns 68 in Ch. 5 and 69 this chapter); General Mills Fun Group Inc. v. Tuxedo Monopoly, Inc., 204 USPQ 396, 401 (TTAB 1979) (see also supra fns 29 in Ch. 5, 98, 125 and 129 this chapter); Barbers Hairstyling for Men & Women, Inc. v. Barber Pole, Inc., 204 USPQ 403, 408 (TTAB 1979) (see also supra fn 35 in Ch. 5 and infra fn 164 this chapter); Times Mirror Magazines, Inc. v. Sutcliffe, 205 USPQ 656, 660 (TTAB 1979) (see also supra fns 7 in Ch. 2, 45 in Ch. 5 and 92 this chapter); Arby's, Inc. v. Abby's Pizza Inns, 205 USPQ 762, 766 (TTAB 1980) (see also supra fns 17 in Ch. 2, 42 in Ch. 5, 47 and 63 this chapter and infra fn 164 this chapter); Finance Co. of America v. Bank America Corp., 205 USPQ 1016, 1022 (TTAB 1980) (see also supra fns 83 in Ch. 5, 49, 121 and 142 this chapter and infra fn 165).

[158] Lacoste Alligator S.A. v. Everlast World's Boxing Headquarters Corp., 204 USPQ 945, 947 (TTAB 1979). See also supra fn 24 in Ch. 5.

[159] Id at 948.

[160] General Electric Co. v. Raychem Co., 204 USPQ 148, 150 (TTAB 1979). See also supra fns 4 and 18 this chapter.

§6.03[2] / Trademark Law

matter with respect to the goods in each class. It would not, however, separate the good from the bad within a class, because it did not view its function, as, in effect, entering ex parte amendments to the recital of goods to salvage what might be registrable.[161]

When an applicant, who sold sets of lead sinkers for fishermen in a container permitting easy selection of the sinkers displayed therein, sought to register the container configuration with the words SINKER SELECTOR thereon, the Board felt that the trademark, if it was one, was identified with the container, not its contents (sinkers).[162]

The Board also held that descriptions of goods (or services) should be changed to correct misspellings and to delete trade or service marks owned by others.[163]

[2] Drawings

Since many marks are used in design form or with a design, they often can be applied for either as a word mark or in the form used. When one applied for a word mark, he could not then argue difference from an opposer's (or cancellation petitioner's) mark on the basis of the design matter, since that was not what was sought to be registered.[164] On the other hand, if one owns a word mark, that may put him in a better offensive position against others later. Ideally, one would apply to register both.

Similarly, in another case, use of a challenged mark on

[161] Electro-Coatings, Inc. v. Precision National Corp., 204 USPQ 410, 420 (TTAB 1979). See also supra fns 32 in Ch. 2, 111 and 146 this chapter.

[162] In re Water Gremlin Co., 204 USPQ 261 (TTAB 1979). See also supra fns 3 and 21 in Ch. 3.

[163] In re Landmark Communications, Inc., 204 USPQ 692, 693 fns 2 and 3 (TTAB 1979). See also supra fn 50 in Ch. 3.

[164] Barbers, Hairstyling for Men & Women, Inc. v. Barber Pole, Inc., 204 USPQ 403, 409 fn 11 (TTAB 1979) (see also supra fns 35 in Ch. 5 and 157 this chapter); H. Sichel Sohne, GmbH v. Michel Monzain Selected Wines, Inc., 202 USPQ 62, 66 (TTAB 1979) (see also supra fns 25 in Ch. 2 and 14 in Ch. 5 and infra fn 168 this chapter); Arby's Inc. v. Abby's Pizza Inns, 205 USPQ 762, 766 (TTAB 1980) (see also supra fns 17 in Ch. 2, 42 in Ch. 5, 47, 63 and 157 this chapter).

## CCPA and PTO Interpretations / §6.03[3]

tires only in association with the company's house mark was irrelevant. The Board pointed out that registration or attempted registration of the mark per se presumed that it performed a trademark function standing alone, and could survive as a source indicator by itself in the market place.[165]

Drawings should reflect the mark as used in the specimen. In an opposition, where the specimen read COASTER-CARD and the drawing read COASTER CARDS, it was recommended that if the applicant prevailed, he should be required to submit either a new drawing or new specimens.[166]

### [3] Miscellaneous

It was too cavalier, said the Board, for an Examiner to blithely assert that he was not bound by past Examiner's mistakes (here, registration of the same mark by the same party, which registration was canceled under Section 8). Demonstration of changed circumstances, new evidence not previously available, or new judicial interpretation of the statute would be valid grounds for failure to follow the precedent, however.[167]

In an opposition in which it appeared that the applicant ordered wine blended in Germany and shipped to a United States distributor, the Board recommended that the Examiner require amendment to recite use by a related company (the distributor).[168] When applicant's ownership derived from assignment from one to whom the mark was licensed

---

[165] Michelin Tire Corp. v. General Tire & Rubber Co., 202 USPQ 294, 298 (TTAB 1979). See also supra fns 34 in Ch. 2, 5 in Ch. 3 and 70 in Ch. 5. Similarly see Finance Co. of America v. BankAmerica Corp., 205 USPQ 1016, 1027 fn 2 (TTAB 1980). See also supra fns 83 in Ch. 5, 49, 121, 142 and 157 this chapter.

[166] In re Bright-Crest Ltd., 204 USPQ 591, 592 (TTAB 1979). See also supra fn 6 in Ch. 3.

[167] In re Hunter Publishing Co., 204 USPQ 957, 960 (TTAB 1979). See also supra fn 18 in Ch. 3.

[168] H. Sichel Sohne, GmbH. v. Michel Monzain Selected Wines, Inc., 202 USPQ 62, 64 fn 2 (TTAB 1979). See also supra fns 25 in Ch. 2, 14 in Ch. 5 and 164 this chapter.

## §6.04 / Trademark Law

back, the Board suggested he should recite current use by a related company rather than by a predecessor in title.[169] First use by the predecessor presumably was an appropriate claim.

Application made under Section 2(f) was held to be an acknowledgment that the mark, when first adopted and used, was merely descriptive (or perhaps otherwise barred by Section 2(e).[170] Interestingly enough, the Board seemed to consider the mark—FLOSSAID for dental floss holders—to be inherently suggestive.

An application statement of geographically limited use was said to have no effect unless the application is for concurrent registration. Any registration to issue would be geographically unrestricted.[171]

## §6.04 Post-Registration Occurrences

### [1] Affidavits, Renewals, Assignments, etc.

The registration analog of abandonment is failure to file a Section 8 affidavit, which results in cancellation of the registration. One registrant filed an affidavit stating that the essential ingredient of its trademarked goods had been unavailable for more than five years from the sole commercial source with whom registrant previously had dealt, but that prospects were favorable for establishing a new commercial source within a few months.[172] The excuse struck the post-registration Examiner as lame, so acceptance of the affidavit

---

[169] Plak-Shack, Inc. v. Continental Studios of Georgia, Inc., 204 USPQ 242, 243 fn 1 (TTAB 1979). See also supra fns 21 in Ch. 2, 73 in Ch. 5, 40, 47 and 136 this chapter.

[170] Floss Aid Corp. v. John O. Butler Co., 205 USPQ 274, 283 (TTAB 1979). See also supra fns 26 in Ch. 2, 23 and 66 in Ch. 5, 54 and 102 this chapter.

[171] Home Federal Savings & Loan Ass'n v. Home Federal Savings & Loan Ass'n of Chicago, 205 USPQ 467 fn 1 (TTAB 1979). See also supra fns 24 in Ch. 2, 19 and 83 this chapter.

[172] In re Moorman Manufacturing Co., 203 USPQ 712 (Comr Pats 1979).

was refused. On appeal, the Commissioner upheld the refusal:

> In fact, the Section 8 affidavit was designed to eliminate from the Register those marks whose nonuse has resulted from ordinary changes in social or economic conditions. In such situations, nonuse may be laid to conscious business decisions of registrants.[173]

On the other hand, prohibition, illness, fire and other catastrophes have sufficed to excuse nonuse. The requirement is that "nonuse be attributable to outside causes." In this case the registrant had failed to set forth "sufficient facts . . . to demonstrate clearly that nonuse is due to circumstances beyond the registrant's control."[174] Bald assertions of commercial unavailability of the necessary ingredient were insufficient. The registrant failed to set forth reasons for being unable (for five years) to find an alternate source, or to indicate what steps, if any, it had taken to promote the mark in the interim.

The lesson is that affidavits of nonuse under Section 8 must both show outside factors causing nonuse, which might have been the case here, and disclose enough details so that the showing of real inability to use is persuasive, which was not the case here.

The Commissioner held that when a Section 8 affidavit for only some classes of a multiple class registration is filed, its acceptance cannot be made conditional upon tendering of the original certificate (or certified copy), for cancellation of the goods in the remaining class(es). Registration in the remaining classes is canceled by operation of law.[175]

Amendment of a registered mark lies within the discretion of the Commissioner. The Board established that permission to amend neither starts running anew the five year period prescribed by Section 14(c) nor can be attacked

---

[173] Id at 713.
[174] Id at 714.
[175] In re Bombardier Ltd., 204 USPQ 943 (Comr Pats 1979).

## §6.05 / Trademark Law

before the Board in the absence of fraud.[176]

### §6.05 Collateral References

Useful information on TTAB practice and procedure can be found in Saul Lefkowitz, Recent Changes in Practice Before the Trademark Trial and Appeal Board, 69 TMR 479 (1979); Rany L. Simms, Tips from the TTAB: Some Interlocutory Hints, 70 TMR 148 (1980); Louise E. Fruge, Tips from the TTAB: Depositions Upon Written Questions, 70 TMR 253 (1980).

[176] Aerco International, Inc. v. Vapor Corp., 608 F2d 518, 203 USPQ 882 (CCPA 1979). See also supra fn 149 this chapter.

PART II

# Trademark Infringement and Unfair Competition

CHAPTER 7

# Infringement and Unfair Competition

### §7.01 Appellate Federal Court Decisions

The review of Appellate Federal decisions this year reconfirms that the factual context of a given case is far more important than legal precedent in determining whether there is an actionable infringement, and that the Circuit Courts of Appeal are likely to reach a conclusion based on ad hoc considerations as much as settled rules of law.

For example, it is generally safe to assume that the use of similar terms on similar goods will give rise to a likelihood of confusion. One might, therefore, have expected the Second Circuit in *McGregor-Doniger, Inc. v. Drizzle Inc.*[1] to enjoin the use of DRIZZLE for women's coats, given the prior appropriation of DRIZZLER for golf jackets. Not so, however, where:

 i. DRIZZLE was adopted in good faith and without knowledge of the DRIZZLER mark;
 ii. The DRIZZLER label prominently featured the plaintiff's McGREGOR mark in striking plaid letters;
 iii. DRIZZLE, on the other hand, was used by defendant solely to identify the producer rather than one of the producer's lines;
 iv. DRIZZLE coats retailed for $100 to $900 and were thus purchased with care; and
 v. the marks coexisted for five years before plaintiff became aware of defendant's use.

[1] 599 F2d 1126, 202 USPQ 81 (CA 2 1979), affg 199 USPQ 466 (SDNY 1978).

§7.01 / Trademark Law

Likewise, one might question the use of an identical term on identical products by major competitors with similar distribution methods who often advertised on adjacent pages of the same magazine. In *Armstrong Cork Co. v. World Carpets, Inc.*,[2] however, the Fifth Circuit reversed a District Court finding of infringement where:

i. the common term was WORLD, a component of eighty-five other marks in the same industry;

ii. WORLD appeared in fine print on defendant's label which was dominated by the ARMSTRONG mark with a circled A:

iii. by contrast, WORLD against the background of a globe was the most prominent feature of the plaintiff's logo; and

iv. the products were "big ticket" floor covering items.

Indeed, courts often skate on thin ice when they mechanically apply precedent in a trademark context. It is generally held, for example, that a junior user/prior registrant of a mark should prevail except in the geographical area occupied by the prior user as of the date the mark is published, the rationale being that the prior user has constructive notice of the junior user/registrant's claim of exclusive rights to use the mark throughout the United States from the date of publication forward.[3] Typically, however, cases in which the rule has been developed have involved a local prior user with a stable, non-expanding business and a junior user/registrant with national ambitions.

[2] 597 F2d 496, 203 USPQ 19 (CA 5 1979), modg 199 USPQ 30 (ND Ga 1978), discussed in 69 TMR 597 fn 219.

[3] Holiday Inns, Inc. v. Holiday Inn, 364 F Supp 775, 177 USPQ 640 (D SC 1973), affd per curiam 498 F2d 1937, 182 USPQ 129 (CA 4 1974); Wrist-Rocket Mfg. Co. Inc. v. Saunders Archery Co., 578 F2d 727, 198 USPQ 257 (CA 8 1978), discussed in 69 TMR 595 fn 213; Old Dutch Foods, Inc. v. Dan Dee Pretzel & Potato Co., 477 F2d 150, 177 USPQ 496 (CA 6 1973), modg 345 F Supp 1399, 173 USPQ 419 (ND Ohio 1972), discussed in 63 TMR 388 fn 246.

## Infringement and Unfair Competition / §7.01[1]

By contrast, the Fourth Circuit in *Armand's Subway, Inc. v. Doctor's Associates, Inc.*[4] was faced with a dormant junior user/prior registrant and a rapidly expanding prior user. For the court to suggest under those circumstances that the prior user's one hundred-twenty-five franchised fast food stores operated in numerous states under the SUBWAY mark "would be vulnerable if plaintiff should [ever decide to] expand" its ARMAND'S SUBWAY sandwich business outside of Washington, D.C.[5] appears questionable. The better approach would have been to emphasize that "the problems of concurrent use issues must ultimately be solved by a comprehensive factual analysis" and to reject a "mechanical approach which always defers to the first to register."[6]

### [1] Descriptiveness and Genericism

Notwithstanding the overriding importance of the facts in an infringement context, courts strive for at least the appearance of legal uniformity as is reflected by the frequency with which the four category formulation of *Abercrombie & Fitch*[7] has been recently repeated in appellate decisions.[8] The distinction between descriptiveness and genericism, at

---

[4] 604 F2d 849, 203 USPQ 241 (CA 4 1979), rmdg 202 USPQ 305 (ED Va 1978). See also infra fn 188 this chapter.

[5] 203 USPQ at 243.

[6] Weiner King, Inc. v. Wiener King Corp., 615 F2d 512, 204 USPQ 820, 831 (CCPA 1980, modg 201 USPQ 894 (TTAB 1979), discussed in 69 TMR 574 fn 151. See also supra fns 23 and 33 in ch. 2, 68 and 143 in ch. 6.

[7] Abercrombie & Fitch Co. v. Hunting World, Inc., 537 F2d 4, 189 USPQ 759 (CA 2 1976), modf 189 USPQ 769 (CA 2 1976), discussed in 66 TMR 394 fn 186. Terms claimed as trademarks may be: (i) generic and unprotectable; (ii) descriptive and protectable with proof of secondary meaning; (iii) suggestive and protectable without proof of secondary meaning; or (iv) arbitrary or fanciful and generally deserving of even broader protection.

[8] See, eg, McGregor-Doniger, supra fn this chapter; Surgicenters of America, Inc. v. Medical Surgeries Co., 601 F2d 1011, 202 USPQ 401 (CA 9 1979), affg 196 USPQ 121 (D Ore 1976), discussed in 68 TMR 807 fn 269; Vision Center v. Opticks, Inc., 596 F2d 111, 202 USPQ 333 (CA 5 1979), revg 461 F Supp 835, 202 USPQ 109 (ED La 1978). See also infra fn 187 this chapter.

§7.01[1] / Trademark Law

least, is easier to state, however, than to apply. For example, in *Vision Center v. Opticks, Inc.*,[9] the Fifth Circuit held VISION CENTER to be merely descriptive of a store where vision defects are corrected through the sale of eyeglasses, but in *Surgicenters of America, Inc. v. Medical Surgeries Co.*,[10] the Ninth Circuit determined SURGICENTER to be generic as applied to facilities for doctors to perform operations. With less difficulty, the Second Circuit in *Reese Publishing Co., v. Hampton International Communications, Inc.*[11] held that VIDEO BUYER'S GUIDE was generic as applied to a publication that reported on and promoted the sale of video products to consumers, and the First Circuit in *S.S. Kresge Co. v. United Factory Outlet, Inc.*[12] concluded that THE MART was generic for a retail discount department store, rejecting plaintiff's argument that the question of genericness is not a question of looking for dictionary definitions, but rather is a question of the public's understanding of the term's meaning.

Questions as to descriptiveness continue, however, to be particularly troublesome and often lead to conflicting results. In *Ideal Industries, Inc. v. Gardner Bender, Inc.*,[13] for example, the plaintiff had originated and others in the industry had also adopted and used the numbers 71B through 76B as size designations for spliced wire connectors. The Seventh Circuit nonetheless affirmed that in granting a preliminary injunction, "the District Court could properly infer that the 71B series numbers had acquired secondary meaning" based in large part on "the fact that Ideal has marketed its connectors with the 71B series designations for over thirty years and that during that period Ideal has been the dominant firm (over 80 percent of the market in 1976)

[9] Id.
[10] Id.
[11] 205 USPQ 585 (CA 2 1980).
[12] 202 USPQ 545 (CA 1 1979).
[13] 612 F2d 1018, 204 USPQ 177 (CA 7 1979), modg 204 USPQ 38 (ED Wisc 1979). See also infra fn 153 this chapter.

## Infringement and Unfair Competition / §7.01[1]

in the market..."[14] The court unfortunately failed to consider the effect of the use of the same designation by others on the issue of acquired distinctiveness.

In *Anti-Monopoly, Inc. v. General Mills Fun Group, Inc.*,[15] on the other hand, the Ninth Circuit rejected the District Court's holding that MONOPOLY was a valid trademark because " 'it is the title of a particular and very popular board game produced by a single company.' "[16] As the Ninth Circuit observed:

> ... if consumers think of MONOPOLY as a unique game, and differentiate it from all other real estate trading games by source-irrelevant characteristics, e.g., length of time it takes to play, or strategy involved, MONOPOLY may [be a generic term].... Again, the crucial determination is...: Do consumers use the term MONOPOLY primarily to denote the product, or instead to denote its producer? The district judge never confronted this issue, because ... he lumped together ... the two critical alternative meanings: "a particular and very popular board game" or instead a game "produced by a single company." He had to differentiate between these latter two alternatives to decide the case properly.[17]

According to the Ninth Circuit, therefore, it is largely irrelevant that consumers identify a term with a source because it is the only readily known producer or is the predominant user of the term. Rather, the nature of the term itself, the consumer's understanding as to its meaning and the context of its use are the more controlling factors.

While it thus represents a more sophisticated approach to genericism, the decision in Anti-Monopoly appears to be

---

[14] 204 USPQ at 183.
[15] 611 F2d 296, 204 USPQ 978 (CA 9 1979), revg 195 USPQ 634 (ND Calif 1977), discussed in 68 TMR 803 fn 264.
[16] 204 USPQ at 985.
[17] Id at 986.

§7.01[2] / Trademark Law

itself flawed. Quoting *Kellogg Co. v. National Biscuit Co.*,[18] for example, the Ninth Circuit strongly suggests that the only question to be answered is whether " 'the primary significance of the term in the minds of the consuming public is . . . the product [or] the producer.' "[19] Kellogg, however, was concerned with the claim that the incipiently descriptive phrase "Shredded Wheat" had acquired sufficient secondary meaning in connection with shredded, pillow-shaped, wheat biscuits to merit protection as a trademark.[20] A different analysis is necessary to determine if an incipiently arbitrary term has so come to identify a product that its use by another will not cause confusion as to source.[21] Principal significance is, therefore, only one element in the equation.

### [2] Standards of Review

Factual variances and the difficulty of applying even accepted trademark principles are not, of course, the only factors frustrating the appearance of legal uniformity. In certain respects, the Courts of Appeal have simply adopted divergent approaches to trademark issues, and in no area is this more apparent than in the standards of review enunciated by the various Circuits.

The Fifth Circuit, for example, has repeatedly held that the issue of infringement presents a question of fact and that the District Court's determination must be affirmed unless it is clearly erroneous.[22] In *Amstar Corp. v. Domino's Pizza,*

---

[18] 305 US 111, 118, 39 USPQ 296, 299 (1938). See also infra fn 7 in ch. 8.

[19] Supra fn 15, 204 USPQ at 983.

[20] Jerre B. Swann, "The Validity of Dual Functioning Trademarks: Genericism Tested by Consumer Understanding Rather Than by Consumer Use," 69 TMR 357, 374 (1979).

[21] See, eg, Jerre B. Swann, "The Economic Approach to Genericism: A Reply to Folsom and Teply," 70 TMR 243, 246–47 (1980).

[22] Armstrong Cork, supra fn 2, 203 USPQ at 24.

## Infringement and Unfair Competition / §7.01[2]

*Inc.*,[23] the Fifth Circuit reiterated, however, that a decision is deemed clearly erroneous when the result "does not reflect the truth and the right of the case." The Fifth Circuit thus reversed the finding that DOMINO'S PIZZA for pizza was confusingly similar to DOMINO for sugar and portion controlled items, the Court observing, inter alia, that:

> i. there had been extensive third party use of the term DOMINO;
> ii. DOMINO was a surname and a common English word;
> iii. DOMINO in possessive form and adjacent to the word PIZZA created an Italian connotation distinct from the use of DOMINO with sugar;
> iv. the only common denominator between pizza and sugar was that both are edible;
> v. the products were distributed through different retail outlets to different types of customers pursuant to different marketing and advertising methods; and
> vi. the marks had coexisted for fifteen years, each with total sales in excess of $100 million, yet there was evidence only as to three debatable instances of confusion, none of which was adduced by the plaintiff.

A literal application of the clearly erroneous rule would have necessitated more attention to the additional District Court findings that:

> i. DOMINO is a famous trademark deserving of wide protection; and
> ii. DOMINO portion control packets of sugar, catsup, mustard and the like were widely distributed in restaurants, including pizza parlors, so that the DOMINO mark was associated with such establishments.[24]

---

[23] 615 F2d 252, 205 USPQ 969, 974 (CA 5 1980), revg 205 USPQ 128 (ND Ga 1979). See also infra fn 103 this chapter.
[24] 205 USPQ at 976–77.

§7.01[2] / Trademark Law

At the very least, therefore, the Fifth Circuit applies the restrictively worded clearly erroneous standard quite liberally.

The Ninth Circuit, on the other hand, applies the clearly erroneous standard only where there are evidentiary disputes as to "foundational facts," e.g., as to the similarity of the marks or the goods, actual confusion, the strength of the first user's mark, intent of the second user and like considerations.[25] Where the foundational facts are not in dispute, the Ninth Circuit considers itself " 'in as good a position as the trial judge to determine the probability of confusion' "[26] and, irrespective of whether there are evidentiary conflicts, the Ninth Circuit holds that "the further determination of likelihood of confusion based on [foundational facts] is a legal conclusion."[27]

It would seem, therefore, that the Ninth Circuit's standard of review is more flexible than the Fifth's, but from a reading of the current cases, the reverse appears to be true. It is difficult to imagine the court which decided *Armstrong Cork* or *Amstar* adopting, as did the Ninth Circuit in *Alpha Industries*,[28] a District finding that ALPHA and ALPHA STEEL are dissimilar or that the second user was principally motivated in adopting its mark by a desire to associate with the positive philosophy of Alpha mind control. Likewise, the tenor of the Fifth Circuit decisions suggests that it would have made short work of a District Court finding, accepted by the Ninth Circuit in *AMF, Inc. v. Sleekcraft Boats,* that there are speed boat submarkets which are sufficiently dis-

[25] AMF, Inc. v. Sleekcraft Board, 599 F2d 341, 204 USPQ 808 (CA 9 1979), revg and rmdg 192 USPQ 231 (CD Calif 1975), discussed in 67 TMR 552 fn 257; Alpha Industries, Inc. v. Alpha Steel Tube & Shapes, Inc., 616 F2d 440, 205 USPQ 981 (CA 9 1980); Faberge, Inc. v. Saxony Products, Inc., 605 F2d 426, 204 USPQ 359 (CA 9 1979); Jockey Club, Inc. v. Jockey Club of Las Vegas, Inc., 595 F2d 1167, 202 USPQ 241 (CA 9 1979).
[26] AMF, supra fn 25, 204 USPQ at 813.
[27] Alpha Industries, supra fn 25, 205 USPQ at 984.
[28] Id at 986.

## Infringement and Unfair Competition / §7.01[2]

tinct to deem them as noncompeting.[29]

This is not to say, of course, that the Ninth Circuit decisions are erroneous; to the contrary, they appear to present close factual and legal questions which were correctly resolved. The finding of noninfringement in *Alpha Industries* was supported by the absence of direct competition between the parties, the sophistication of their customers and the weakness of the ALPHA mark. And the differentiation in AMF between general family speed boats and such boats primarily designed for racing and water skiing was substantially negated by the court's later conclusion that "the general class of boat purchasers exposed to the products overlap."[30] Nevertheless, the difference between the Fifth and Ninth Circuits in the application of their respective standards of review is even more stark than the formulation of the standards themselves.

Divergent approaches to the standard of review do not end, of course, with the Fifth and Ninth Circuits. In the Second Circuit, the clearly erroneous rule applies only to a District Court's acceptance or rejection of testimony on credibility grounds.[31] Inferences to be drawn from the testimony are subject to a "more searching review" and a "stricter standard of review is also applied where the district judge's inferences were drawn in part from documentary evidence available for inspection" at the appellate level.[32] Where the analysis turns on a review of the marks themselves, the Second Circuit considers that "it is in as good a position as the district court to determine whether they are confusingly similar."[33] Unquestionably, still other variations

---

[29] AMF, supra fn 25, 204 USPQ at 814.

[30] Id at 818.

[31] RJR Foods, Inc. v. White Rock Corp., 603 F2d 1058, 203 USPQ 401, 403 (CA 2 1979), affg 201 USPQ 578 (SDNY 1978), discussed in 69 TMR 600 fn 227.

[32] Ibid.

[33] Perfect Fit Industries, Inc. v. Acme Quilting Co., Inc., 205 USPQ 297, 302 fn 6 (CA 2 1980), modg 484 F Supp 643, 203 USPQ 481 (SDNY 1979). See also infra fn 99 this chapter.

§7.01[3] / Trademark Law

would have been enunciated had other Circuits directly faced the issue.

### [3] Intent

Conflicts can exist, of course, within a Circuit as well as between Circuits. In *American Footwear Corp. v. General Footwear Co. Ltd.*,[34] for example, the Second Circuit rejected evidence that the public associated the word "Bionic" with the "Six Million Dollar Man" and "Bionic Woman" television series despite an admission by the junior user that it had adopted the mark for boots to capitalize on the public receptiveness to the word which the senior user had created. In *RJR Foods, Inc. v. White Rock Corp.*, on the other hand, the Second Circuit held that "intentional simulation on the part of the defendant supports plaintiff's argument that it had succeeded in creating consumer recognition and good will for its product's dress"[35] and in *Perfect Fit Industries, Inc. v. Acme Quilting Co.*, the Second Circuit added that "[i]f there was intentional copying, the second comer will be presumed to have intended to create a confusing similarity of appearance and will be presumed to have succeeded."[36] Still further, the result in *American Footwear* appears inconsistent with the Second Circuit's observation in *Dallas Cowboys Cheerleaders, Inc. v. Pussycat Cinema, Ltd.* that:

> In order to be confused, a consumer need not believe that the owner of the mark actually produced the item and placed it on the market ... The public's belief that the mark's owner sponsored or otherwise approved the use of the trademark satisfies the confusion requirement.[37]

[34] 609 F2d 655, 204 USPQ 609 (CA 2 1979), modg 199 USPQ 531 (SDNY 1978), cert denied 205 USPQ 680 (US 1980).
[35] Supra fn 31, 203 USPQ at 402.
[36] Supra fn 33 at 301.
[37] 604 F2d 200, 203 USPQ 161, 164 (CA 2 1979) (citations omitted), affg 201 USPQ 740 (SDNY 1979), discussed in 69 TMR 611 fn 264.

## [4] Actual Confusion

In one area, the recent appellate decisions are in agreement, i.e., while likelihood of confusion is generally the test, proof of actual confusion may be required where the marks have coexisted in the market place for an appreciable period of time.[38] As the Second Circuit stated in *McGregor-Doniger*:

> McGregor's conceded ignorance of Drizzle's existence during the years 1969–1974 would seem to us to further buttress both the trial court's finding that no actual confusion had been proven and its ultimate conclusion that confusion is not likely. . . . Had customers, suppliers, or middlemen ever misdirected inquiries, complaints, raw materials, or finished goods, presumably the Drizzle company and its mark could not have escaped McGregor's attention for five years.[39]

## [5] Damages, Accounting and Attorneys' Fees

In other areas divergencies among the circuits also appear. The Fifth Circuit, for example, appears to be far more hospitable to an award of damages, accounting and attorneys fees than does the Ninth. In *Maltina Corp. v. Cawy Bottling Co., Inc.*,[40] the Fifth Circuit affirmed the award of an accounting not as compensation for diverted sales, but to prevent the defendant's unjust enrichment, and in *Boston Professional Hockey Ass'n v. Dallas Cap & Emblem Mfg., Inc.*,[41] the Fifth Circuit implicitly held that it was within the District Court's discretion to double the damage decree by

---

Those whose technical (rather than prurient) interests are aroused by this case will be interested in "Dallas Cowboys Cheerleaders, Inc. v. Pussycat Cinema, Ltd.: The Trademark Doctrines of Fair Use and Dilution," 9 Cap L Rev 343 (1979).

[38] McGregor-Doniger, supra fn 1, 202 USPQ at 91; Amstar Corp., supra fn 23, 205 USPQ at 979; AMF, supra fn 25, 204 USPQ at 819.
[39] Supra fn 1, 202 USPQ at 91 fn 6 (citations omitted).
[40] 205 USPQ 489 (CA 5 1980).
[41] 202 USPQ 536 (CA 5 1979).

§7.01[6] / Trademark Law

reason of defendant's "bad faith,"[42] despite the admonition of Section 35 of the Lanham Act that awards "shall constitute compensation and not a penalty."[43] In *Faberge, Inc. v. Saxony Products, Inc.*,[44] on the other hand, the Ninth Circuit affirmed what it apparently views as the unfettered discretion of the District Court to deny an accounting even though the defendant "had intentionally simulated the Brut trade dress in developing its packaging for Bravado,"[45] and in *New West Corp. v. NYM Co. of California, Inc.*,[46] the Ninth Circuit inexplicably cited its 1966 ruling[47] that "attorneys fees are not recoverable in trademark infringement cases under the Lanham Act,"[48] notwithstanding the 1975 amendment of the Act authorizing attorneys fees "in exceptional cases."[49]

[6] Color Combinations

For its part, the Second Circuit rendered multiple endorsements of the proposition that "a combination of colors together with a distinctive arbitrary design may serve as a trademark."[50] In *RJR Foods, Inc. v. White Rock Corp.*,[51] for

---

[42] The Fifth Circuit remanded the doubling of damages, but only because the District Court had failed to sufficiently detail its findings of bad faith and the reasons for its exercise of discretion.

[43] 15 USC §1117. A bad faith infringement can, of course, exacerbate the plaintiff's damages to an unquantifiable degree so that a doubling or even a trebling of ascertainable damages is appropriate to more accurately reflect the plaintiff's injury. The Fifth Circuit does not appear, however, to have limited an exercise of the District Court's discretion to such circumstances.

[44] Supra fn 25.
[45] 204 USPQ at 360.
[46] 595 F2d 1194, 202 USPQ 643 (CA 9 1979).
[47] Maier Brewing Co. v. Fleischmann Distilling Corp., 359 F2d 156, 149 USPQ 89 (CA 9 1966), affd 386 US 714, 153 USPQ 432 (1967), discussed in 56 TMR 754 fn 283 and 57 TMR 700 fn 298. See also infra fn 585.
[48] Supra fn 46, 202 USPQ at 650.
[49] 15 USC §1117.
[50] Dallas Cowboys Cheerleaders, supra fn 37, 203 USPQ at 164 fn 6.
[51] Supra fn 31.

## Infringement and Unfair Competition / §7.01[6]

example, the Second Circuit affirmed the finding below that the design of the HAWAIIAN PUNCH fruit drink can had attained a secondary meaning apart from the mark itself. In *Ives Laboratories, Inc. v. Darby Drug Co., Inc.*,[52] a thoughtful contribution by Judge Friendly to the continuing erosion of *Sears* and *Compco* and a thorough exposition of the extent to which competing pharmaceutical concerns must at least identify the source of their products, the Court observed that:

> The argument that, like functional elements, color ought to be automatically denied protection because of the risk of creating monopolies through tying up all available colors . . . does not seem persuasive; the evidence showed that, in addition to the other primary colors, an endless number of color combinations was available to the defendants.[53]

In a similar vein, the Second Circuit held in *Perfect Fit Industries, Inc. v. Acme Quilting Co. Inc.*[54] that "monopolization is not a problem in the realm of trade dress, because the possible varieties of advertising display and packaging are virtually endless,"[55] and in *Dallas Cowboys Cheerleaders*,[56] the Second Circuit spent an inordinate number of pages in expressing what any Sunday afternoon armchair quarterback could have stated in twenty-five words or less: the design and coloration of a Dallas Cowboys Cheerleaders' uniform are not purely functional.

---

[52] 601 F2d 631, 202 USPQ 548 (CA 2 1979), affg 455 F Supp 939, 200 USPQ 724 (EDNY 1978). See also infra fns 135 this chapter, 1 and 8 in Ch. 8.

See also J. S. Kahan, "Recent Developments Regarding Look-Alike Drugs," 35 Food Drug Cosm L J 35 (1980) and Iver P. Cooper, "Trademark Aspects of Pharmaceutical Product Design," 70 TMR 1 and 152 (1980).

[53] 202 USPQ at 558.
[54] Supra fn 33.
[55] Id at 300.
[56] Supra fn 37.

§7.01[7] / Trademark Law

[7] **Miscellaneous**

Otherwise, the recent appellate decisions are a series of vignettes. *Clairol, Inc. v. Boston Discount Center of Berkeley, Inc.*[57] reflects the continuing potential for conflict between unfair competition and antitrust concepts. The Sixth Circuit enjoined the sale of plaintiff's "professional" hair coloring to the general public even though its formulation was substantially identical to, and its price substantially lower than, its "retail" product. The Sixth Circuit's trademark analysis may have been correct. But it would seem unfortunate that the result is to permit an action for unfair competition to be the tool by which a vendor can successfully increase sales through price discrimination.[58] Indeed, to do so may be inconsistent with the spirit of Section 33(b)(7)

---

[57] 608 F2d 1114, 204 USPQ 89 (CA 6 1979), affg 191 USPQ 632 (ED Mich 1976), discussed in 65 TMR 549 fn 243.

[58] As Professor Lawrence Sullivan has observed in his treatise, *Handbook of the Law of Antitrust* at 89 (1977):

A firm will not discriminate unless it has market power. In a competitive market, a firm cannot sell above the competitive price and has no reason to sell below it; all its sales will cluster at its costs (including a reasonable return). Differences in price between one group or category of sales and another will be reflective of differences in associated costs. For a firm with power, however, this is not necessarily so. We can assume that if it must set a single price to all that the price will be at the profit maximizing level. To lower price further would mean more sales, but the added (the "marginal") revenue would be less than the added cost of making and supplying the additional product. The additional sales add to revenue, even at the lowered price, since but for the reduction, these sales would not be made at all. But these sales can only be made if the price is reduced to all, including those who would buy at the higher price. The net increase in revenue will thus be less than the revenue yielded by the additional sales. But if discrimination is possible, price can be reduced to pick up new customers, thus adding to total revenue, without reducing price to all customers. The total contribution to revenue of the new sales will thus be higher. A firm with power may thus have a motive to discriminate. Of course, to successfully do so it will have to be able to segregate its customers into separate categories for price purposes and keep those in the low price category from reselling to those in the higher price category at some intermediate price.

## Infringement and Unfair Competition / §7.01[7]

of the Lanham Act[59] and it would seem that the court could have worked out a better accommodation of the duty to protect the public from injury and the right of the defendants to sell its property at the lowest possible price.

*Miller Brewing Co. v. Jos. Schlitz Brewing Co.*,[60] a sequel in the Miller "Lite" controversy, contains a comprehensive analysis of the collateral estoppel doctrine in a trademark context and *R.G. Barry Corp. v. Mushroom Makers, Inc.*,[61] a sequel in the Mushroom(s) controversy, holds that a carefully worded trademark dilution claim which does not allege consumer confusion cannot be removed from a state to a federal forum on the ground that the complaint states a cause of action within the District Court's original jurisdiction.[62] In *SSP Agricultural Equipment, Inc. v. Orchard-Rite Ltd.*, the Ninth Circuit reiterated its position that the "use of competitor's trademark for purposes of comparative advertising is not trademark infringement 'so long as it does not contain misrepresentations or create a reasonable likelihood that purchasers will be confused . . .' "[63] and in *In re Vuitton et Fils S.A.*,[64] trademark counsel, confronted with infringers who would transfer counterfeit merchandise to confederates when served with a complaint, demonstrated both ingenuity and persistence in obtaining from the Second Circuit a direction that the District Court issue an ex parte restraining order without notice to the defendant. The unique order award goes, however, to the district judge in *Miss Universe, Inc. v. Flesher* who enjoined further use of

[59] 15 USC §1115(b)(7).

[60] 605 F2d 990, 203 USPQ 642 (CA 7 1979), modg 449 F Supp 852, 203 USPQ 620 (ED Wisc 1978), cert denied 205 USPQ 96 (US 1980). See also infra fn 162 this chapter.

[61] 204 USPQ 521 (CA 2 1979), revg 204 USPQ 113 (SDNY 1979). See also infra fn 156 this chapter.

[62] See, Beech-Nut, Inc. v. Warner-Lambert Co., 480 F2d 801, 178 USPQ 385 (CA 2 1973), discussed in 64 TMR 410 fn 329. It could, of course, still be removed if there was diversity of citizenship and the defendant did not reside within the district.

[63] 202 USPQ 1, 6 (CA 9 1979).

[64] 606 F2d 1, 204 USPQ 1 (CA 2 1979).

§7.02 / Trademark Law

"Miss Nude USA" but would have permitted defendant to use "Miss Nude-USA," requiring that in oral expressions of the mark, defendant say "Miss Nude hyphen USA."[65] Neither party was happy with the result and the Ninth Circuit agreed with the plaintiff that the hyphen was a difference without distinction.

§7.02 Federal District Court Decisions

The increase in trademark litigation in recent years has continued and this trend is evident in the number of reported District Court decisions this past year. The range of issues dealt with in these cases was equally broad. The doctrine of aesthetic functionality received some support in decisions from courts in the Ninth Circuit and the fledgling theory of the right to protect developing secondary meaning received both support and some limiting holding in cases in the Southern District of New York. Of special interest was the continuing tussle between proponents of the doctrine of misappropriation and backers of a more limited scope of protection for industrial property rights.

[1] Misappropriation Doctrine and Preemption

The misappropriation doctrine of the *International News Service*[66] case formed the bases, in part, for an award of damages for copying a copyrighted bank form in *Professional Systems & Supplies Inc. v. Databank Supplies & Equipment Co., Inc.*[67] The court found that plaintiff had expended money and skill in devising the form and that plaintiff was injured by the use of the form by its competitor, the defendant. The propriety of applying that doctrine in a case when the copied work was also in copyright is questionable. Nevertheless, there are persistent signs that the impact of this

---

[65] 605 F2d 1130, 204 USPQ 354, 358 fn 10 (CA 9 1979), modg 433 F Supp 271, 200 USPQ 330 (CD Calif 1977), discussed in 69 TMR 598 fn 220.
[66] International News Service v. Associated Press, 248 US 215 (1918).
[67] 202 USPQ 693 (WD Okla 1979).

landmark decision is still to be reckoned within appropriate cases of unfair competition.

The *INS* case also formed, in part, the basis for the grant of an injunction in *Traditional Living Inc. v. Energy Log Homes Inc.*[68] In this case, the parties were competitors in the log home business. Plaintiff supplied packets containing simple plans and information, in the form of written questions and answers. In copying these materials, the defendant was found by the court to have intended to misappropriate to itself plaintiff's advertising and promotional efforts and its efforts in creating its designs. Finding that the packets, including their—unspecified—nonfunctional aspects had acquired distinctiveness in the geographic area where defendant engaged in business, the court entered a preliminary injunction based upon common law unfair competition as well as copyright infringement.

In the case of *Synercom Technology Inc. v. University Computing Co.*,[69] the court considered the extent of the application of the doctrine of misappropriation and held it not to be applicable where to hold otherwise would have had a materially adverse effect on competition. In an earlier decision,[70] the court had found that the defendants had infringed plaintiff's copyright in certain user manuals for computer programs which it had developed, but denied copyright infringement based upon the defendants' copying of plaintiff's input methodology for the reason that the inputs were essentially ideas, not expressions. The most recent decision dealt with plaintiff's alternative claim that the use of its input methodology was actionable as an act of misappropriation. In a carefully drafted opinion, the court traced the history of the doctrine of misappropriation and held that even if the use of these input methods constituted misappropriation—as to which conclusion the court was manifestly uncertain—the application of the state unfair competition law in this case would have been in conflict with the pur-

[68] 464 F Supp 1024, 202 USPQ 703 (ND Ala 1978).
[69] 474 F Supp 37, 204 USPQ 29 (ND Tex 1979).
[70] 199 USPQ 537 (ND Tex 1978).

§7.02[1] / Trademark Law

poses of the federal copyright and patent statutes. Here, the court reasoned, to restrict use of the input methods developed by plaintiff would be effectively to grant a monopoly of the kind contemplated in the copyright laws—but without limit in time—and would effectively block competition for an extended period. Due to the economics of the business, competitors would be forced to develop a competitive system which would have to be sold for a considerably higher price since substituting a competitive program with different inputs would necessitate an expensive retraining of the customer's employees. It appears that the court decided essentially based upon its belief that the results of applying the plaintiff's legal theory would be to prevent effective competition, notwithstanding that the relief sought would not have prevented the defendants from devising its own equally effective system.

The doctrine of misappropriation surfaced in another context in the decision in *Mitchell v. Penton/Industrial Publishing Co., Inc.*[71] While nominally a copyright case, the decision is noteworthy here for the court applied the preemption clause of the 1976 Copyright Act to preclude the assertion of a common law misappropriation claim based upon the misuse by the defendant of the information contained in plaintiff's copyrighted book. The court held that if the misappropriation count lay because of the copying of the copyrighted work, the claim was banned by Section 301(a) of the Copyright Act, and if it did not lie because the copyright did not cover the copied matter, the doctrine of the *Sears* and *Compco* cases[72] precluded the enforcement of the rights claimed by plaintiff in respect of matter in the public domain.

The opposite result, however, was reached in what was also essentially a copyright infringement case, *Bi-Rite Enter-*

[71] 486 F Supp 22, 205 USPQ 242 (ND Ohio 1979).
[72] Sears, Roebuck & Co. v. Stiffel Co., 376 US 225, 54 TMR 217, 140 USPQ 524 (1964) and Compco Corp. v. Day-Brite Lighting Inc., 376 US 234, 54 TMR 223, 140 USPQ 528 (1964).

*prises Inc. v. Dan Barrett, Inc.*,[73] in which the court enjoined defendant's sale of a copy of plaintiff's copyrighted poster of STARSKY & HUTCH on the additional ground that the sale of the identical poster was a kind of palming off based on an implied representation that the copied prints were those of plaintiff's and were sold with authorization. Insofar as the only operative fact in the case was the sale of the infringing copy, this additional theory of liability would seem to fall within the provisions of Section 301(a) of the Copyright Act preempting state unfair competition claims so based.

In *Frederick Warne & Co., Inc. v. Book Sales, Inc.*[74] the court denied cross motions for summary judgment in a most unusual case. Plaintiff claimed that defendant's use of its cover illustrations for books which plaintiff published, but which were not in copyright, was trademark infringement and violated Section 43(a) of the Lanham Act. Defendant's book was a republication of seven public domain stories in a single volume. Defendant's book contained reproductions which appeared on the cover, but not in the text, of the original works. Plaintiff, which has used at least one of these illustrations is an extensive licensing program and had registered three as trademarks, asserted that the cover illustrations were valued trademarks despite the fact that the books had fallen into the public domain. The court easily disposed of plaintiff's motion for summary judgment, holding that whether the cover illustrations identified plaintiff as the source of the books was a question of fact which could not be resolved on motion. In denying defendant's motion, the court addressed the issue of defendant's right to publish public domain works in their entirety. The court noted that the right was limited to publication unaccompanied by conduct which amounted to unfair competition. It held that while the covers were copyrightable, and thus entitled to protection under the book's copyright, the lapse of that right did not necessarily throw the covers into the public domain. Noting the difference in the purposes of the copyright and

[73] 203 USPQ 574 (ND Ill 1978).
[74] 481 F Supp 1191, 205 USPQ 444 (SDNY 1979).

## §7.02[2] / Trademark Law

trademark laws, the court held that the right to copy the covers should be governed by the same standards as govern trade dress and packaging cases. Thus, the correct question was not, as contended by defendant, whether the cover had fallen into the public domain, but whether, having done so, had the illustrations thereon acquired secondary meaning. That, clearly was a question of material fact.

### [2] Protection of Developing Secondary Meaning

In an unfair competition case where the question of developing secondary meaning was raised, the district judge in *Orion Pictures Co., Inc. v. Dell Publishing Co., Inc.*[75] enjoined defendant's publication of a book under a title identical to that of plaintiff's motion picture, basing its decision primarily on notions of fairness under New York State decisions. In this interesting case, the plaintiff's film was based upon, but radically departed from, an underlying novel. Prior to release of the motion picture, defendant acquired the right to republish the novel under any name it chose. It elected to use the motion picture title as the name, and, relying heavily on the motion picture's promotion, printed "Now a Major Motion Picture" on the book cover. The court had no difficulty in holding that it was unfair to misappropriate plaintiff's efforts and good will in this fashion.

On the basic claim of unfair competition, the court also rejected defendant's argument that plaintiff's pre-release publicity was insufficient to establish the requisite secondary meaning. The District Court held that an injunction would permit plaintiff the opportunity to attain such significance:

> Moreover, there appears to be growing support for the proposition that a secondary meaning "in the making" should be protected, at least to the extent of preventing

---

[75] 471 F Supp 392, 202 USPQ 819 (SDNY 1979). See also infra fn 101 this chapter.

intentional attempts, as by the defendant here, to capitalize on the efforts and goodwill of others.[76]

The court also found, from defendant's deliberate attempts to capitalize upon the good will of the motion picture's title, that an inference of secondary meaning could be drawn. In this, at least, the court was probably in error in that the defendant's conduct appears to have been equally attributable to the hope that the film would in the future acquire great renown. The decision, however, reflects a welcome trend toward examining the morality of the defendant's conduct in such cases and to adapting the law to meet the facts. The law of unfair competition ought to be as ingenious in preventing unfair conduct as the defendants are in designing means to take a free ride on the good will or efforts of others.

A similar rationale, illustrating the emergence of the theory of protecting developing secondary meaning in the Southern District of New York, is found in another case decided in that court. The District Court, in *Blake Publishing Corp. v. O'Quinn Studios Inc.*,[77] enjoined the proposed use of FANTASTICA as a magazine title in view of plaintiff's prior use of FANTASTIC FILMS as a title for a competitive magazine directed to the same, rather limited, public. Noting that the title FANTASTIC FILMS was "more nearly" descriptive than suggestive, the court nevertheless found it entitled to protection, both because it believed the title had acquired recognition among the group of readers to whom it was addressed and because the court believed the title was entitled to protection for its "emerging" secondary meaning. The decision represents, to some extent, an extension of the theory that when the efforts of the plaintiff are in the process of achieving trademark status for a mark, that result ought not to be frustrated merely because an "infringer" comes along before distinctiveness can be demonstrated with certainty.

In *Perfect Fit Industries, Inc. v. Acme Quilting Co.*,

---

[76] 202 USPQ at 823.
[77] 202 USPQ 848 (SDNY 1979).

§7.02[3] / Trademark Law

*Inc.*,[78] however, the court unfortunately refused to extend the doctrine of protecting incipient secondary meaning to a case involving copying of trade dress. Four months after plaintiff brought out its new, but unpatented product, defendant began to sell its copy in packages which bore an insert which was concededly copied from and simulated that used by plaintiff. The court held that secondary meaning had not been proved, and noted that the acquisition of distinctiveness was unlikely because defendant brought out its copy within four months. The court also declined to protect plaintiff's right to develop a secondary meaning, noting that no Second Circuit decision sanctioning the protection of incipient secondary meaning had been cited. The court also denied relief under New York State unfair competition cases. Although conceding that the law of New York in some cases dispenses with the requirements for a showing of secondary meaning, no New York case involving the conduct in issue was cited and the district judge declined to extend the law. The total absence of any reference to the defendant's intent and to the cases raising a presumption of secondary meaning where intent to pass off is shown is remarkable. The extremely narrow reading of the state law of unfair competition is equally regrettable. As noted above, this decision was reversed in the Second Circuit.

[3] Incontestability Affidavits

In an unusual case involving the complex legal and factual issues raised by the expansion of service businesses into new geographic areas, *Armand's Subway Inc. v. Doctor's Associates, Inc.*,[79] the District Court dismissed defendant's counterclaims attacking plaintiff's pleaded registration predicated on the allegation that plaintiff, when it filed its Section 15 affidavit of incontestability, had failed to note the pendency of defendant's concurrent use application as a

[78] 484 F Supp 643, 203 USPQ 481 (SDNY 1979), mofd 205 USPQ 297 (CA 2 1980). See also supra fn 33.
[79] 202 USPQ 129 (ED Va 1978).

## Infringement and Unfair Competition / §7.02[4]

pending "proceeding." Analogizing a concurrent use proceeding to an interference, the court held that no "proceeding" was pending until one was formally declared by the Commissioner of Patents and Trademarks. Since that apparently had not occurred, as of the date of the Section 15 affidavit, the attack on the registration was dismissed.

### [4] Miscellaneous Likelihood of Confusion Cases

In *Motor Master Products Corp. v. Motor Masters Warehouse Inc.*,[80] the District Court unaccountably held that the trademark MOTOR MASTER and design for automotive replacement products was not infringed by the use of the trade name MOTOR MASTERS WAREHOUSE for the business of distributing automotive parts, which were in part identical to the products sold by the plaintiff. The court, in addition to finding no likelihood of confusion, also rejected plaintiff's argument that the relevant trade would mistakenly believe that defendant was a division of, or related to, plaintiff or distributed plaintiff's products. Perhaps the court was influenced by the fact that the names had coexisted since 1954 and no actual confusion appeared to have surfaced, although this was in part explained by the relatively small sales effected by plaintiff in defendant's trading area.

*Uniroyal Inc. v. Kinney Shoe Corp.*,[81] saw the court deny protection to the Famous KEDS trademark by refusing to enjoin use of "Kinney KiDS" for identical products, notwithstanding that defendant, trading under the name KINNEY, had previously distributed KEDS shoes and showed by use of the registered trademark symbol that KINNEY was a separate mark. The court reasoned that the word "Kids," considering its significance and that its use by defendant was for shoes for children, was not unduly similar to KEDS and that, when used as part of the composite mark, confusion was unlikely. One would perhaps agree with the court more

[80] 463 F Supp 232, 202 USPQ 213 (ED Pa 1978).
[81] 453 F Supp 1352, 202 USPQ 273 (SDNY 1978).

### §7.02[4] / Trademark Law

readily if the defendants were not attempting to use "KiDS" as part of a trademark. The existence of several other "Kid" trademarks for shoes, however, seemed to tip the balance.

Summary judgment was granted against both plaintiff and the counterclaiming defendant in *Continental Corrugated Container Corp. v. Continental Group, Inc.*[82] Plaintiff, a small local distributor of corrugated paper products, claiming that it was known in its market area as CONTINENTAL CORRUGATED, a name it had never used, sought to enjoin defendant's use of CONTINENTAL CORRUGATED as the name of one of its divisions which competed with plaintiff. The defendant had adopted its name in 1968, some ten years before the dispute. Defendant sought, in its counterclaim, to enjoin plaintiff's use of "Continental" for paper products, based on its previous use of that term as a trade name in the packaging industry. In granting defendant's motion for summary judgment, the court found that the plaintiff could not prove the acquisition of secondary meaning which was required to succeed both in its claims for federal and state trademark infringement and unfair competition. Additionally its dilution claims fell due to the total lack of distinctiveness of the term in issue. The court, after reviewing some of the cases, declined to rule on the question of whether plaintiff could in all events predicate its claim on a nickname which it never used or whose use it never encouraged.

Similarly, the court granted plaintiff's motion to dismiss the counterclaim on the considerably more doubtful theory that a geographic term such as "Continental" could not be the basis for a claim of trademark infringement by reason of its use on goods other than those in respect of which the first user had actually appropriated it. In short, the court held as a matter of law that the common word "Continental" was entitled to but the narrowest scope of protection.

In *Mego Corp. v. Mattel, Inc.*[83] the court found that defendant's mark BATTLESTAR GALACTICA, for space toys,

---

[82] 462 F Supp 200, 203 USPQ 993 (SDNY 1978).
[83] 203 USPQ 377 (SDNY 1978).

was not so similar to plaintiff's GALACTIC CRUISER or GALACTIC WARRIOR as to constitute a clear showing of likely success on the merits, and therefore warrant a preliminary injunction. The court noted the significance of the term "Galactica" as applied to "space" toys and extensive evidence of third party uses, federal applications and registrations. The court also rejected plaintiff's claim that defendant copied its dress of goods and found that the balance of hardships was greatly in defendant's favor. Accordingly, the preliminary injunction was denied.

In *Bethom Corp. v. Meredity Corp.*[84] the court denied plaintiff a preliminary injunction enjoining the entry of defendant into the real estate franchise business in California under the name BETTER HOMES AND GARDENS REAL ESTATE SERVICE. Plaintiff had used the service mark BETTER HOMES for real estate services in California since 1964 and, commencing in 1975, had franchised sixty others to do the same. In denying the motion, the court noted that there were numerous other parties in similar businesses in California and elsewhere who utilized the words "Better Homes" as part of their trade names. Not only were those words not protectable absent proof of secondary meaning, but the plaintiff had wholly failed to prove that such significance had been achieved.

In *Meredith Corp. v. Bouschard*,[85] the tables were turned on the magazine owner when the District Court unaccountably denied its motion for summary judgment seeking to enjoin continued maintenance by defendant of the corporate name, BETTER HOMES & GARDENS REALTY INC., for the reason that plaintiff had failed to prove that defendants had incorporated under that name "for fraudulent purpose." It is difficult to fathom what non-fraudulent purposes defendant could have had in incorporating under plaintiff's famous mark within a few months of plaintiff's announcement of its intention to engage in the real estate business through franchisees in various states.

[84] 203 USPQ 819 (ND Calif 1978).
[85] 205 USPQ 513 (ND Ill 1979).

§7.02[4] / Trademark Law

The district judge in *General Foods Corp. v. General Foods Inc.*[86] had little difficulty in finding fraudulent intent in defendant's incorporating as "General Foods Inc." in the Virgin Islands, and engaging in the sale of foods at wholesale and retail under that name. In granting summary judgment to plaintiff the court rejected defendant's argument that the granting of its corporate charter somehow created a right to use the name vis-à-vis plaintiff, as well as a series of other defenses asserted by it. The court found defendant's conduct to be trademark infringement, unfair competition, false designation of origin or deception, dilution and a violation of the local statute prohibiting infringement with intent to cause confusion.

The case of *Ashe v. PepsiCo, Inc.*[87] involved the question of whether PepsiCo's trademark ADVANTAGE, registered for tennis, golf and other equipment, infringed plaintiff's ADVANTAGE ASHE for tennis glasses. In finding no infringement existed the court held that while the plaintiff's mark was suggestive and thus protectable absent proof of secondary meaning, the plaintiff's failure to prove such meaning left the court with but a weak mark to consider. In light of this non-distinctiveness of the mark, proof of numerous third party marks containing the term both in tennis as well as other fields and the differences in the products, it was held that confusion was unlikely. The court took particular note of the frame of plaintiff and that plaintiff's mark was dominated by the word ASHE.

In *Transamerica Corp. v. Trans-American Collections, Inc.*[88] the District Court held that defendant's name and service mark, dominated by the words TRANS-AMERICAN, and TRANS-AMERICAN COLLECTIONS for collection agency services was confusingly similar to plaintiff's prior mark, TRANSAMERICA, for a variety of financial services. The use of the plaintiff's name and mark by a number of plaintiff's subsidiaries in various areas of the financial and

[86] 205 USPQ 538 (D VI 1979).
[87] 205 USPQ 451 (SDNY 1979).
[88] 205 USPQ 1231 (ND Calif 1979).

## Infringement and Unfair Competition / §7.02[4]

insurance business was held to inure to the plaintiff's benefit.

In *Russ Berrie & Co., Inc. v. Jerry Elsner Co., Inc.*[89] the District Court dismissed plaintiff's claim that defendant had infringed the copyright in plaintiff's stuffed dolls, but held that plaintiff's trademark GONGA, for its gorilla doll, was infringed by the name CONGO, adopted by defendant. Holding that the mark was fanciful and strong, the court held that no showing of secondary meaning was necessary, and concluded that confusion was likely based on the similarity of marks alone.

In *General Electric Co. v. Alumpa Coal Co. Inc.*[90] the court enjoined the sale by defendant of teeshirts bearing a reproduction of plaintiff's famous GE monogram in which the words "Genital Electric" were substituted for GENERAL ELECTRIC. Following the decision in the nearly identical case of *The Coca-Cola Co. v. Gemini Rising Inc.*,[91] the court held that the substantial similarity of the marks would be likely to result in consumer confusion.

In *Park 'N Fly, Inc. v. Park & Fly, Inc.*[92] the District Court held that plaintiff's incontestable registration was impervious to defendant's attack on the ground of descriptiveness. In this case, the registered mark of plaintiff was PARK 'N FLY for auto parking services in the vicinity of airports. Defendant subsequently adopted the mark PARK & FLY and plaintiff sued. Defendant claimed that since incontestability pertains only to the mark as registered and since its mark differed from the registered mark by excluding a logo used by plaintiff, the protection from attack did not apply. The court rejected this argument as simplistic, recognizing that acceptance of the argument would mean that the mere act of making small and inconsequential changes in a registered mark would destroy the benefits of incontestability

---

[89] 482 F Supp 980, 205 USPQ 320 (SDNY 1980).

[90] 205 USPQ 1036 (D Mass 1979).

[91] 346 F Supp 1183, 175 USPQ 56 (EDNY 1972), discussed in 63 TMR 392 fn 264.

[92] 204 USPQ 204 (D Mass 1979).

§7.02[4] / Trademark Law

which Congress intended to bestow. The court declined to limit the right in the fashion contended.

District Judge Brieant's decision in *Ferrara v. Scharf*[93] gave further impetus to the doctrine that doubts on the issue of likelihood of confusion should be resolved against the later user. In holding that plaintiff's prior trade name and trademark rights in the designations J & C FERRARA CO and FERRARA, used in the low-priced jewelry business were infringed by defendant's use of FERRARA CREATIONS in a directly competitive business, the court gave especial weight to numerous instances of actual confusion. Especially noteworthy was the court's finding, based upon defendant's failure to engage in its own advertising, that defendant was trading on plaintiff's good will and the court's deduction that defendant's rapid expansion without advertising was evidence that defendant was benefiting from plaintiff's renown in the trade. Such a holding, of course, was dependent upon a finding that the name FERRARA had acquired distinctiveness. In so holding, the court articulated the standard of proof applicable to this most difficult of factual conclusions as proof sufficient to establish "more likely than not" that the mark or name had come to stand in the mind of the public or trade, "even if merely subconsciously" as the name or identification of a firm or its products.

In *Johnson v. Heilman*[94] the District Court held that plaintiff's federally registered mark COLLECTORS EXTRAVAGANZA and design of an eagle was not infringed by defendant's use of such names as "Penna. Antique & Collectors Extravaganza" for the services of operating markets at which collectors and dealers displayed and sold antiques to the public. The court held COLLECTORS EXTRAVAGANZA to be descriptive and that plaintiff had failed to prove the acquisition of secondary meaning. The court likewise noted the geographic diversity of the parties and held that in all events, confusion was thereby unlikely. This latter

[93] 466 F Supp 125, 204 USPQ 118 (SDNY 1979).
[94] 204 USPQ 655 (ED Pa 1979).

conclusion seems somewhat doubtful since the parties advertised in the same publications, so that the opportunity for confusion, if otherwise likely, would appear also to have been present.

In an exceptionally well-reasoned and thorough opinion, the District Court in *Decatur Federal Savings & Loan Ass'n. v. Peach State Federal Savings & Loan Ass'n*[95] held that the service mark SAVING SHOP was infringed by the mark THE SAVINGS SPOT, both used for banking services. The court first rejected defendant's attack on plaintiff's mark as being generic, or merely descriptive, of small banking booths located in shopping malls and the like. Conceding that both "Savings" and "Shop" were separately generic, the court found that the mark as a whole was different, unique and required the exercise of some thought to disclose what the services were. In considering the ultimate question of likelihood of confusion, the court stressed that substantially the only means of distinguishing the services of savings and loan associations was by way of catchy advertising slogans and marks and for that reason the public was more likely to be confused by similar marks. In addition, in response to defendant's assertion that use of their full names by both parties avoided confusion, the court declined to adopt a fixed rule regarding the use of trade names with marks. Whether such accompanying uses exacerbated or diminished a likelihood of confusion should depend on the facts of each case. In this case, the use of the bank names with the service marks was held to increase the probability of confusion because of the similarities in the trade names themselves since both contained the word "federal" and because the public's choices here were likely to be motivated more by advertising than by more rational reasons. Additionally both parties did not uniformly use their names with their marks. Conceding the closeness and difficulty of the case, the court ultimately noted that the rights of first users should prevail in doubtful cases.

In a battle on the drug scene, the court, in *Trans-High*

[95] 203 USPQ 406 (Na Ga 1978).

## §7.02[4] / Trademark Law

*Corp. v. Alshar Corp.*[96] was not persuaded that defendant's HILIFE name for its magazine was selected because of its similarity to plaintiff's HIGH TIMES magazine—with which it was directly competitive—as opposed to its desire to take advantage of the immediate identification anticipated of its prospective audience with the word "High." The court was concerned by the closeness of the case, but in the last analysis, felt that the disproportionate impact of the injunction on the defendant, which was not shown to the court's satisfaction to have been acting in a predatory manner, militated a denial of the preliminary injunction sought.

In a well-reasoned opinion in *American Home Products Corp. v. Morton-Norwich Products, Inc.*,[97] the District Court enjoined the use by defendant of the trademark OVAL, or ENCARE OVAL, for vaginal suppositories in light of the similarity of the word OVAL to plaintiff's prior OVRAL and LO/OVRAL marks for birth control pills. The court rejected the argument that the differences in the packaging should be considered, for the reason that the purchaser would not be likely to see the products in juxtaposition. Additionally, the court found that the addition of the trademark ENCARE did not distinguish the marks, for the public might well believe that the owner of the ENCARE mark was a licensee or authorized user of plaintiff's mark. The court appears to have been particularly impressed with the potentially harmful effects of confusion with regard to the effectiveness of birth control products, as well as unfavorable comments on defendant's products by the FDA.

A case having significant impact on trademark maintenance programs is *Procter & Gamble Co. v. Johnson & Johnson, Inc.*[98] In this case the court held that plaintiff's trademarks SURE for underarm anti-perspirant and a woman's tampon, and ASSURE for mouthwash and shampoo, were not infringed by defendant's use of ASSURE! for a woman's tampon, and SURE & NATURAL for an external

---

[96] 204 USPQ 567 (SDNY 1978).
[97] 202 USPQ 824 (SDNY 1978).
[98] 205 USPQ 697 (SDNY 1979).

## Infringement and Unfair Competition / §7.02[4]

menstrual protection shield. In addition, the court sustained defendant's counterclaim for cancellation of plaintiff's federal registrations for SURE for women's tampons, and ASSURE for mouthwash and shampoo on the ground that they did not represent existing trademark rights. While plaintiff was able to prove extensive use of SURE in respect of personal deodorants, its use of that mark on tampons as well as its use of ASSURE, had for a number of years been confined to its "Minor Brands" program.

In this factually complex case, defendant had become aware of plaintiff's above-noted registrations when seeking a mark for its new line of tampons. However, based on an investigation which revealed no instance of actual use, defendant concluded that plaintiff's registrations "were no legal obstacle" to its use of ASSURE! and it commenced a cancellation action in the Patent and Trademark Office. During the pendency of the cancellation proceeding the civil action was commenced. Defendant failed to submit evidence during its testimony period in the cancellation, relying on the "practice" of suspension of Patent and Trademark Office proceedings when litigation eventuates. A default was entered which the Trademark Trial and Appeal Board failed to vacate. A review of the failure to vacate the default in the Patent and Trademark Office was incorporated as an issue in the pending litigation by an appeal to the District Court.

In a long and carefully drafted opinion, the District Court found that there was no likelihood of confusion between SURE for an anti-perspirant on the one hand, and ASSURE! for a tampon or SURE & NATURAL for a protection shield on the other, and ordered cancellation of the plaintiff's registrations—except that for SURE for anti-perspirants—on the ground of nonuse. In finding for defendant, the court noted that, while suggestive rather than descriptive, the word SURE was not entitled to a very broad ambit of protection, "falling in the weakest end of the suggestive range." Plaintiff was hoist by its own petard, for support for this weakness of the mark was found in plaintiff's successful de-

§7.02[4] / Trademark Law

fense of a suit by a third party seeking to enjoin plaintiff's use of SURE on the basis of the prior use of the word "Sure" descriptively in advertisements for deodorants by that third party. In a perhaps less defensible part of the opinion, in addition to weakness of the mark the court held that the differences between SURE on the one hand and ASSURE! and SURE & NATURAL on the other were "marked and prominent."

Of particular interest is the court's finding that defendant, despite its knowledge of plaintiff's registrations and its failed attempt to purchase them, had not acted in bad faith in later adopting the mark ASSURE! The honest (and correct) belief that there was no conflict and that the registrations did not represent valid trademark rights were held to be consistent with a good faith adoption.

The court went on to order cancellation of plaintiff's "Minor Brand" marks, on the ground that, notwithstanding token sales of fifty units a year, nonuse for ten and twelve years indicated that no genuine commercial use had occurred or was intended. It stated that, whatever the case might be where there is a present intent to commence use, the keeping of a series of marks in a "Trademark Bank" over an extended period of time, no matter how sound the motivation or justifiable the reasoning, would not result in the creation or maintenance of actual trademark rights. The court reasoned that the filing of a Section 15 declaration of incontestability in such a case would not alter the facts or create rights where no trademark exists as a matter of law.

The similarity of the service marks UNITED STATES AUTO CLUB and UNITED STATES MOTOR CLUB, as well as the defendant's use of a device "amazingly" similar to plaintiff's famous shield device, led the court to grant an injunction in *United States Auto Club Inc. v. United States Motor Club Corp.*[99] The court noted that the parties were direct competitors in the conduct of their motoring clubs and sought to attract members in exactly the same ways.

[99] 205 USPQ 150 (ED La 1979).

## Infringement and Unfair Competition / §7.02[6]

### [5] Misrepresentation

In a delightfully written opinion in *Scott & Fetzer Co. v. Dile*,[100] the court had no difficulty in holding that defendant's offering of rebuilt and used KIRBY vacuum cleaners as new constituted both trademark infringement and unfair competition. The court deplored the fact that it took over one year for the plaintiff to obtain a hearing on its motion for a preliminary injunction.

### [6] Confusion of Sponsorship

In another case involving an attempt to take advantage of the good will anticipated from the publicity accompanying a motion picture, the producer's rights were also upheld in *Walt Disney Productions v. Kusan, Inc.*,[101] where the District Court enjoined defendant's use of BLACK HOLE IN SPACE as the trademark for a game, notwithstanding that plaintiff's game entitled THE BLACK HOLE had not then yet been sold. The court found that defendant's promotion of its game was intended to take advantage of Disney's extensive promotion of its forthcoming movie, entitled THE BLACK HOLE, and that defendant's first "trademark" use of the BLACK HOLE IN SPACE occurred after the announcements of the forthcoming movie. The court held that defendant's earlier shipment of a game to a potential manufacturer was insufficiently "public" use to create trademark rights. It similarly rejected defendant's claim that rights arose when a game was displayed to an employee of Sears with a view to its inclusion in Sears' catalog on the somewhat dubious ground that use of the name on an accompanying production sheet was not trademark use as there was no affixation to the goods. The court rejected defendant's argument that the printing of the words "Hole in Space" on a

---

[100] 204 USPQ 838 (D Ariz 1979).
[101] 204 USPQ 284 (CD Calif 1979). See also supra fn 75 this chapter.

On protection of merchandising properties flowing from motion pictures, etc, see Charles W. Grimes and Gregory J. Battersby, "The Protection of Merchandising Properties," 69 TMR 431 (1979).

§7.02[6] / Trademark Law

black background was the visual equivalent of the words BLACK HOLE IN SPACE.

It appears that the defendant was indeed the first to use the name BLACK HOLE IN SPACE. But that use was disregarded by the district judge who apparently felt quite strongly that defendant's attempt to take a free ride on the Disney movie, coupled with the substantial balance of hardships in Disney's favor, called for ignoring the defendant's earlier and minimal use.

The court, in *Foxfire Fund Inc. v. Burke*,[102] preliminarily enjoined defendant's use of FOXFIRE for its sales of rustic homes in Rabun County, Georgia, in view of plaintiff's prior rights in FOXFIRE stemming from its publication of THE FOXFIRE magazine, books dealing with rustic living in the area encompassing Rabun County, Georgia, and its construction and maintenance of a restoration village in that county. The court rejected for lack of proof defendant's assertion that the area in question was known as the "Foxfire Area" and also held that the numerous proffered third party uses were either geographically irrelevant, or were unaccompanied by evidence of use which would have had an effect on the public's perception of the word "Foxfire" in Rabun County.

In *Amstar Corp. v. Domino's Pizza Inc.*[103] the District Court enjoined the use by defendants of the name DOMINO'S or DOMINO'S PIZZA as a trade name and trademark for its pizza shops as well as the products sold therefrom. The court adopted verbatim the extensive findings of fact and conclusions of law proposed by the plaintiff, which recited the fame of plaintiff's mark, the extent of its use and advertising and the relationship of its products—sugar and portion controlled foods—to the rendering of restaurant services as well as in the preparation of food products sold for both on- and off-premises consumption. The manifest one-sidedness of the findings, however, makes it difficult to ana-

[102] 203 USPQ 416 (ND Ga 1978).
[103] 205 USPQ 128 (ND Ga 1979), revd 615 F2d 252, 205 USPQ 969 (CA 5 1980). See also supra fn 23 this chapter.

lyze what, if anything, the case stands for. It seems clear, however, that at a minimum, the court felt that there would be an association in the public mind of defendant's pizza parlors and products sold under plaintiff's famous mark.

In *Inner Circle Inc. v. Holiday Inns, Inc.*[104] the court rejected plaintiff's claim that defendant's use of INNER CIRCLE and HOLIDAY INN INNER CIRCLE for a special privilege (noncredit) card in the Columbus, Ohio, area infringed its prior rights in the service mark INNER CIRCLE for its restaurant and lounge business. Based on evidence of numerous third party uses, the court found INNER CIRCLE to be a weak mark, and that no secondary meaning had been achieved by plaintiff. In all events, no likelihood of confusion was believed to be present due to the differences in the nature of the businesses and the good faith adoption by defendant. The court elected to disbelieve plaintiff's testimony of numerous instances of actual confusion and attributed that which did perhaps occur to inattention on the part of recipients of defendant's card.

The name of a well-known television science program, NOVA, was the subject of the decision in *WGBH Educational Foundation, Inc. v. Penthouse International Ltd.*[105] Defendant was in the course of preparing to use that word as the name for a magazine devoted to "science, science, fiction, UFO's and occult matters." The District Court found there existed a likelihood that the public would assume that there was a relationship between defendant's magazine and plaintiff's television program. The distinctiveness of the name and the fact that plaintiff's program was distributed via cassetts for use in schools and was the subject of printed materials published by plaintiff or under its authority were all deemed to be persuasive factors. The court was apparently equally impressed with the potential negative impact of defendant's use of NOVA as the name for a titillating magazine on plaintiff's reputation as a serious scientific endeavor and concerned at the potential loss of sponsorship resulting

[104] 203 USPQ 427 (SD Ohio 1978).
[105] 453 F Supp 1347, 203 USPQ 432 (SDNY 1978).

§7.02[6] / Trademark Law

from it. It is equally apparent that the court disbelieved the defendant's testimony as to the dire consequences which would flow from the injunction sought. In another context, the court took particular pains to comment on the likelihood of confusion survey conducted by defendants pointing out defects in the universe selected and the slanted nature of the questions asked. Of particular note is the court's candid acknowledgment that, while it did not know the correct universe, it knew that the one selected was incorrect and that this fact detracted from the persuasiveness of the evidence.

In *Reddy Communications, Inc. v. Environmental Action Foundation*[106] the court denied plaintiff relief from defendant's use of a caricature of plaintiff's service mark—a stick-like figure known as REDDY KILOWATT. Defendant, an environmental group, used copies of REDDY in unflattering poses as part of its materials critical of the electric utility industry. Plaintiff attempted to show a likelihood of confusion by means of an extensive survey which posed questions based on the unusual appearance of the figures used by both parties. The court gave little weight to the survey results because the methodology ignored the realities of the market place. In fact, the survey did not seek to reproduce the circumstances under which the public might see defendant's uses and thus was entitled to little, if any, weight on the question of likelihood of confusion. The survey did, however, show a close identification of the REDDY KILOWATT figure with the electric utility industry generally; and the court concluded that the sophisticated readers of defendant's materials would recognize the defendant's use as a form of satire and would not be confused as to origin, sponsorship or relationship to plaintiff.

In *General Foods Corp. v. Mellis*,[107] the District Court enjoined defendant's use of the name I'M THE POP ROCK KING for phonograph recordings based on plaintiff's use of POP ROCKS for an effervescent candy. The defendant had

[106] 477 F Supp 936, 203 USPQ 144 (DC DC 1979).
[107] 203 USPQ 261 (SDNY 1979).

## Infringement and Unfair Competition / §7.02[6]

attached bags of plaintiff's candy to the record jackets and the photos thereon showed him consuming plaintiff's products. Even the recordings contained the sounds associated with plaintiff's candy. In these circumstances the court found a likelihood that the public would be confused as to the source or sponsorship of defendant's recording.

In a case which illustrates certain of the pitfalls in trials by a magistrate, *Johnny Carson Apparel Inc. v. Zeeman Mfg. Co., Inc.*[108] the court found for defendant, notwithstanding that it found an intent to trade on plaintiff's good will. In this case, the defendant copied a distinctive suit design popularized by plaintiff (which the court held it clearly had a right to do). Not satisfied with copying the suit, however, defendant affixed labels identifying the suit as defendant's JOHNNY model and used a television ad which introduced the suit with the words "Here's the JOHNNY model suit from Zeeman Manufacturing," and showed a model on a golf course who ended the ad with a simulated golf swing—all indicia associated with Johnny Carson. While rejecting the masters finding that there was no intent to wrongfully associate its goods with the plaintiff, the court held that because of the many references to defendant's name in the television ad, defendant had failed to achieve its wrongful goal and that, notwithstanding its efforts to the contrary, no likelihood of confusion existed. It is remarkable that the court never addressed the probability that the association intentionally created with Johnny Carson would be likely to induce the belief that defendant's suits were licensed or authorized by plaintiff or Johnny Carson. One can only conclude that defendant's swift abandonment of the ad and labels colored the court's view of the result.

In *Volkswagenwerk AG v. Smith*,[109] the District Court held that defendant's use of the trade names BUG AND BEETLE CLINIC INC. and INDEPENDENT VW SERVICE constituted unfair competition and trademark infringement in that they would tend to confuse the public

---

[108] 203 USPQ 585 (ND Ga 1978).
[109] 417 F Supp 385, 203 USPQ 891 (D NM 1979).

§7.02[7] / Trademark Law

into the belief that defendant was an authorized dealer in plaintiff's car or repair services. The mere use of another trademark in the defendant's firm name was sufficient. The court entered an extremely broad injunction enjoining inter alia, use of VW, BUG, BEETLE, VOLKS, the color blue, or use of such phrases as "VW Repair" and so forth, except as an adjective to describe plaintiff's cars and to tell what kind of services he specialized in and even then, close restrictions in the form, content and color of the use were imposed.

In *Victoria Station Inc. v. Clarefield Inc.*,[110] the District Court entered a preliminary injunction enjoining defendant's use of the name VICTORIA STATION MALL for its shopping center by reason of its similarity to plaintiff's VICTORIA STATION restaurants. The court, relying on certain unspecified instances of actual confusion and on the fact that defendant intended to rent space to a restaurant, if possible, found that a likelihood of confusion existed sufficient to warrant provisional relief.

[7] **Owner's Right to Restrict Distributor's Use of Trademark**

While essentially an antitrust test case, *Edward J. Sweeney & Sons, Inc. v. Texaco, Inc.*[111] dealt with trademarks in two pertinent respects. First, the court held that the existence of a trademark did not constitute the trademarked product of one producer as a market, i.e., a trademark does not define a market for purposes of Section 2 of the Sherman Act. More significantly, the court followed an increasingly longer line of cases holding that trademark owners have the right to determine what products will bear their marks and that those who arrogate that right to themselves are infringers. This aspect of the case dealt with the plaintiff Texaco's distributor's conduct in selling non-Texaco gas as TEXACO gas, which he attempted to justify on the ground that Texaco

[110] 458 F Supp 199, 203 USPQ 956 (WD Pa 1978).
[111] 478 F Supp 243, 204 USPQ 906 (ED Pa 1979). See also infra fn 1 in ch. 10.

## Infringement and Unfair Competition / §7.02[7]

itself purchased gasoline made by others which it sold as TEXACO gas. The Court disposed of this argument cogently:

> Clearly, Texaco had the right to put its trademark on whatever gasoline it deemed suitable. The crucial point, which apparently escapes Sweeney, is that just because Texaco, the owner of the trademark, could decide what gasoline to market under that trademark does not mean that Sweeney, who had only the right to sell gasoline so marked, had a like right to decide which gasoline to call Texaco. Any perceived unfairness in this disparity evaporates with the realization that it is precisely what the trademark laws are supposed to accomplish. Indeed, if anyone could decide what goods to market under a given trademark, the value of that trademark and therefore its identity as a trademark would disappear.[112]

Gulf, the plaintiff in *Gulf Oil Corp. v. Heller*,[113] did not fare as well as Texaco in a case which presented a somewhat similar fact pattern. In compliance with a Massachusetts law which requires that unbranded gasoline be identified at the pump as NO BRAND, the defendant, an authorized GULF dealer, sold gasoline so identified from pumps at his GULF service station. The GULF sign at the station identified it as a GULF station and GULF gasoline was dispensed from GULF-labeled pumps as well.

Plaintiff, asserting that the identification of the service station as a GULF station indicated to the public that all gasoline on sale there was GULF gasoline, sought a preliminary injunction. In denying the motion, the District Court held that in the absence of any proof that the public was actually confused, the defendant was entitled to the presumption that the clear NO BRAND labeling on the pump was sufficient to tell the public that the gasoline was not

[112] 204 USPQ at 934.
[113] 204 USPQ 1051 (D Mass 1980).

§7.02[7] / Trademark Law

GULF gasoline. On these facts alone plaintiff was found to have failed to prove a likelihood of success on any of its Section 43(a), passing-off or trademark infringement theories.

In a case which presented several of the same issues as in the *Texaco* case, *Memorex Corp. v. Sound/Pro*,[114] the District Court held that a retailer who purchased unbranded tape from the Memorex Corporation could not place MEMOREX trademarks on his packages. In a somewhat more dubious advisory opinion to the defendant, appearing pro se, the court also stated that the defendant could not state in his packaging who made the product. That statement, at least, seems to be at variance with a long list of cases involving ingredients, for example, and one can see no injury to plaintiff in having its product identified as being its product.

The case of *Hank Thorp, Inc. v. Minilite Incorporated*[115] raised the question of ownership of an incontestable registration as between a British manufacturer and a domestic distributor. The plaintiff-distributor sued the defendant-manufacturer for infringement of its incontestable trademark MINILITE by reason of defendant's use of MINILITE and MAXILITE as marks for automobile wheels. Plaintiff had been defendant's exclusive United States distributor for some eleven years, and had disclosed the fact that it had registered the mark to the defendant some six years prior to the commencement of the lawsuit. Holding that the ownership of the marks as between the parties was one of agreement, the court held that not only was there no agreement giving ownership to plaintiff, but that the facts were inconsistent with such an intent. Deducing from the transitory and "at will" nature of the distributorship arrangement, the court reasoned that neither party intended a permanent assignment of defendant's rights in the United States, and since plaintiff was aware of that fact when it applied to register the mark, its registration had been procured by fraud, and thus should be canceled. The court also rejected

[114] 204 USPQ 350 (CD Calif 1978).
[115] 474 F Supp 228, 205 USPQ 598 (D Del 1979).

plaintiff's claim of laches and estoppel for the reason that there had been neither adverse use nor detrimental reliance by plaintiff on defendant's failure to object to its registration. Additionally, no estoppel arose since the party asserting it did not act in good faith and was not misled in any way by the defendant's silence.

### [8] Personal Names

The name PIERRE CATTIER and CATTIER used for cosmetics were found to be too close to CARTIER in *Cartier Inc. v. Three Sheaves Co., Inc.*[116] Defendant's principal defense, that it was using the real name of its licensor, was undercut by the absence of any evidence that the licensor actually existed or was actually in business in France and by the fact that the license appeared to be invalid as lacking in quality control provisions. In all events, the district judge noted that the right to use one's own name is limited to uses which do not constitute unfair competition or trademark infringement.

In another case involving the use of surnames, the district judge in *General Outlet Corp. v. Acronite Corp.*[117] denied an injunction which would have forever precluded a jewelry designer from using her full name in the jewelry business. With the designer's permission while employed by plaintiff, it secured a registration for the trademark EDITIONS BY HELEN Z for jewelry. It then sought to enjoin the use of HELEN ZELLERMAIER FOR ACRONITE by the defendants on the theory that in the trade the marks HELEN Z and HELEN ZELLERMAIER were synonymous. Citing the need to protect the rights of persons to use their own names, provided such use is fair, and noting that the injunction sought would in effect prevent the individual defendant from using her own name ever again, the court denied the preliminary injunction sought. In doing so, the court distinguished those "personal name" cases in which the defen-

[116] 465 F Supp 123, 204 USPQ 377 (SDNY 1979).
[117] 467 F Supp 269, 204 USPQ 494 (SDNY 1979).

§7.02[9] / Trademark Law

dant had sold a business identified with the name. Here, the plaintiff sought, by means of a trademark registration to foreclose the use of someone's own name forever, a result which struck the judge as unfair and inappropriate to the employer-employee relationship.

In still another "surname" case, the District Court in *Markel v. Scovill Mfg. Co.*[118] enjoined plaintiff's use of MARKEL HEATER for heaters and related goods in light of defendant's rights in the same mark and trade name. Plaintiffs were dissatisfied shareholders of defendants' predecessor in interest. When that predecessor sold the assets of its heater distribution business, including all rights in the MARKEL name and mark, to defendants, plaintiffs formed a company named MARKEL HEATER, originally to forestall the sale, but subsequently to compete with defendants. The District Court found that the MARKEL name had achieved a secondary meaning prior to plaintiffs' announcement of use of that name and that confusion was likely. The court relied primarily upon plaintiffs' intent which, in the surrounding circumstances, was clearly to take advantage of the good will in the assets sold to defendants. The court rejected plaintiffs' argument that defendants, by using the MARKEL name with its "NuTone" and SCOVILL marks, had abandoned the MARKEL mark. The court, in granting the preliminary injunction, also found that defendant was likely to prevail on the merits with regard to its dilution claim as well.

### [9] Use of Another's Trademark

The court, in *Norton Co. v. Newage Industries Inc.*[119] enjoined defendant's act of identifying its products as TYGON-TYPE, TYGON being plaintiff's trademark. In addition to finding a likelihood of confusion as to the characteristics of the defendant's products, or their origin, the court found that such references to plaintiff's mark threatened its dis-

---

[118] 471 F Supp 1244, 204 USPQ 641 (WDNY 1979).
[119] 204 USPQ 382 (ED Pa 1979).

### Infringement and Unfair Competition / §7.02[10]

tinctiveness as a trademark. The Court found that the defendant's "usage is calculated or likely to cause the mark to lose its significance as a source of origin,"[120] and thus was actionable in this regard.

In yet another of the infamous perfume copy cases,[121] copier Sherrell was found guilty of false advertising under Section 43(a) on a motion for summary judgment. In the case, originally filed in 1976 by Sherrell claiming antitrust violations by a number of manufacturers, the court found sufficient evidence in affidavits and documents to determine that Sherrell's perfumes were in fact not "equivalent fragrances," "superb copies," "deluxe fragrances copies which are equal to the originals," and that "you can't tell the difference from the originals." While the fact that differences in fragrance existed was proven by gas chromatograph and damaging admissions in Sherrell's chief perfumist's notebook, the court also relied on the testimony of Chanel's chief chemists' undisputed "expert nose." Discussing the earlier cases, the court stressed the requirement of truth in comparative advertising claims, indicating that a false claim can be actionable even without regard to public reaction and an examination of how the public would interpret or be damaged by the claims. Instead of claiming similarity, a vague term commonly used in past cases, Sherrell had gone further and made statements which could be reasonably viewed as claims of absolute identity. As a result, Chanel came out (with apologies for the falsity of comparison) "smelling like a rose."

### [10] National Bank Name Preemption

In a novel case presenting questions of first impression, the court in *State of North Dakota v. Merchants National*

---

[120] Id at 384.

[121] Sherrell Perfumers, Inc. v. Revlon Inc., 483 F Supp 188, 205 USPQ 250 (SDNY 1980).

§7.02[10] / Trademark Law

*Bank & Trust Co.*,[122] held that a state cause of action to enjoin the change of the name of a national bank which had been approved by the Controller of the Currency pursuant to 12 USC Section 30, was barred by the doctrine of federal preemption. In an earlier appeal,[123] the Court of Appeals had held that there was no federal ground to enjoin the Controller of the Currency from authorizing a change of name and that no federal claim was stated. It remanded the case for consideration of the state unfair competition claim which was based on the contention that the new name of the national bank was unduly similar to that of a pre-existing state bank.

In holding that the state cause of action was barred, the court found no direct congressional authority for preempting the states in this area. It held, rather, that the applicable federal statutes created a scheme of total federal control of national banks and a pattern of specific authorization of state power in certain areas, e.g., services or interest rates. Finding no authorization in the federal statute for the state action with regard to bank names, the district judge held that the field was preempted.

The decision appears to be in error on several grounds. In the first instance, the court failed to analyze whether the proposed state action was inconsistent with the federal scheme of regulation[124] or whether the Congress deliberately left the area open to state concurrent jurisdiction. It seems clear that the prior Eighth Circuit decision merely confirmed the authority of the Controller to approve or disapprove of names and did not purport to authorize him to decide disputes relating to non-banking matters which are only incidental to the power to control the names of national banks. There appears to be neither Congressional authority or practical need to confer such power upon the Controller nor any national purpose served by permitting

[122] 466 F Supp 953, 204 USPQ 500 (D ND 1979).
[123] 579 F2d 1112 (CA 8 1978).
[124] See Goldstein v. State of California, 412 US 546, 178 USPQ 129 (1973), discussed in 63 TMR 413–14 fn 341 and 64 TMR 342 fn 13.

national banks to adopt with impunity names which are confusingly similar to prior state names.

The effect of the decision is to insulate all national banks from the laws of trade name unfair competition and no rational reason to do so is seen. It is equally clear that the function of the Controller in name authorization is merely to approve or disapprove of a name in much the same fashion as a Secretary of State approves or disapproves a corporate name. It is well settled, however, that the right to adopt and use a name is not conferred by governmental fiat exclusively, but depends also on its availability vis-à-vis the prior rights of others as well. Perhaps this apparently gratuitous extension of federal power will be reversed upon appeal.

### [11] Trademark "Fair Use" Defense

The infrequently considered effect of a Lanham Act Section 33 (b)(4) "fair use" defense was the subject of the opinion in *Clarke v. Joseph H. Dahlkemper Inc.*[125] Plaintiff's trademark for its target ball games was SAFE-T-BALL. Defendant sold a substantially identical game under the trademark FLINGER CLINGER. Beneath that mark appeared the words "The Safety Ball Target Game." Such descriptive use of the plaintiff's mark was permissible since "Safety Ball" was the common descriptive name of the products and the term was not used by defendant as a trademark, but merely to describe its products. The court was influenced by other clearly descriptive uses of "Safe" and "Safety" elsewhere in the defendant's products, and the prominent display of defendant's FLINGER CLINGER trademark. The judge took note of defendant's change of the language to "Safety Ball" from "Safety Dart," but held that wrongful intent did not convert an otherwise permissible use to one which was impermissible.

The popularity of ball and target games produced another trademark case concerning that toy in which the plaintiff

[125] 468 F Supp 441, 204 USPQ 505 (WD Pa 1979).

§7.02[11] / Trademark Law

was again unsuccessful. In *Clarke v. K-Mart*[126] the District Court held that SAFE-T-BALL was merely descriptive of a game in which balls were thrown against a target. The court found that plaintiff's sales and advertising were so meager that as a matter of law no secondary meaning could have been created and granted defendant's motion for summary judgment.

The "fair use" defense was also sustained in *Robert B. Vance & Associates Inc. v. Baronet Corp.*[127] In that case, the court held that the words "CHECK CLUTCH" were merely descriptive of a clutch purse with a built in checkbook holder, and that defendant's use thereof was fairly made only to describe its products and thus avoided the presumptions flowing from plaintiff's incontestable registration of CHECK CLUTCH for the same goods. The court declined to order plaintiff's registration canceled, however, holding CHECK CLUTCH to be descriptive but not generic of the goods. The descriptiveness of the mark also precluded finding for plaintiff under Section 43(a) as well and also defeated plaintiff's dilution argument.

The question of "fair use" was also the principal issue in *Salton Inc. v. Cornwall Corp.*[128] Plaintiff, owner of an incontestable registration for the trademark HOTRAY for electric food warmers, sued to enjoin defendant's use of HOT TRAY in publicity materials published by defendant, a direct competitor. The court rejected the contention that HOT TRAY had become the generic name for the goods principally for the reason that only one of perhaps a dozen competitors used that term and the others all used other generic names —principally, electric food warmer—as did prominent retailers. Moreover, the court found defendant's witnesses' testimony not credible and noted that sales of the product had not been inhibited by the use of other generic names. Why defendants failed to adduce survey evidence as to the

[126] 473 F Supp 1129, 205 USPQ 1237 (WD Pa 1979).
[127] 205 USPQ 24 (ND Ga 1979).
[128] 477 F Supp 975, 205 USPQ 428 (D NJ 1979). See also infra fn 193 this chapter.

public's understanding of the term is difficult to understand. Having found the term HOT TRAY, or HOTRAY, not generic and the issue of descriptiveness foreclosed by the incontestable status of plaintiff's registration, the court turned to defendant's claim that its use was a use other than as a trademark, fairly to describe its products. In rejecting this defense, the court noted that at least one of defendant's uses of HOT TRAY was a trademark use and that the arguably descriptive use was not fair, but was motivated by an intent to take advantage of plaintiff's efforts in popularizing its HOTRAY mark. Fairness, as used in Section 1115(b)(4), was equated with an intent to describe the product as opposed to an attempt to trade upon plaintiff's good will. This seems preferable to the opinion in the Clarke case. Indeed, the court questioned, but did not hold, whether the fair use defense should ever be available where the plaintiff's mark had acquired distinctiveness. It seems clear that the defense should be available in appropriate cases, for to hold otherwise would seem to nullify the intent of Congress in enacting that defense.

### [12] Section 43(a) of the Lanham Act

The judge in *Lee Pharmaceuticals v. Den-Mat, Inc.*[129] gave an exceptionally limited reading to Section 43(a) of the Lanham Act, holding, on a motion for summary judgment, that the Section reaches only misrepresentations as to the source of the products of the defendant and that defendants' clear labeling of their products obviated application of the statute. Equally surprising was the rare event of a claim for trademark infringement being dismissed on summary judgment, the court holding as a matter of law that there could be no likelihood of confusion between ENAMEL BOND, DRY BOND and PRECEDENT on the one hand and ENAMELITE, PREP-DRY, PROSTHODENT, RESTODENT and PRESTIGE on the other.

In *DCA Food Industries Inc. v. Hawthorn Mellody,*

[129] 203 USPQ 546 (CD Calif 1978).

§7.02[13] / Trademark Law

*Inc.*,[130] the District Court held that common law trademark infringement, even where the products were clearly labeled with the name of the manufacturer, constituted a violation of Section 43(a). The court went on to hold that, where a common law trademark was established, a false representation occurred by reason of the origin-indicating impact of the trademark. An indication of origin is one part of the bundle of information carried by a trademark, the court noted. No secondary meaning was required to be pleaded in order to sustain a claim for relief for the reason that suggestive marks—YOZERT for frozen yogurt—require no acquired distinctiveness to be protectable. Such marks ipso facto indicate origin. In rejecting defendants' contention based on their truthful display of their name and address, the Court held:

> Surely one reason to adopt a trademark is to avoid asking the consumer to resort to footnotes in order to trigger the desired cognitive responses.[131]

### [13] Ownership of Entertainment Group Names

The difficult question of ownership of service marks used by entertainment groups continues to be litigated. The case of *Capetola v. Orlando*[132] involved ownership of the service mark DAWN, used by two singing groups as their names. Plaintiff was a partnership which owned a federal registration for the mark, but which did not render the entertainment services. Rather, it managed the group identified by the name and its rights stemmed from an oral assignment of the name by one of the performers in the group who had been professionally known by that designation for several years.

Defendants had commenced use of the name long after plaintiff's activities had begun and in response to plaintiff's

---

[130] 470 F Supp 574, 202 USPQ 739 (SDNY 1979).
[131] 202 USPQ at 743–44.
[132] 463 F Supp 498, 204 USPQ 21 (ED Pa 1978).

objection had employed plaintiff to promote defendants' records using the DAWN mark. Defendants moved for summary judgment asserting that since the group name identified the group, not the registered owner, that the use of the name inured to the performer rather than the manager. While the court did not reject this theory out of hand, it did indicate that the issue would turn on the relationship intended to be created by the parties—a factual issue—and thus was not suitable for resolution on summary judgment. But it is apparent that the court was willing to look beyond the external fact that the managing partnership owned the registration and to examine the actual intent and conduct of the parties.

### [14] Pharmaceutical Product Simulation

The question of product substitution by pharmacists was the subject of *Pennwalt Corp. v. Zenith Laboratories, Inc.*[133] in which the Michigan District Court entered a preliminary injunction prohibiting the defendant pharmaceutical manufacturer from selling its products in capsules identical to those used by plaintiff for its therapeutically similar product to pharmacists, but not enjoining such sales to dispensing physicians. The court did not examine the question of the function of color on such capsules, nor did it find that a secondary meaning had been acquired. It enjoined the defendant, based upon evidence that pharmacists were wrongfully substituting the defendant's products for those of plaintiff, on the theory that the defendant had placed an instrument of fraud in the hands of retailers:

> More specifically, when a defendant markets a product, that defendant's accountability for his customer's wrongful use of that product turns on the issue of whether a reasonable person in the defendant's position would realize either that he himself had created a situation which afforded a temptation or an opportuni-

[133] 472 F Supp 413, 203 USPQ 52 (ED Mich 1979).

§7.02[15] / Trademark Law

ty to act wrongfully to the average person or was dealing with a customer whom he should know would be peculiarly likely to use the defendant's product wrongfully.[134]

The court found support for its conclusion of inducing wrongful conduct on defendant's part in an advertising brochure in which defendant referred to its product as "similar to" plaintiff's. Such language presumably suggested to pharmacists that the products could be substituted. The court found no support of defendant's action in the Michigan generic drug laws, which authorized substitution with the prescribing physician's permission and full disclosure, because here the products were not "generic equivalents." The court did not discuss the "need" of the defendant to use similarly colored capsules in order to compete effectively or whether the "need" to use different colors would inhibit competition. The court noted the contrary decision of the New York Federal District Court in *Ives Laboratories, Inc. v. Darby Drug Co., Inc.*,[135] but declined to follow it. However, the court paid lip service to the *Ives* case by declining to extend the injunction to capsules sold to dispensing physicians on the theory that they could not be confused and that to extend the injunction absent confusion would be a great restraint on competition. Nowhere did the court address what seems to be the underlying question: what is the function of the colors and thus what is the effect, both competitively and on the consumer, of the use of the same color schemes on two different medications.

[15] Functionality

In *Famolare Inc. v. Melville Corp.*[136] the District Court

[134] 203 USPQ at 55.
[135] 455 F Supp 939, 200 USPQ 724 (EDNY 1978, affd 601 F2d 631, 202 USPQ 548 (CA 2 1979). See also supra fn 52 this chapter and infra fns 1 and 8 in ch. 8.
[136] 472 F Supp 738, 203 USPQ 68 (D Hi 1979).

## Infringement and Unfair Competition / §7.02[15]

found that the wavy soles of the plaintiff's shoe were functional in nature, since they were a motivating factor in the decision of the consumer to purchase the shoe. Following the rationale of the Ninth Circuit in *Pagliero v. Wallace China Co.*[137] that where products are purchased because of their aesthetic appearance, features of appearance are functional and thus incapable of exclusive ownership absent a patent or copyright, the court found that the wavy sole design was aesthetically functional and thus freely copyable. Since all of plaintiff's other claims for passing off, misappropriation, and trademark infringement were dependent on a holding that the appearance of the soles served as a trademark, or had acquired protectable status, each was held to have failed and summary judgment was awarded defendant.

In *Magor Pool Equipment Corp. v. Ideal Pool Corp.*,[138] the court held that the tile design which was used as a border around the upper edge of plaintiff's pool liner was incapable of functioning as a trademark having been adopted and used as mere ornamentation where such ornamentation is commonly used in the trade so that the public would look upon it as having been applied to achieve nothing more than aesthetic appeal. A repeated pattern is not protectable even if arbitrary the court held. Alternatively, the court held that the design had not been used as a trademark and that there had been a complete failure to show that any member of the public had come to associate that particular design with a specific source. Finally, the court also found the design to be functional in the sense that it contributed to the visual appeal and desirablility of the liner, and thus contributed to the consumer's decision to purchase, wholly apart from any alleged origin-indicating function.

In *Trak Inc. v. Franz Kneissl Skifabrik Gesellschaft mbH*[139] the court preliminarily enjoined defendant's sale of a ski which had reproduced on the bottom a silk screen

---

[137] 198 F2d 339, 95 USPQ 45 (CA 9 1952), discussed in 43 TMR 829 fn 154. See also infra fn 5 in ch. 8.
[138] 203 USPQ 577 (ND Ga 1979).
[139] 205 USPQ 35 (D NH 1979).

§7.02[15] / Trademark Law

design which duplicated the appearance of the design used by plaintiff for some time on its variable depth fish scale cross country skis. The court, based on counsel's representations that plaintiff was the sole ski maker to employ such a design held it likely that plaintiff would prove that the design had acquired distinctiveness. The judge, in rejecting defendant's claim that the design was descriptive in that it merely reproduced the design of the fish scale base of plaintiff's ski, noted that the silk screen design exaggerated and emphasized the fish scale design and conveyed only a "general" idea of the actual base. The court distinguished between those cases where the design copied was primarily functional and where the function was merely incidental, as in the case at bar. The court was clearly motivated by the apparent attempt of the defendant to ride on the good will created by the plaintiff as well as the success of its ski.

In *Fisher Stoves Inc. v. All Nighter Stove Works Inc.*[140] the District Court declined to enjoin defendant's sales of stoves which copied the configurations of those of plaintiff in many respects. After examining the difference between features which are " primarily" functional and those which were only "incidentally" functional, the court found that the double tier configuration was intended to provide a dual combustion chamber and surfaces with two different temperatures. Such a feature was "primarily" functional in nature and thus not protectable absent a patent. Moreover, the plaintiff had in all events failed to prove the acquisition of secondary meaning. In that regard, the court pointed out that the configuration of plaintiff's stove was not constantly the same and was similar to several other stoves on the market.

The question of the right to sell luggage copied from that of plaintiff was the issue in *Le Sportsac, Inc. v. Dockside Research Inc.*[141] While the court held that many of the copied features were non-functional or at least not primarily functional and that, in all probability, plaintiff would suc-

[140] 205 USPQ 1009 (D NH 1979).
[141] 478 F Supp 602, 205 USPQ 1055 (SDNY 1979).

ceed in proving that the appearance of its bags had acquired secondary meaning, nevertheless, the preliminary injunction sought was denied because of defendant's prominent use of its own name and trademark on its copies as well as the inordinate delay of eight months between plaintiff's discovery of the existence of defendant's copies and the motion for temporary relief. While the court's rejection of the automatic application of the *Sears* and *Compco* cases is welcome, one cannot help being discouraged by the reaffirmation of the holding in *Bose Corporation v. Linear Design Labs Inc.*[142] that a likelihood of confusion in a case involving the copying of the configuration of goods is obviated when the copier puts its own name or mark on its copy. That doctrine ignores the fact that many persons familiar with the trademark function of the copied features of the orginial product may be wholly unaware of the name of the actual source. In such a case, the use of the defendant's own name or mark not only does not clarify the source of origin but also may cause the public to believe that the copier is actually the source of the original, thus compounding the effect of confusion. Adding one's own mark or name to what is, in effect, someone else's trademark does not eliminate confusion which is otherwise likely to occur.

### [16] Former Licensee's Duties

The doctrine that a former licensee has an affirmative duty to take all reasonable steps to avoid possible confusion was reaffirmed in *Holiday Inns Inc. v. Alberding*.[143] In that case, the court found that the former Holiday Inn franchisee's continued use of a modified "great sign" was unacceptable. The deletion of the words "Holiday Inn," the arrowhead and star elements and the repainting of the sign in yellow rather than the usual green were not sufficient to distinguish the former licensee's business.

---

[142] 467 F2d 304, 175 USPQ 385 (CA 2 1972), discussed in 63 TMR 409 fn 325.
[143] 203 USPQ 273 (ND Tx 1978).

§7.02[17] / Trademark Law

The duty of a former licensee to distinguish his products from those of his erstwhile licensor was also noted in *Thought Factory, Inc. v. Idea Factory, Inc.*[144] Defendant's name and trademark IDEA FACTORY was held to be unduly similar to plaintiff's THOUGHT FACTORY also used in the creation and sale of greeting cards, by reason of the substantial identity of meaning. The court also found that, in addition to copyright infringement, the defendant's copying of certain of plaintiff's cards amounted to unfair competition in that the stylized and consistent format used by plaintiff on all of its cards had achieved the status of a "dress of goods" which defendant deliberately copied. While not clearly articulated, it appears that the court was convinced that the elements of the appearance of plaintiff's cards had acquired distinctiveness in an extremely short period of time.

In *Or Da Industies, Ltd. v. Leisure Learning Products Inc.*,[145] the court entered a preliminary injunction enjoining defendant's sales of a game copied from plaintiff's BRAINY BLOCKS—which defendant initially distributed—under the trademark MR. BRAIN BUILDER. Finding an intent on defendant's part to take advantage of plaintiff's good will, the court had little difficulty in finding that the marks were so similar in connotation as well as sound that confusion of purchasers—youngsters for the most part—was likely. In finding the requisite element of irreparable injury, the court held that the element was present either because the likelihood of confusion inherently created lost sales and confusion which were unmeasurable, or that defendant's mark would dilute the distinctive quality of plaintiff's mark.

[17] **Genericism**

The decision in *Johnson & Johnson v. Carter-Wallace, Inc.*[146] rejected the plaintiff's contention that it had acquired

---

[144] 203 USPQ 331 (CD Calif 1978).

[145] 479 F Supp 710, 205 USPQ 1128 (SDNY 1979).

[146] 487 F Supp 740, 205 USPQ 827 (SDNY 1979). See also infra fn 11 in ch. 8.

exclusive rights to the display of the words "Baby Oil" on cosmetic products, notwithstanding the existence of extensive survey evidence that the public in fact associated products described as containing that substance with Johnson & Johnson. Finding that the words were the generic name for mineral oil used by a number of personal products manfacturers, the court distinguished between de facto recognition or association of the term with plaintiff and true secondary meaning. Accordingly, the court was not concerned with the benefit the defendant received by reason of plaintiff's extensive advertising:

> In a situation in which a generic term has acquired de facto secondary meaning, a second manufacturer can benefit from a "free ride" due to the first manufacturer's efforts at promoting public acceptance of the product known by a generic name.[147]

Finding no palming off or other practices which would have caused public confusion, the court denied the requested preliminary injunction.

In *Carcione v. Greengrocer, Inc.*,[148] the District Court denied defendant's motion for summary judgment holding that an issue of fact existed as to whether plaintiff's registerd mark GREENGROCER or what appear to have been grocery store services or products was generic. While the term was held to be generic in Britain, the question of its significance when used in the United States was to be determined at trial where the issue was the significance of the term to the public, not its dictionary definition. The court was to some extent influenced by the fact that a registration had issued on the Principal Register. Moreover, clearly influenced by the substantial investment plaintiff had made in its mark, the court granted plaintiff's motion for a preliminary injunction, but restricted the relief to requiring the

---

[147] 205 USPQ at 831.
[148] 205 USPQ 1075 (ED Calif 1979).

§7.02[17] / Trademark Law

defendant to use a term with the accused mark which would distinguish its business from plaintiff's. The presumption of validity flowing from registration supported the plaintiff's showing of a likelihood of ultimate success on the merits.

In *Funwood, Inc. v. Cutting Corners*,[149] the court declined to enter a preliminary injunction against defendant's alleged unfair competition. Defendant, whose principal had applied for and been denied a franchise to operate a CALICO CORNERS piece goods store in San Diego, proceeded to open a similar store called CUTTING CORNERS ("Cutting Corners" being a phrase long associated with plaintiff) and adopted a number of features common to plaintiff's stores. The court disregarded and minimized defendant's conduct copied from that of plaintiff, and found distinctly different connotations in the names of the parties. The decision seems to be questionable since there was a clear attempt on defendant's part to copy those aspects of plaintiff's successful business upon which its success was based and which were known to the public. One detects that a failure to prove secondary meaning was influential in this case, notwithstanding what appears to have been an obvious intent to trade on plaintiff's good will. The court was clearly not convinced that an attempt to copy a successful business method or format, as opposed to copying a series of features with which the public was familiar, had taken place. The court was also influenced by the fact that plaintiff's nearest store was over one hundred miles distant. No geographic analysis of the businesses, however, appears in the decision.

The distinction between descriptive and generic words continued to cause confusion in the courts. In *Leon Finker, Inc., v. Schlussel*,[150] the District Court held that the designation "Trillion," as applied to triangular cut diamonds, was not a valid trademark in light of its similarity to the concededly generic term "Trilliant." While recognizing that "Trillion" was specifically different from "Trilliant," the court, noting the similarity in sound to the generic term and that

[149] 205 USPQ 1978 (SD Calif 1978).
[150] 469 F Supp 674, 202 USPQ 452 (SDNY 1979).

diamonds are generally traded over the telephone, found that the similarity to the generic term was so close that had the terms been trademarks, a likelihood of confusion would exist and thus, it concluded, "Trillion" was not a valid mark. While the holding may have been correct for other reasons relating to the trade's perception of the term's significance, the court's holding that a term which is aurally similar to a generic term is not a valid trademark seems doubtful. The correct test woud appear to be the significance of the term to the trade ( or public) in which it was used, an area of inquiry the court unaccountably avoided.[151]

Notwithstanding the failure of its trademark claims, however, the plaintiff prevailed on theories of common law unfair competition. The court found that defendant's wide dissemination of false claims of exclusivity in its advertising, as well as other misleading uses of "Trillion," injured plaintiff and were actionable under New York's broad unfair competition decisions.

### [18] Related Goods

In *Gioia Macaroni Co., Inc. v. Joseph Victori Wines*[152] the District Court enjoined defendant's use of the trademark GIOIA for wine in view of plaintiff's long use of the same mark on a variety of Italian food specialties including wine vinegar, pasta and other similar foods. Plaintiff adduced testimony of its intent to expand into the wine business and, in all events, the court found—as had the Trademark Trial and Appeal Board in an opposition between the parties—that the goods were so closely related that confusion was likely to ensue from the use of the identical marks thereon.

### [19] Irreparable Harm

The district judge in *Ideal Industries Inc. v. Gardner*

---
[151] See Bayer Co. v. United Drug Co., 272 Fed 505, 509 (SDNY 1921) (L. Hand, DJ).
[152] 205 USPQ 986 (EDNY 1979).

§7.02[20] / Trademark Law

*Bender, Inc.*,[153] entered a preliminary injunction enjoining defendant's use, on its electrical connectors, of model designations first used by plaintiff. After finding that the model or size designations had acquired distinctiveness the court considerd the issue of irreparable harm. It granted the motion principally because of the effect on the use of these terms by other competitors:

> There is also evidence tending to show beginning use of the 71B-74B, 76B, and 78B series by manufacturers other than Gardner Bender at or about subsequent to the time that Gardner Bender commenced using the series on its connectors. In the Court's opinion, the fair implication of both such types of evidence is that the plaintiff is presently in danger of losing business and of losing in the future is presently held identification as the source of the 71B-74B, 76B, 78B connectors, and, further, that should plaintiff ultimately prevail on the merits of the suit, its burden of eradicating impermissible uses of its trademarks will be substantially increased if the present use by the defendant, which is the major present infringer, is not enjoined.[154]

[20] Res Judicata

The opinions this year were replete with complex procedural questions, the usual number of cases raising intricate and often difficult questions of jurisdiction and venue, and questions of the relation between federal and state claims for relief.[155]

The continuing saga of the MUSHROOMS trademark,

---

[153] 204 USPQ 38 (ED Wisc 1979), mofd 612 F2d 1018, 204 USPQ 177 (CA 7 1979). See also supra fn 13 this chapter.

[154] 204 USPQ at 40.

[155] Another procedural topic of great interest is discussed in Gary M. Ropski, "The Federal Trademark Jury Trial—Awakening of a Dormant Constitutional Right," 70 TMR 177 (1980).

## Infringement and Unfair Competition / §7.02[20]

*R.G. Barry Corp. v. Mushroom Makers, Inc.*,[156] goes on. In a prior decision, the District Court had held that the use by defendant of the trademark MUSHROOM on women's garments did not infringe plaintiff's rights in MUSHROOMS acquired by reason of its prior use on ladies' footwear. That decision was upheld on appeal[157] where the Second Circuit, in a startling and incomprehensible decision, held that injunctive relief was not warranted—notwithstanding that a likelihood of confusion existed and notwithstanding that the Lanham Act specifically provides for relief in such circumstances. In plaintiff's original complaint, it had failed to assert a claim under New York's anti-dilution statute. A motion for leave to amend made after trial had been denied.

In the next go round, the plaintiff commenced an action in the New York State Courts seeking a permanent injunction based entirely on the state anti-dilution statute. Defendant removed the action to the federal court on the basis of diversity of citizenship and moved for summary judgment on the ground of res judicata. The District Court sustained the motion on the proffered ground and also held that the denial of the requested injunction in the prior case foreclosed the second suit. The doctrine of res judicata was found to be applicable since the plaintiff sought to obtain the same relief on the same set of facts adjudicated in the first action. Its new action, it was held, was merely an effort to set forth a new theory to support its claims made and litigated previously. Barry argued, however, that since defendant had committed new acts subsequent to the prior litigation that the prior judgment could not apply thereto. The doctrine of res judicata was held to bar relitigation of these new acts which were essentially identical to the condut which was the subject of the first action. Thus, offered a second chance to alter a manifestly wrong decision, the District

---

[156] 204 USPQ 113 (SDNY 1979), revd 204 USPQ 521 (CA 2 1979). See also supra fn 61 this chapter.

[157] 580 F2d 44, 199 USPQ 65, 68 (CA 2 1978), cert denied 439 US 1116, 200 USPQ 832 (1979), discussed in 69 TMR 591 fn 201.

§7.02[21] / Trademark Law

Court elected to follow the Court of Appeals and not buck the higher court. Barry filed an appeal.

While the appeal was pending, Barry tried again, by commencing still another state court action, this time naming an officer of defendant a party—thereby destroying diversity. A different district judge, the third one invloved, in *R.G. Barry v. Mushroom Makers, Inc.*,[158] sustained removal to the District Court on the theory that, although the complaint was couched in terms of the New York anti-dilution statute only, that this was merely a screen to camouflage a federal claim for relief as a state cause of action. Relying on prior Second Court decisions that a state complaint asserting unfair competition and trademark infringement could have been brought under Section 43(a) of the Lanham Act, the District Court held this to be in effect a federal claim and thus removable on federal question grounds. It then proceeded to apply the doctrine of res judicata to sustain defendants' summary judgment motion.

After this loss, Barry finally won a round in the Court of Appeals.[159] The Second Circuit reversed the removal of the first state court action on two grounds: (1) that there was, in fact, no diversity of citizenship; and (2) that a complaint based entirely on the state anti-dilution statute "fails to state a claim under the Lanham Act, and does not give rise to a federal question within the original jurisdiction of the district court."[160]

## [21] Collateral Estoppel

The doctrine of collateral estoppel expressed in *Blonder-Tongue Laboratories, Inc. v. University of Illinois Foundation*[161] was applied to dismiss plaintiff's case on the merits in

[158] 204 USPQ 116 (SDNY 1979).
[159] 612 F2d 651, 204 USPQ 521 (CA 2 1979), revg 204 USPQ 113 (SDNY 1979).
[160] 204 USPQ at 527.
[161] 402 US 313, 169 USPQ 513 (1971).

*Miller Brewing Co. v. Jos. Schlitz Brewing Co.*[162] In sustaining defendant's motion to dismiss plaintiff's action, insofar as it was based on the alleged validity of its trademark LITE for beer, the court held that the prior decision of the Seventh Circuit in *Miller Brewing Co. v. G. Heileman Brewing Co., Inc.*,[163] holding that the word "Light" or its equivalent "Lite" was incapable of serving as a trademark, estopped plaintiff from again litigating the issue. The court rejected plaintiff's argument that it had not had a full and fair opportunity to litigate the issue of genericness because the earlier decision was on a motion for preliminary relief, and in all events no trial had been had. In rejecting this argument, the district judge asserted that by reason of the nature of the issue plaintiff had had a fair opportunity to submit proof in the prior action.

[22] **Jurisdiction and Venue**

Note should be taken of the decision in *Holiday Rambler Corp. v. Arlington Park Dodge, Inc.*[164] While the case involved only issues relating to jurisdiction and venue, the court held that sales of $200,000 over a seven-year period, notwithstanding they amounted to less than 1/10th of one percent of defendant's sales, were not "miniscule," and thus they could be the predicate of jurisdiction based on acts of infringement within the state. Of equal note, however, is the court's holding that in testing the balance of convenience, especial weight in trademark cases should be given to the place of the location of defendant's advertising and sales records, since most of the evidence will concern itself with these activities of the defendant.

The court in *True Form Foundations, Inc. v. Strouse,*

---

[162] 449 F Supp 852, 203 USPQ 620 (ED Wisc 1978), mofd 605 F2d 990, 203 USPQ 642 (CA 7 1979), cert denied 205 USPQ 96 (US 1980). See also supra fn 60 this chapter.

[163] 561 F2d 75, 195 USPQ 281 (CA 7 1977), cert denied 434 US 1025, 196 USPQ 592 (1977), discussed in 68 TMR 783 fn 223.

[164] 204 USPQ 750 (ND Ill 1979).

§7.02[22] / Trademark Law

*Adler Co.*,[165] upheld venue of a trademark infringement action in the Eastern District of Pennsylvania on a finding that the cause of action arose within that district where from two to three percent of the alleged infringer's sales occurred in the district and defendant had salesmen call on stores in the district. Additionally, it engaged in cooperative advertising with stores in the district and certain stores sent order forms to their customers in the district.

In *Metropa Co., Ltd v. Choi*[166] the court found that a claim for relief based on trademark infringement did not arise in New York, for venue purposes, where defendants only contact with the state was the effecting of two sales at a gross sales price of $28.99. Such miniscule contact, even where sufficient support of in personam jurisdiction under the New York long arm statute was insufficient to support venue over defendant's objection.

*Griffin v. Gates*[167] presented the question of the proper venue for an action in which plaintiff asserted that defendant was seeking to appropriate to itself the service mark owned by a corporation in which the plaintiff owned all of the stock. Plaintiff and defendant were members of a musical group known as BREAD. The mark was registered by a California corporation owned by the parties. Defendant allegedly set out on a course of conduct to appropriate that mark to himself. In the course of this conduct, defendant gave a concert in Chicago and appeared in a television program from Chicago. Venue in such a case lies in the district in which the claim arises under Section 1391(b).[168] In cases involving such "transitory" claims for relief, the court held that the "weight of the contacts" rule should apply and that, notwithstanding the defendant's activity in Illinois, the real dispute centered in California to which the case was transferred.

The district judge in *Leaf Confectionery, Inc. v. Life Sav-*

---

[165] 203 USPQ 1081 (ED Pa 1978).
[166] 458 F Supp 1052, 203 USPQ 938 (SDNY 1978).
[167] 205 USPQ 1150 (ND Ill 1979).
[168] 28 USC §1391(b).

## Infringement and Unfair Competition / §7.02[23]

*ers, Inc.*,[169] declined to enjoin the prosecution by a Canadian company of a Canadian trademark infringement suit. Plaintiff had brought a declaratory judgment action, based on defendant's assertions that plaintiff's sale of BUBBLE FUN bubble gum both in Canada and in the United States constituted trademark infringement in both countries of defendant's BUBBLE YUM mark. The court held that the complaint pleaded facts (supported only by counsel's affidavit) that gave rise, prima facie, to an actual controversy in the United States; but the court could find no basis for jurisdiction over the person of the Canadian defendant and thus dimissed as to it. The court also declined to enjoin the prosecution of the Canadian suit started by the dismissed defendant both because it had no jurisdiction over that party, which was the Canadian plaintiff, and because the court clearly felt that the issue of infringement under Canadian law in Canada should be litigated there regardless of the effect such a litigation might have upon the domestic dispute.

*Lubrizol Corp. v. Neville Chemical Co.*[170] involved the question of the correct venue for an action which was commenced as an appeal from a decision of the Trademark Trial and Appeal Board.[171] The court held that for purposes of the application of the tests of Section 1391,[172] such an action did not have any particular connection with Ohio, apparently on the theory that an opposition does not have a situs within a particular state. Accordingly, the action was transferred to the district in which defendant resided.

### [23] Bankruptcy Transfers

The vexatious question of the transfer of trademarks by a trustee in bankruptcy was the subject of the opinion in

[169] 204 USPQ 363 (ND Ill 1979).
[170] 463 F Supp 33, 203 USPQ 500 (ND Ohio 1978).
[171] 196 USPQ 756 (TTAB 1977), discussed in 68 TMR 730 fn 116.
[172] 28 USC §1391.

§7.02[24] / Trademark Law

*Hough Mfg. Corp. v. Virginia Metal Industries, Inc.*[173] The contestants in this case were two companies which each purchased a different portion of the assets of the bankrupt trademark owner. Neither purchased the trademark VMP or the trade name VIRGINIA METAL PRODUCTS. Several months after the trustee sold the assets and ceased all operations, defendant commenced use of the name VIRGINIA METAL INDUSTRIES and the use of VMI as a trademark. Some three months thereafter, plaintiff, for separate consideration, purchased the trademark VMP from the trustee and commenced to use it. The outcome hinged on the validity of this assignment. After a review of the cases, the court found that the trustee, by ceasing the operation of the bankrupt and selling the non-trademark assets separately, had extinguished those rights, for there was no business to which the marks were appurtenant for some six months prior to the assignment to plaintiff:

> The Court therefore holds that where, as here, all business operations cease and the tangible assets necessary for the resumption of business operations are separated from the good will of the business, the trade names and trademarks of that business cease to be protectible, exclusive property rights.[174]

[24] Assignment of Infringement Claims

The unusual question of the right to assign a claim for trademark infringement without the assignment of the underlying trademark was dealt with in *International Society for Krishna Consciousness of Western Pennsylvania, Inc. v. Stadium Authority of the City of Pittsburgh.*[175] The plaintiff, a religious organization, brought suit to compel the Stadium Authority to permit it access to the Three Rivers Stadium in Pittsburgh. Defendant, as assignee of the chose-

[173] 453 F Supp 496, 203 USPQ 436 (ED Va 1978).
[174] 203 USPQ at 440.
[175] 479 F Supp 792, 204 USPQ 660 (D Pa 1979).

## Infringement and Unfair Competition / §7.02[25]

in-action of the Pirates baseball team counterclaimed for trademark infringement and unfair competition arising out of the sale by plaintiff's devotees of materials bearing the logo of the Pittsburgh Pirates baseball team. Plaintiff's motion to dismiss the counterclaim was granted on the theory that a claim for relief for trademark infringement—as well as for unfair competition arising from the same acts—could only be prosecuted by the owner of the mar. Finding no direct authority in trademark cases, the court reviewed patent cases which held that, because a patent is a unique property created by statute, the right to sue is governed by the statute which created the right, which statute limits the right to sue to the patent owner. The court then—palpably in error—stated that, like patents, the property—trademarks—exist solely by virtue of federal statutory law, and thus by analogy only the "owner" of a federally registered trademark may sue.

That trademarks do not exist by virtue of federal or even state statutory laws is manifest. Both trademark infringement and unfair competition are common law torts and the Lanham Act, at least, is not (with but limited exceptions) intended to create rights as opposed to creating remedies. At common law, a chose-in-action could be freely assigned with the exception of certain claims for relief which were peculiarly personal in nature. It is regrettable that the court did not deal with the issue on its merits as opposed to deciding by way of a faulty analogy to patent law. It is clear that Section 31 of the Lanham Act[176] does provide that an action may be brought by the registrant, but nowhere does it preclude an assignment of that claim without the mark. It may, indeed, be that the result here is correct, but some analysis of the issues would have been welcome.

### [25] Exhaustion of Administrative Remedies

In *Schwinn Bicycle Co. v. Abikaran*,[177] the District Court

---
[176] 15 USC §1114.
[177] 453 F Supp 57, 202 USPQ 284 (D PR 1978).

§7.02[26] / Trademark Law

rejected the defense of failure to exhaust adminstrative remedies to a claim for trademark infringement. In this case, the plaintff sued for infringement of its federally registered mark. As additional relief, it also sought cancellation of defendant's Puerto Rican registration for a similar mark. The previously registered similar mark was already the subject of an administrative proceeding for cancellation before the Puerto Rico Secretary of State.

The District Court denied defendant's motion for summary judgment of the ground of failure to exhaust administrative remedies, reasoning that the nature of the proceeding and of the rights being pursued by the plaintiff in the infringement suit differed from those in the proceeding before the Secretary of State of the Commonwealth. The court did, however, preclude the plaintiff from seeking cancellation of the Puerto Rican registration by way of relief in the federal court prior to the completion of the proceeding before the Secretary of State.

### [26] Laches Defense

In *Underwriters Laboratories, Inc. v. United Laboratories, Inc.*,[178] the court had little difficulty in finding that defendant's use of its initials UL in a seal-like design was an intentional infringement of plaintiff's UL certification mark and even less in holding that the defense of laches was inapplicable despite defendant's ten years of use prior to commencement of the litigation. The court noted that laches does not exist where plaintiff is ignorant of defendant's use; and in all events, the defense does not apply to an intentional infringement. Moreover, here its application would be inconsistent with the court's duty to protect the public from confusion.

### [27] Adoption of Trademarks

In *Daytona Automotive Fiberglass v. Fiberfab, Inc.*[179] the

[178] 203 USPQ 180 (ND Ill 1978).
[179] 475 F Supp 33, 205 USPQ 1245 (WD Pa 1979).

court held that the purported assignment of trademark rights by an individual to the plaintiff did not convey any rights because the assignor had made no use of the mark in her own business. The assignor (apparently a stockholder of the corporation which used the mark) never engaged in any business of her own. All of the uses of the mark were by the corporation with which she was associated. In the absence of the conduct of any business, the court reasoned, there could be no trademark and thus nothing to convey by assignment. It was irrelevant that the purported assignor had conceived of the mark, authorized its use by the corporation, had her name used in association with the mark on the corporation's products and was otherwise intimately connected with the products bearing it. In the absence of any business it was held that there could have been no rights in the assignor.

### [28] Post-Registration Procedures

In a case involving post-registration procedures, *Le Cordon Bleu, S.A. v. BPC Publishing Ltd.*,[180] the court ordered plaintiff's registration of the trademark LE CORDON BLEU for magazines canceled by reason of abandonment. While the registrant had not published a magazine as such for some time, it did disseminate materials bearing the mark during cooking courses. The distribution of sixteen-page spiral bound course materials identified by the mark was held not to be use of the mark on magazines. The court rested on the finding that these materials were distinguished from magazines because they were not issued periodically, had no editorial content and were not offered for sale to the general public. As an alternative holding, the court noted that the registration had been fraudulently obtained within the meaning of Section 1064[181] on the theory that the specimen filed with the registrant's Section 8 declaration in order to "obtain" the full twenty-year term was a dummied up copy

---

[180] 451 F Supp 63, 202 USPQ 147 (SDNY 1978).
[181] 15 USC §1064.

§7.02[29] / Trademark Law

of the course recipe booklet which registrant's officer knew was not a magazine when she executed the required affidavit.

### [29] Abandonment

The question of abandonment arose in other cases as well. The effect of the presumption of abandonment from proof of two years of nonuse of a mark set forth in Section 45 of the Lanham Act[182] was the subject of the decision in *Poncy v. Johnson & Johnson*,[183] in which the court construed the statutory prima facie abandonment provision. Applying Federal Rule of Evidence 301, the court held that the statutory presumption of abandonment does not shift the burden of proof as such as it is merely an evidential presumption which is easily rebutted. In the absence of other evidence, a showing of two years nonuse is sufficient to survive a motion directed to the defense, but the offer of proof of a lack of intent to abandon by the trademark owner was held sufficient to overcome that presumption. The Court held:

> Treating two-year non-use as a statutory presumption, the court considers the inferences from the underlying fact to be weak. Since intention to abandon is the test, with non-use merely a mode of trying to prove intent, and since circumstances vary widely from case to case, an assertion of continued intent to use, coupled with evidence showing a reasonable explanation for non-use, is sufficient to support the conclusion that abandonment has not been established by a preponderance, and the claim of abandonment must fail.[184]

The facts of the case established that Johnson & Johnson had purchased the trademark STERITEMP from the defendant (with good will, patented machinery and customer

[182] 15 USC §1127.
[183] 460 F Supp 795, 202 USPQ 199 (D NJ 1978).
[184] 202 USPQ at 206.

## Infringement and Unfair Competition / §7.02[29]

lists). The purchaser ceased using the mark, however, due to doubts that the product was in fact sterile, an attribute suggested by the prefix STERI. Crediting Johnson & Johnson's explanation of its discontinuance of use as being unaccompanied by intent to abandon, as satisfying the requirement for a showing of some reason for the discontinuance, the court found the mark not abandoned despite a number of years of nonuse. It is not clear, however, that the statutory presumption should be overcome merely because the owner's reasons for disontinuance seem valid, in the absence of evidence of the owner's efforts to solve the problems which led to the nonuse with a view to recommencing use. Apparently recognizing this defect, the court concluded that, plaintiff having explained its nonuse, the burden of going forward remained with the party asserting abandonment. Such a ruling places an almost insuperable burden upon a party asserting abandonment and seems to emasculate the very purpose of the statutory presumption. One would be happier with the decision if the court had considered the question of intent to resume use as significant as the alleged reasons for the cessation of use.

Another abandonment case was *Sunbeam Corp. v. Merit Enterprises, Inc.*[185] in which the District Court denied defendant's motion for a preliminary injunction on the ground that defendant had failed to show that it was the earlier user of the mark LE CHEF for food processors or for a hamburger cooker. Defendant's claim that it was entitled to the earlier use of a predecessor company was rejected for the reason that the use by the predecessor had halted for six years before defendant began again to use the mark. The court rejected defendant's claim that its servicing of the products sold by its predecessor during the six year hiatus was evidence of lack of intent to abandon. The issue of abandonment was left for determination at trial.

*Anvil Brand, Inc. v. Consolidated Foods Corp.*[186] presented the case of two users of the same mark, RUGGER, which

[185] 451 F Supp 571, 203 USPQ 494 (SDNY 1978).
[186] 464 F Supp 474, 204 USPQ 209 (SDNY 1978).

§7.02[30] / Trademark Law

the court held to be merely descriptive of rugby type sport shirts. Plaintiff had been the first to adopt the mark for shirts in the 1930s and was the owner of a federal registration therefor. In 1970, plaintiff decided to discontinue the use of the mark and some one hundred thousand extra RUGGER labels were thereafter used up by sewing the same on promotional and close-out merchandise. Sales of small quantities of shirts so labeled were made in 1971, 1972, and 1973. Some labels were still on hand as late as 1975. In 1975 defendant decided to use RUGGER as a trademark on its line of rugby type shirts, and between 1977 and 1978 expended over one and one-half million dollars in promoting the same. In 1975, defendant became aware of plaintiff's registration. When plaintiff protested in 1976, defendant declined to desist based on plaintiff's apparent abandonment and on defendant's belief that the word RUGGER was generic for the kind of shirts in issue. After holding RUGGER to be generic and thus incapable of exclusive appropriation, the court nevertheless went on to consider the question of abandonment because defendant had used that mark on clothing not associated with the game of rugger or rugby. That seems to have been clear error since plaintiff's registration, being for goods associated with rugby was invalid and thus defendant's use on other goods could not in all events have constituted an act of infringement. The court went on to sustain the defense of abandonment finding that the intent to abandon had been established and that the incidental use of the excess labels was not intended to be trademark use as such but merely to use up a supply of labels on goods on which the label was immaterial.

[30] Expansion of Trade Area

The increasing number of cases which arise when geographically remote users expand into each other's territory continued to present vexing questions for decision. In *Vision Center v. Opticks, Inc.*,[187] it was held that the trade

## Infringement and Unfair Competition / §7.02[30]

name and service mark THE VISION CENTER was suggestive rather than merely descriptive. In granting plaintiff the preliminary injunction which it sought, the court noted that defendant's incontestable registration for the identical term, VISION CENTER (which post-dated plaintiff's use), was prima facie evidence that the term was a valued trademark when used by plaintiff for the same services. Holding that plaintiff's use in New Orleans was continous from a date prior to defendant's registration, the court enjoined defendant's expansion into New Orleans where THE VISION CENTER had been used by plaintiff for some thirty-three years. As an additional holding, the court found that, in the New Orleans market, THE VISION CENTER had acquired distinctiveness prior to defendant's proposed expansion.

In *Armand's Subway, Inc. v. Doctors' Associates, Inc.*,[188] a decision notable for the apparent confusion of the court, plaintiff was denied relief on the holding that the service mark ARMAND'S SUBWAY for restaurant services was not infringed by SUBWAY, for identical services. In order to reach this conclusion, the court appears to have found notwithstanding the absence of any evidence to support the holding, that the designation SUBWAY was merely descriptive of a restaurant selling "submarine" sandwiches. Moreover, assuming the descriptiveness of the word SUBWAY, there is no discussion of whether that term had acquired distinctiveness, although the court appears to recognize that plaintiff's earlier use in the Washington, D.C. area had created some renown, at least within one and one-half miles of each of its restaurants. The court appears to have been confounded by plaintiff's registration and defendant's honest adoption and earlier use of what appear to be two suggestive but confusingly similar marks.

The case does present a somewhat unusual fact pattern in that the first user of the mark SUBWAY, the defendant,

---

[187] 461 F Supp 835, 202 USPQ 109 (ED La 1978), revd 596 F2d 111, 202 USPQ 333 (CA 5 1979). See also supra fn 8 this chapter.

[188] 202 USPQ 305 (ED Va 1978), rmd 604 F2d 849, 203 USPQ 241 (CA 4 1979). See also supra fn 4 this chapter.

## §7.02[30] / Trademark Law

expanded its chain of restaurants rapidly through the East without any federal registration. Plaintiff, while geographically restricted in area to metropolitan Washington, D.C., and the second user, was armed with an incontestable federal service mark registration. Without discussing the Seventh Circuit's holding in the *Eveready* case,[189] the court held that incontestability was but a shield and not a sword—at least when the defendant was the earlier user. In effect, the court held that, as against a prior user, incontestability is not a factor and that it was not the intent of Congress to interfere with common law rights vis-à-vis a prior user in any geographic location. The court did recognize, however, that plaintiff, the later user overall, did have a right to use its mark in its area of first use. Apparently, rather than fact the apparently difficult task of parcelling out the parties' rights, the court found the two marks sufficiently dissimilar that confusion was unlikely to occur.

Faced with existing actual confusion on the part of the public which had become entrenched over a period of years, the District Court in *Pizitz, Inc. v. Pizitz Mercantile Co. of Tuscaloosa, Inc.*,[190] devised an order compelling the plaintiff, as the price for opening a store in defendant's trade area, to engage in a wide variety of educational advertising programs intended to minimize confusion. In this case, the plaintiff, operators of department stores in Alabama under the PIZITZ name, were well-known throughout Alabama, including Tuscaloosa. Defendant, originally a member of the same family, had for many years operated ladies ready-to-wear stores in Tuscaloosa, also under the PIZITZ name. Because of the fame of plaintiff's Birmingham store, the largest in the state, and its extensive advertising, many of defendant's customers apparently believed that there was a connection between the stores of the parties. The issue presented to the court was whether plaintiff—which sought a

---

[189] Union Carbide Corp. v. Ever-Ready, Inc., 531 F2d 366, 66 TMR 59, 188 USPQ 623 (CA 7 1976), cert denied 191 USPQ 416 (US 1976), discussed in 66 TMR 391 fn 173.

[190] 204 USPQ 707 (ND Ala 1979).

## Infringement and Unfair Competition / §7.02[30]

declaratory judgment—could directly invade the Tuscaloosa market.

Apparently motivated by the existence of confusion in all events, and plaintiff's expectation of conducting extensive advertising in connection with the opening of its stores in Tuscaloosa, the court approved the plaintiff's expansion conditioned upon plaintiff's following an advertising scheme devised by the court intended to reduce both prospective and existing confusion to an irreducible minimum. The decision is noteworthy not only for the flexibility of the remedy devised but also by the court's repeated reliance on surveys of consumer attitudes made by both parties.

*Country Properties, Inc. v. Bill's Country Kitchen*[191] presented graphically the classic case for federal registration of trademarks. Plaintiff was a franchisor of COUNTRY KITCHEN restaurants with a franchise in Tampa, near defendant's place of business. (The opinion is unclear as to who opened first in Tampa, but it would appear that defendant was the first user in that area.) Plaintiff's incontestable registration, conclusively establishing plaintiff's exclusive right, was cited as nullifying defendant's claims of innocent adoption and lack of secondary meaning. The court held that the defendant's claim of laches was no bar to injunctive relief, even if proved (which it was not). The court also held that the burden of proving a likelihood of confusion was met by conceded evidence of actual confusion.

In *A. S. & W. Products, Inc. v. Atlantic Steel Co.*[192] the court enjoined plaintiff's use of the trademark and name ATLANTIC for steel buildings and structural parts thereof in light of defendant's prior use of ATLANTIC and ATLANTIC STEEL COMPANY in respect of its steel business, which also encompassed the sale of steel structures. The court held that it was immaterial that defendant's early use was as a trade name and recognized that steel buildings were, in all events, an area of natural expansion from the steel business generally. The court also rejected plaintiff's

[191] 204 USPQ 548 (MD Fla 1979).
[192] 205 USPQ 1037 (WDNY 1979).

§7.02[31] / Trademark Law

assertion that the parties' businesses were geographically remote in light of defendant's early sales in the upstate New York area in which plaintiff conducted its business. Additionally, the court noted that plaintiff had been aware of defendant's existence when it adopted the ATLANTIC name and held that a junior user with knowledge, no matter how remote its business, could not prevail over the senior user.

### [31] Damages, Profits and Attorneys' Fees

Perhaps among the least understood and most difficult questions in trademark law is the entitlement to and computation of damages, profits and attorney fees. A number of cases dealt with these issues in this past year.

In *Salton Inc. v. Cornwall Corp.*,[193] after denying the plaintiff's demand for counsel fees under the Lanham Act, the court awarded them under the New Jersey common law claims for relief, holding that the Supreme Court decision in *Fleischmann Distilling Corp. v. Maier Brewing Co.*[194] was inapplicable under the decisions of the New Jersey Supreme Court. An award was made because of the perceived intent of defendants to take a free ride on plaintiff's efforts and the "unfairness" of such conduct.

The District Court, in *Jordan v. ABC Records, Inc.*,[195] dealt with the award of attorneys' fees in a common law unfair competition case. The question arose after the defendant's motion for summary judgment dismissing the complaint was granted on the ground that plaintiff's song titles had not acquired secondary meaning. Notwithstanding the finding that plaintiff had no reason to believe that its song titles had become distinctive and that it was "doubtful" plaintiff had commenced the action in good faith, no "exceptional circumstances" warranting the award of counsel

---

[193] 477 F Supp 975, 205 USPQ 428 (D NJ 1979). See also supra fn 128 this chapter.
[194] 386 US 714, 153 USPQ 432 (1967). See also supra fn 47 this chapter.
[195] 202 USPQ 74 (ND Ill 1978).

fees were found to exist. It should be noted that this case did not purport to construe Section 40 of the Lanham Act, although, no doubt, the court would have held the same way if a federal claim had been asserted.

The correct measure of damages for unfair competition under Section 43(a) of the Lanham Act was considered in *Donsco, Inc. v. Casper Corp.*[196] Having found that plaintiff had established the existence of a trend of steadily rising sales of its penny banks which was interrupted upon the advent of defendant's infringing copies in 1974, the court held that the difference in profit between 1974 and the prior year was an accurate measure of plaintiff's damages. It declined to accept plaintiff's assertion that it was entitled to the increase that it normally would have expected in 1974 or thereafter based on the prior trends, for the reason that "other" market factors intervened and there was no evidence that the decrease in sales after 1974 was attributable to defendant's sales. Of considerable interest, however, was the court's willingness to assume that the fact of damage was established by the showing that an upward trend in plaintiff's sales ended contemporaneously with the advent of defendant's wrongful sales in the absence at least of any showing of other pertinent factors.

In *Aalba-Dent, Inc. v. Certified Alloy Products, Inc.*[197] the issue decided also related to the calculation of damages, based upon a decline in profits, but the court reached an opposite conclusion. Conceding that its use of VERIBOND for a dental alloy infringed plaintiff's prior VERABOND for the same product, defendant's claim was that plaintiff's proof of damages in the nature of lost profits was inadequate because its witness failed to limit his testimony to lost sales of the VERABOND product and had failed to make all proper deductions for administrative costs. The court, in disallowing any damages, accepted defendant's arguments and also noted that there was evidence that a number of other competitive products had appeared in the market during

[196] 205 USPQ 246 (ED Pa 1980).
[197] 203 USPQ 326 (ND Calif 1979).

§7.02[31] / Trademark Law

the period in question and, presumably, contributed to the decline in plaintiff's sales.

While the case of *Flashmaps Publications, Inc. v. Geographia Map Co., Inc.*[198] dealt with unfair competition arising from defendant's copying of the size, appearance, content and concept of plaintiff's unique guide book, accompanied by the copying of other features, all of which were held to constitute a false representation of origin under Section 43(a), the case, in the form of an extract from the transcript of the record, is perhaps most noteworthy because of the coloquy relating to the amount of the bond to be posted. The district judge directed that a bond in the amount of $15,000 be posted. Defendant sought a penalty sum of $100,000, on the ground that $15,000 was manifestly insufficient to make defendant whole in the event it proved to be successful on the trial of the merits and thus that the injunction had been improvidently granted. The court questioned the right to such a recovery as a matter of law, and seemed to address the issue as one of reasonableness considering the size of the plaintiff and its ability to respond to the requirement for security.

The issue presented in *Jones Apparel Group, Inc. v. Steinman*[199] was whether the losses sustained by the defendant in respect of certain infringing sales could be offset against the profits made on other such sales when computing plaintiff's entitlement to defendant's profits. Nothing that the award of damages and profits in such cases is subject to the rules of equity, the court held that there should be no offset. The court reached this conclusion by the somewhat odd reasoning that if the defendant had removed the false labels on the goods in the sales at a loss, those sales would have been non-infringing, whereas leaving the labels on resulted in an infringing sale. Because that sale was at a loss, the defendant would thereby profit from the act of infringement in the sense that the sale at a loss would reduce its liability to the plaintiff. Under such a theory, no sales at a loss would ever

[198] 204 USPQ 552 (SDNY 1979).
[199] 466 F Supp 560, 203 USPQ 1002 (ED Pa 1979).

be offset against profitable sales for such purposes. The better rule would appear to be an inquiry as to whether the sales were related or connected in some fashion. If so, then the total profit should be the measure of damages; and if unrelated, as here, no offset should be permitted. The court, however, denied plaintiff's claim for attorney's fees, holding that such an award was warranted only in cases of "malicious," "fraudulent," "deliberate" or "willful" infringement.

CHAPTER 8

# Section 43(a) of the Lanham Act

In *Ives Laboratories, Inc. v. Darby Drug Co., Inc.*,[1] the color of a product was deemed the key ingredient of its commercial success. Plaintiff Ives, manufactured and distributed the prescription drug cyclandelate under the registered trademark CYCLOSPASMOL. For over twenty years Ives had successfully marketed and sold the drug in two specific kinds of packages, pale blue capsules containing a 200 mg. dosage and red and blue capsules containing a 400 mg. dosage. Defendants were several manufacturers and wholesalers of generic cyclandelate who, in their ordinary course of business, purchased powder and empty capsules for subsequent assembly and sale of the product. Two of the defendants sold the 200 mg. and 400 mg. capsules in colors identical to those marketed by Ives, and the third defendant did so but only with the 200 mg. dosages. Ives commenced action against the three defendants for trademark infringement and unfair competition.

Ives claimed that defendants were guilty of contributory infringement under Section 32 of the Lanham Act in that their use of identical colors for their capsules invited druggists to mislabel their capsules with Ives' trademark CYCLOSPASMOL. The District Court denied a preliminary injunction which was affirmed on appeal. On remand the District Court found no contributory infringement. Although some mislabeling had occurred, the court found that it stemmed from druggists' misunderstanding of the generic

[1] 455 F Supp 939, 200 USPQ 724 (EDNY 1978), affd 601 F2d 631, 202 USPQ 548 (CA 2 1979), remand for trial 488 F Supp 394, 206 USPQ 238 (EDNY 1980), revd 638 F2d 538 (CA 2 1981). See also supra fns 52 and 135 ch. 7 and infra fn 8 this chapter.

## Trademark Law

drug law's labeling requirements rather than any conscious effort by druggists to pass defendants' capsules off as the Ives product.[2]

Ives' principal claim according to the court, was that the defendants' use of identical colors for their capsules was a "false designation of origin" and a "false description or representation"[3] of their products in violation of Section 43(a) of the Lanham Act, contending that it was entitled to have the exclusive use of the blue and red colors in selling the cyclandelate. In response to the Ives' claim the court resolved that the defendant's imitation of the product's trade dress would be actionable if the particular features imitated were "non-functional" and had acquired "secondary meaning."

The Court cited the Ninth Circuit case[4] of *Pagliero v. Wallace China Co. Ltd.* for the test of "functionality":[5]

> [i]f the particular feature is an important ingredient in the commercial success of the product, the interest in free competition permits its imitation in the absence of a patent or copyright.

To establish "functionality, the defendant had to prove that copying this particular feature of the product served a utilitarian purpose essential to effective competition. At trial, the defendant's witnesses testified that some of their patients refused to take generic cyclandelate packaged in a different color despite a physician's assurance of the drug's absolute equivalence. The Court determined that the colors of the pill capsules were functional to its commercial success because of the patient's emphatic association between the appearance of the drug and its therapeutic effect, saying that "to insist that defendants' use a different color would

---

[2] Supra fn 1, 206 USPQ at 240–241.
[3] 15 USC §1125(a).
[4] Supra fn 1, 206 USPQ at 241.
[5] 198 F2d 339, 343, 95 USPQ 45, 48 (CA 9 1952). See also supra fn 137 in Ch 7.

## Infringement and Unfair Competition

unjustifiably put them at a competitive disadvantage."[6]

The court went on to hold that even if the colors were not functional to the success of the product, the plaintiff had failed to show that the colors were indicative of the product's origin in the sense that it had acquired a secondary meaning.[7] This conclusion was based on the testimony of defendant's expert witnesses who claimed that the patients associated the color of the drug only with its effect on their disability. They further vowed that no association was made in the patients' minds between the color of the drug and its origin, Ives Laboratories. The court resolved the case in favor of the defendants[8] and on a final note made reference[9] to *Kellogg Co. v. National Biscuit Co.* wherein Justice Brandeis proclaimed that "(s)haring in the goodwill of an article unprotected by patent or trade mark is the exercise of a right possessed by all—and in the free exercise of which the consuming public is deeply interested."[10]

In *Johnson & Johnson v. Carter-Wallace, Inc.*[11] the District Court for the Southern District of New York also declined to recognize a plaintiff's claim for unfair competition under Section 43(a) of the Act. Plaintiff Johnson & Johnson is the manufacturer of a product widely known as "Johnson's Baby Oil." Johnson & Johnson began marketing the product in 1935 and since that time had been the major producer of baby oil with approximately a seventy-five percent share of

---

[6] Supra fn 1, 206 USPQ at 242.

[7] To establish secondary meaning a plaintiff must show that the "primary significance of the term in the minds of the consuming public is not the product but the producer." Kellogg Co. v. National Biscuit Co., 305 US 111, 118, 39 USPQ 296, 299 (1938). See also supra fn 18 in ch. 7.

[8] EDITOR'S NOTE: The Second Circuit Court of Appeals later reversed the District Court. 638 F2d 538 (CA 2 1981). The Second Circuit held that the evidence supported a claim of contributory infringement against defendants. 638 F2d at 540. The court expressed no view on the Section 43(a) issue, although it found that the District Court's finding of functionality was not supported by the evidence. 638 F2d at 544–45.

[9] Supra fn 1, 206 USPQ at 242.

[10] Supra fn 7, at 122, 39 USPQ at 300–01.

[11] 487 F Supp 740, 205 USPQ 827 (SDNY 1979). See also supra fn 146 in ch. 7.

## Trademark Law

the market for the twelve years prior to trial.[12] Since the 1940s, defendant Carter-Wallace had distributed NAIR depilatory, and in 1975 inaugurated a new advertising campaign which emphasized the fact that NAIR contained baby oil.

Johnson & Johnson alleged that Carter's new packaging and marketing techniques were conducted in such a way as to give consumers the false impression that NAIR was a Johnson & Johnson product. It specifically claimed that Carter's use of a banner device on the new NAIR bottle combined with the use of the words "with baby oil" falsely designated the origin of the product as Johnson & Johnson. Although Johnson & Johnson had a registered trademark for its flag device, it did not allege that Carter had infringed this mark, i.e., urging instead that it was the combined effect of the "baby oil concept" and the alleged similar banner device which constituted a violation of the Lanham Act.

The court found that the trade dress of the NAIR product, taken as a whole, did not confuse the average observer as to its origin. Its conclusion was based on the belief that the different color schemes of the product's labels rendered the overall impression of the products "substantially different."[13] In addition, the court observed that the use of banners, flags and ribbons of various shapes and colors is common to the toiletries and pharmaceuticals industry where such banners are used to highlight salient ingredients or features of the product.[14]

Furthermore, the court insisted that although Johnson &

[12] 205 USPQ at 831. Twelve other companies market mineral oil under the name baby oil. Johnson & Johnson does not claim that it has any legally protectable right in the name "baby oil."

[13] Id at 830. See Combe Inc. v. Scholl Inc., 453 F Supp 961, 201 USPQ 760 (SDNY 1978), discussed in 69 TMR 614 fn 270.

[14] Ibid. The rule is that "common basic shapes such as circles, diamonds, triangles, squares, ovals, arrows, and the like have been so commonly adopted as marks or as a part of marks . . . that whatever rights one possesses in such a design are confined to (that) particular design." Hupp Co. v. AER Corp., 157 USPQ 537, 540 (TTAB 1968), discussed in 58 TMR 657 fn 217.

## Infringement and Unfair Competition

Johnson was the dominant producer of baby oil for many years and as such the product might have acquired an association with the manufacturer in the minds of the public, "de facto secondary meaning" was not legally protectible under the Lanham Act.[15] Quoting from the Second Circuit decision[16] in *Abercrombie & Fitch Co. v. Hunting World, Inc.*, the Court noted that:[17]

> While ... the Lanham Act makes an important exception with respect to those merely descriptive terms which have acquired secondary meaning ... it offers no such exception for generic marks ... no matter how much money and effort the user of a generic term has poured into promoting the sale of its merchandise and what success it has achieved in securing public identification, it cannot deprive competing manufacturers of the product of the right to call an article by its name.

The Court concluded that in a situation where a generic term has acquired a de facto secondary meaning, "a second manufacturer can benefit from a 'free ride' due to the first manufacturer's efforts at promoting public acceptance of a product known by its generic name."[18]

Balanced against these restrictive applications of Section 43(a) is the recent decision of *DC Comics, Inc. v. Filmation Associates*.[19] Plaintiff DC Comics, Inc., had been marketing comic books since 1941 featuring a fictional character known as Aquaman, and in 1967, extended this to include an Aquaman animated television series over a major network. In 1973 it produced a second animated television series which included the Aquaman character. Plaintiff also licensed others to market toys and games based on its Aqua-

---

[15] Id at 831. See 1 J. Thomas McCarthy, *Trademarks and Unfair Competition* §12.15, pp 432–33 (1973).

[16] Ibid.

[17] 537 F2d 4, 10, 189 USPQ 759, 764 (CA 2 1976), discussed in 66 TMR 394 fn 186.

[18] Supra fn 11, 205 USPQ at 831.

[19] 486 F Supp 1273, 206 USPQ 112 (SDNY 1980).

## Trademark Law

man character. Since 1967, the plaintiff had also marketed comic books using a fictional character known as Plastic Man, and in 1979 began exhibiting a Plastic Man animated series over the same network that featured its Aquaman character.

Defendant Filmation Associates made live and animated television film series. In 1967 Filmation entered into a contractual agreement with DC Comics to create the Aquaman series. In 1976 DC Comics additionally granted Filmation an option to produce the Plastic Man series but it declined the offer. In 1978 Filmation produced two animated television series over a competing network featuring fictional characters with essentially the same distinct characteristics and abilities as those exhibited by the plaintiff's characters. Shortly thereafter DC Comics brought suit against Filmation claiming, among other things, that Filmation was guilty of trademark infringement under Section 43(a) of the Lanham Act. A jury trial resulted in a favorable verdict for DC Comics. Filmation subsequently petitioned the court for a judgment notwithstanding the verdict or in the alternative, a new trial.

The plaintiff's primary contention in regard to its Section 43(a) claim was that the Lanham Act protected its characters, including all their traits and abilities, from copying and imitation by others.[20] Filmation, on the other hand, insisted that the scope of the Act is much narrower since it was directed "primarily at false advertising and palming off through the use of misleading packaging, labeling or naming of the product sold."[21] Accordingly, Filmation asserted that since its series were not being "palmed off" as originating in the plaintiff, it could not be held liable under the Act.

Although the court felt that the defendant's interpreta-

---

[20] Section 43(a) (15 USC §1125(a)) provides in relevant part: "Any person who shall . . . use in connection with any goods or services . . . a false designation of origin, or any false description or representation, including words or other symbols tending falsely to describe or represent the same, and shall cause such goods or services to enter commerce . . . shall be liable to a civil action. . . ."

[21] Supra fn 18, 206 USPQ at 114.

## Infringement and Unfair Competition

tion of legislative intent was largely correct, it nonetheless found that the plaintiff could claim protection under Section 43(a) because the product being sold was "entertainment." The Court reasoned that where the product for sale is entertainment in one form or another, then "not only the advertising of the product but also an ingredient of the product itself can amount to a trademark protectable under 43(a) because the ingredient can come to symbolize the plaintiff or its product in the public mind."[22] Holding that protectable "ingedients" recognized by the Second Circuit Court of Appeals include the names of characters as well as their physical appearances and costumes, the court granted DC Comics' reques for an injunction based on its Lanham Act claims.[23]

In the famous *Westinghouse Uranium* case[24] the District Court for the Northern District of Illinois applied a broad brush to the limits of protection afforded by Section 43(a). The subject of dispute at this particular stage of the litigation was Westinghouse's motion to dismiss various counterclaims by several of the defendants including counts alleging violations of the Lanham Act. One of the defendants, Utah International, Inc., specifically claimed that Westinghouse had made two false representations to its customers: First, "that

[22] Ibid. See American Footwear Corp. v. General Footwear Co., 609 F2d 655, 199 USPQ 531 (CA 2 1979); Dallas Cowboy Cheerleaders, Inc. v. Pussycat Cinema, Ltd., 604 F2d 200, 201 USPQ 740 (CA 2 1979), discussed in 69 TMR 611 fn 264; Ideal Toy Corp. v. Kenner Products Division General Mills Fun Group, Inc., 443 F Supp 291, 197 USPQ 738 (SDNY 1977).

[23] The similarities between the plaintiff's and defendant's characters were blatantly obvious. Aquaman is an underwater hero who with his female companion fights villains and assorted forces of evil. Aquaman has a walrus-like companion, Tusky. Defendant's Manta is also an underwater hero who has a female companion. Whiskers is their walrus-like companion.

"Plaintiff's Plastic Man character has the ability to stretch and assume the shape of inanimate objects. Defendant's Superstretch character has essentially the same abilities and characteristics as Plastic Man.

[24] Westinghouse Corp. v. Rio Algom, Ltd., 473 F Supp 393, 204 USPQ 449 (ND Ill 1979).

## Trademark Law

it had the capability to carry through its commitments to make future deliveries of uranium to the utilities [companies], when it knew or should have known that it had no such capability," and second, that Westinghouse said it owned sufficient uranium or would be able to obtain sufficient uranium to enable it to meet its commitments to make future deliveries of 80 million pounds "when [actually] it owned only 15 million pounds of uranium . . . and had no such ability" to meet such a commitment.[25]

In its motion to dismiss the counterclaims Westinghouse maintained that Utah's allegations fell beyond the parameters of Section 43(a) which, in Westinghouse's opinion, was aimed primarily at misuse of a trademark or conduct of a similar nature. Westinghouse predicated its claim on the Seventh Circuit decision in *Bernard Food Industries, Inc. v. Dietene Co.*,[26] which held that the correct interpretation of Section 43(a) embraces "only such false descriptions or representations as are of substantially the same economic nature as those which involve trademark infringement or other improper use of trademarks."[27] Westinghouse thus argued that its alleged misrepresentations were not of Bernard character since they only involved its ability to supply goods to its various customers. Utah, on the other hand, insisted that Section 43(a) has a broad scope and as such covers any false representation that a party uses in connection with its goods or services.

The court agreed with Utah that the statute was not limited to false advertising in connection with competing products. Rather, the court interpreted Section 43(a) as including a prohibition against misrepresentations about the quality of one's own goods "even where the misrepresentations do not tend to confuse [his] goods with those of a

---

[25] 204 USPQ at 459.
[26] 415 F2d 1279, 163 USPQ 264 (CA 7 1969), discussed in 60 TMR 460 fns 280 and 281.
[27] 163 USPQ at 267, quoting Samson Crane Co. v. Union Sales, Inc., 87 F Supp 218, 222, 83 USPQ 507, 509 (D Mass 1949). See Alberto-Culver Co. v. Gillette Co., 408 F Supp 1160, 1163, 194 USPQ 84, 86 (ND Ill 1976), discussed in 68 TMR 831 fn 342.

## Infringement and Unfair Competition

competitor or otherwise misstate the origin of the goods."[28] The court held that the Act should be read as one that protects competitors from misrepresentations that a party makes about its own products and which relates to the principal basis of competition among sellers. Holding that Utah had framed an actionable claim for misrepresentation under Section 43(a) by alleging that Westinghouse had misrepresented its uranium supply capabilities to its customers, Westinghouse's motion to dismiss Utah's counterclaim was denied.

The Northern District of Illinois in *Dawn Associates v. Links*[29] held that a film title is entitled to protection under the doctrine of unfair competition as codified in Section 43(a) assuming the title has acquired the requisite secondary meaning. While the "infringing" title alone may not have been sufficiently close to warrant relief, the court held that defendant's various promotional activities surrounding its film *Return of the Living Dead* violated plaintiff's rights in its earlier film *Night of the Living Dead.* Included in the list of aggravating factors were indications that defendant used promotional materials, still photographs and advertising phrases from the earlier film, possibly represented their film as a sequel to the earlier film, and copied advertising lettering style. Even though defendants had discontinued some of these additional activities, the court still entered a preliminary injunction.

In *Wolf v. Louis Marx & Co., Inc.,*[30] the Southern District of New York took a stand against Section 43(a) as an absolute catchall for every conceivable type of unfair competition claim. Plaintiff claimed trade secret misappropriation and unfair competition violations under state law and diversity jurisdiction but threw in Lanham Act claims on the basis of defendant's advertisement that its toy is "new and novel."

---

[28] Supra fn 24, 204 USPQ at 460, quoting Universal Athletic Sales Co. v. American Gym, Recreational & Athletic Equipment Corp., 397 F Supp 1063, 1072, 187 USPQ 104, 111 (WD Pa 1975), discussed in 66 TMR 414 fn 250.
[29] 203 USPQ 831 (ND Ill 1978).
[30] 203 USPQ 856 (SDNY 1978).

## Trademark Law

Plaintiff argued that such a claim impliedly represented that defendant did not steal the toy design but invented it itself. The court refused to extend Section 43(a) to cover "mere puffing," distinguishing a claim of "new and novel" from far more substantive claims on which consumers could rely, e.g., tar content of cigarettes, strength of pain-relieving drugs, etc. The court was undoubtedly influenced by the probability that the Lanham Act claims merely served to bring in a defendant against whom there was no diversity and who would otherwise could not be joined in the federal court action.

In *Ebeling & Reuss Co. v. International Collectors Guild, Ltd.*,[31] the defendant was preliminarily enjoined against distribution of a fortune-telling teacup/saucer set that was not protected by any patent or copyright. Defendant deliberately set out to copy the otherwise unprotected product and purchased several of plaintiff's sets to do so. The end product was close, but the painted decal was altered in a manner that made it readily distinguishable from the original. Unfortunately for defendant, its advertising photographs utilized plaintiff's original set and not the set defendant ultimately marketed. The court refused to believe defendant's explanations for the advertising mix-up and defendant's failure to substitute actual photographs and, pointing to several instances of actual confusion, held that the substitution of photographs was a false description or representation actionable under Section 43(a).

In *Benson v. Paul Winley Record Sales Corp.*,[32] the defendant took recordings made years ago when the internationally acclaimed jazz musician George Benson was an unknown member of a small combo, repackaged them in an LP entitled "George Benson, Erotic Moods" and prominently featured Benson on the jacket cover. On the basis of certain dubbing and mixing changes, defendants also called it a "new" LP. The court had no difficulty in finding that defendants intended to, and most likely did, mislead the

[31] 462 F Supp 716, 204 USPQ 139 (ED Pa 1978).
[32] 452 F Supp 516, 204 USPQ 498 (SDNY 1978).

## Infringement and Unfair Competition

public into believing that the album contained recent recordings by Benson as the principal performer. While some earlier cases had refused relief in analogous situations, the fact that Benson was not a principal performer in the original recording and the erotic or suggestive advertising and dubbing/mixing modifications were sufficient additional factors to warrant the granting of a preliminary injunction.

In *Klockner-Humboldt-Deutz Ak, Kohn v. Hewitt-Robins Division of Litton Systems, Inc.*,[33] defendant was a former licensee of plaintiff in the manufacture of heavy rock-crushing machinery. Under the terms of the license, several machines bearing plaintiff's trademark but manufactured by defendant under license from plaintiff were installed around the country. After the license terminated, defendant began marketing its own machine, allegedly using misappropriated trade secrets and drawings. Defendant's product, allegedly substantially identical to plaintiff's, was advertised by referring to various successful installations of machines previously made by defendant under license from plaintiff. Since the crushers were actually plaintiff's products (albeit manufactured under license by defendant) defendant's use of the descriptions and designations was held to be false, misleading and deceptive and in violation of Section 43(a). Defendant had urged the court to narrowly interpret Section 43(a) by finding that there was no false designation of origin, false description or false representation. However, the court found the allegations to state a sufficient false designation of origin to defeat a motion to dismiss.

On Section 43(a) generally, see: J. E. Maslow, "Droit Moral and Sections 43(a) and 44(i) of the Lanham Act—A Judicial Shell Game?" 48 Geo Wash L Rev 48 (1979); John E. Stiner, "Lanham Trade-Mark Act Offers Relief for Implied Advertising Claims: American Home Products Corp. v. Johnson & Johnson," 11 Conn L Rev 692 (1979).

[33] 205 USPQ 257 (D SC 1978).

CHAPTER 9

# State Court Decisions

In *Cebu Association of California, Inc. v. Santo Nino de Cebu Association of U.S.A.*,[1] a California Appellate Court reviewed a claim to an exclusive right to use trade names denoting a geographic location and a patron saint. Plaintiff Cebu Association of California, Inc., is a quasi-religious and charitable service organization founded in 1968 and headquartered in San Francisco. Since 1968 they have employed the phrase CEBU ASSOCIATION OF CALIFORNIA and generally CEBU ASSOCIATION, as their trade name. Each year the Association sponsors the annual Fiesta of the Santo Nino de Cebu held in San Francisco.

In March of 1976 a number of the members of the Cebu Association, the defendant-appellants in this case, left the organization and formed a new non-profit organization entitled SANTO NINO DE CEBU ASSOCIATION, U.S.A. The defendants chose that particular name because most of its members were from Cebu and they worshipped the patron saint. Later that year defendants planned their own event called "Fiesta of the Santo Nino de Cebu" and scheduled its commencement one week prior to plaintiff's annual "Fiesta of the Santo Nino de Cebu."[2] Cebu Association filed suit charging the defendant with unfair competition and infringement of their common law rights in three trade names —CEBU ASSOCIATION OF CALIFORNIA, CEBU ASSOCIATION and FIESTA OF THE SANTO NINO DE CEBU. The trial court issued a preliminary injunction.

On appeal the critical question was whether an organiza-

[1] 95 Cal App3d 129, 205 USPQ 362 (Calif Ct App 1979).

[2] Not only was the event given the same title, but it was also to be held at the same church.

tion can be the owner of common law trade names which designate a geographic location and a patron saint. The Court of Appeals concluded that such a claim could not be maintained.[3] Initially it noted that the word "Cebu" denotes one of many islands in the Philippines. The court agreed with the defendants that "Cebu" was a nonprotectable geographic term, and that the trade name CEBU ASSOCIATION was simply descriptive of the Association's individuals and their area of interest, to wit, an association of persons having some connection with the island of Cebu. As such, the Court specifically denounced the injunction against the use of the word "Cebu" because a nonprotectable geographic term:[4]

> ... remains such regardless of the extent to which it is known or unknown throughout the country . . . (a)ll persons with a legitimate claim to the same geographical designation have the right to use that designation ... No one is allowed to have exclusive rights in a mark which others can employ with equal truth for the same purpose.

Turning to the question of whether Cebu Association could exclusively use the name "Santo Nino de Cebu" the Court ruled that an organization could not appropriate the name of a patron saint to the exclusion of others.

On the issue of whether there existed any rights to the name "Fiesta of the Santo Nino de Cebu" the court initially noted that it could only be protected as a service mark, but held that the plaintiff had never used "Fiesta of the Santo Nino de Cebu" as a service mark merely sponsoring an annual event so named. Highlighting the fact that the Fiesta of the Santo Nino de Cebu had been celebrated in the Philippines for hundreds of years, and in Los Angeles since 1934,

[3] 205 USPQ at 365.
[4] Id at 366. See In re Westgate Sea Products Co., 154 F2d 1010, 1011, 69 USPQ 438, 438–39 (CCPA 1946); In re Kraft-Phenix Cheese Corp., 120 F2d 391, 392, 49 USPQ 650, 651–52 (CCPA 1941).

## Infringement and Unfair Competition

the court concluded that Cebu Association had failed to establish the requisite originality for a successful suit based on trade name infringement.

In *Hirsch v. S. C. Johnson & Son, Inc*,[5] Elroy Hirsch, a sports figure of national prominence, sought damages for the unauthorized use of his nickname "Crazylegs" on shaving gel manufactured by the defendant, S. C. Johnson & Son, Inc.[6] On the key issue of whether Hirsch could establish a prima facie case of common law trademark/trade name infringement, the court held as a matter of law, that the action could not be maintained where there was no allegation or evidence that the name had ever been used to identify a product or service.

On appeal, however, the Wisconsin Supreme Court concluded that it was a misstatement of the law to hold that no cause of action for trade name infringement will lie unless a party alleges and proves that the name had been used to identify and distinguish a product or service. The Court quoted[7] *J. I. Case Plow Works v. J. I. Case Threshing Machine Co.*, which held that the law of unfair competition is based on the simple maxim that "[o]ne man may not reap where another has sown nor gather where another has strewn,"[8] as well as the Restatement of Torts definition of a trade name: "(a) trade name is a designation which is used by a person to identify his business, vocation or occupation . . . "[9] The court held that for Hirsch to establish a trade name infringement, there was no necessity as a matter of law to show that

---

[5] 90 Wis 379, 280 NW2d 129, 205 USPQ 920 (Wisc Sup Ct 1979).

[6] Hirsch was a star athlete at the Wausau (Wisconsin) High School, he thereafter attended the University of Wisconsin. In his first season as a superstar at Wisconsin he acquired the name "Crazylegs" due to his unique running style. It was a Chicago Daily News sportswriter who tagged Hirsch with the nickname. It is undisputed that Hirsch has been known by the nickname ever since that first season at Wisconsin. The court took judicial notice of the fact that as recently as June of 1979 he was referred to as "Crazylegs" in the Madison newspaper, the Wisconsin State Journal. 205 USPQ at 923.

[7] Id at 929.

[8] 162 Wisc 185, 201, 155 NW 128 (1916).

[9] Restatement (Second) of Torts §716 (Tent Draft No. 8, 1963).

## Trademark Law

the name functioned to identify a service or product. The court decided that it would be enough if Hirsch could show that the name was one used to identify him in his business or occupation and that the use of the name was likely to cause confusion or mistake in the public's mind with respect to the sponsorship of the defendant's goods. Accordingly, the court reversed and remanded the case for a determination of the claim under a less restricitve interpretation of the protections afforded by the law of unfair competition.

The right of states to regulate trade names and some constitutional problems with that regulation are discussed in "Reuniting Commercial Speech and Due Process Analysis: The Standard for Deceptiveness in Friedman v. Rogers." 57 Tex L Rev 1456 (1979); "Constitutional Law—Commercial Speech—Trade Names Are Not a Protected Form of Commercial Speech," 11 Tex Tech L Rev 717 (1980); "Constitutional Law—First Amendment—Narrowing the Scope of First Amendment Protection for Commercial Expression," 13 Suffold U L Rev 13 (1979); "Professional Trade Names: Unprotected Commercial Speech," 59 Neb LR 482 (1980).

CHAPTER 10

# Trademarks and the Antitrust Laws

This year again most of the cases considering the relationship between trademarks and the antitrust laws arose out of claims that the trademark owner had illegally tied the use of one product, its trademark, to the required purchase of other products. In *Edward J. Sweeney & Sons, Inc. v. Texaco, Inc.*,[1] a terminated gasoline distributor sued Texaco, its supplier, for antitrust violations and Texaco counterclaimed for trademark infringement arising out of the distributor's sale under the TEXACO trademark of gasoline not purchased from Texaco or of such gasoline commingled with TEXACO gasoline. Following prior decisions such as *Redd v. Shell Oil Co.*,[2] the court entered judgment for Texaco on its counterclaim.

In *Sweeney*, the distributor attempted to defend its conduct on the ground that Texaco purchased gasoline from other refiners which it then sold as TEXACO gasoline. In rejecting this defense, the Court stated:

> Thus, the validity of Texaco's position does not depend on whether the gasoline it bought from other refiners contained additives or not. Clearly, Texaco had the right to put its trademark on whatever gasoline it deemed suitable. The crucial point, which apparently escapes Sweeney, is that just because Texaco, the owner of the trademark, could decide what gasoline to market under that trademark does not mean that

[1] 478 F Supp 243, 204 USPQ 906 (ED Pa 1979). See also supra fn 111 in ch. 7.
[2] 524 F2d 1054, 188 USPQ 1 (CA 10 1975), discussed in 66 TMR 419 fn 270.

225

## Trademark Law

Sweeney, who had only the right to sell gasoline so marked, had a like right to decide which gasoline to call Texaco. Any perceived unfairness in this disparity evaporates with the realization that it is precisely what the trademark laws are supposed to accomplish. Indeed, if anyone could decide what goods to market under a given trademark, the value of that trademark and therefore its identity as a trademark would disappear. This is truly a case where what is good for the goose is not good for the gander—that Texaco could and did lawfully decide what gasoline to sell under its trademark does not change the illegality of the same actions when done by Sweeney. It is Texaco's trademark, not Sweeney's.[3]

*Bogosian v. Gulf Oil Corporation, et al.,*[4] is a class action suit between a group of former and present lessee service station dealers and most of the oil companies. In 1977, the Court of Appeals for the Third Circuit had denied motions to dismiss and motions for summary judgment against a complaint alleging in part that it is illegal for the oil companies to require their dealers to sell only gasoline supplied by the oil companies from pumps bearing their trademarks. On March 31, 1980, the District Court (the same court as in Sweeney but a different judge) denied motions to dismiss or for summary judgment directed against this trademark tying claim, holding that the prior decision of the Third Circuit precluded it from following cases such as *Redd v. Shell Oil Co.* and *Sweeney,* and that the question of whether the trademark/franchise and the gasoline were a single product or separate products was an issue of fact for trial.

Several cases raised the question of whether sufficient economic power to render a trademark tie per se illegal could be presumed from the fact a trademark was involved.

[3] Supra fn 1 at 279–80, 204 USPQ at 934 (citation omitted).
[4] 561 F2d 434, 451–53 (CA 3 1977).

## Infringement and Unfair Competition

In *Cash v. Artic Circle, Inc.*,[5] the court narrowly construed *Siegel v. Chicken Delight, Inc.*,[6] and refused to presume from the mere existence of a registered trademark the existence of the requisite economic power for per se illegal tying purposes. The Artic Circle franchises alleged that they were victims of a contractual tie of syrups and toppings products to the trademark/franchise and a tie of accounting services to the mark. While agreeing with Chicken Delight that registered trademarks are entitled to statutory protection against conflicting use, the court distinguished Chicken Delight on the ground that the CHICKEN DELIGHT trademark was presumed to have sufficient economic power in the relevant product market because of evidence establishing its uniqueness.

Artic Circle arose in the Ninth Circuit where the economic power of trademarks has usually been presumed. In the Second Circuit, on the other hand, no such presumption has existed because a trademark does not preclude competition but only infringement.[7] In a case in the Second Circuit, *Esposito v. Mister Softee, Inc.*,[8] the District Court found that the MISTER SOFTEE trademark did have sufficient economic power. The court noted that the francisor was the only mobile soft ice cream franchisor in the relevant geographic area and that of one hundred ten mobile ice cream vendors, ninety four were the franchisor's dealers. It then determined that there was adequate strength in and public acceptance of the franchisor's mark to give it market position sufficient to compel many people desirous of obtaining its franchise to purchase all tied supplies from designated sources and thus significantly restraining competition in the market for the tied products.

In *AMF, Inc. v. Bandage, Inc.*,[9] a competing supplier of radial tire retreading equipment sued a retreading franchi-

---

[5] 204 USPQ 902 (ED Wash 1979).
[6] 448 F2d 43, 171 USPQ 269 (CA 9 1971), discussed in 62 TMR 500 fn 467.
[7] See 68 TMR 834.
[8] 1980-1 Trade Cases ¶63,089 (EDNY 1979).
[9] 1980-1 Trade Cases ¶63,080 (D Md 1979).

## Trademark Law

sor alleging that the franchisor's refusual to permit its franchisees to use the competing supplier's equipment in connection with the franchisor's equipment constituted illegal exclusive dealing. In granting a preliminary injunction to the competing supplier, the court paid little heed to the claim that this would adversely affect the franchisor's ability to control quality of the tires sold from outlets bearing its name.

Avid antitrusters (pro and con) will also enjoy: Elliot R. Zinger, "The McDonald's Antitrust Litigation: Real Estate Tying Agreements in Trademark Franchising," 13 John Marshall L Rev 603 (1980); J. Thomas McCarthy, "Trademarks, Antitrust and the Federal Trade Commission," 13 John Marshall L Rev 151 (1979); B. G. Katz, "Competition in the Soft Drink Industry," 24 Antitrust Bull 263 (1979); Neil W. Averitt, "The Meaning of 'Unfair Methods of Competition' in Section 5 of the Federal Trade Commission Act," 21 BC L Rev 227 (1980); A. R. Kamp, "In re Borden: The FTC Goes Sour on Trademarks," 35 Bus Law 501 (1980).

# Index

References are to pages

**Infringement and Unfair Competition**
  Antitrust Laws, 168, 225-28
  Damages and Attorneys' Fees, 141-42, 145, 204-07
  Defenses, 154-56, 159-61, 175-77, 190-93, 195-96, 203
  Evidence, 171, 176-77, 205-06, 210
  Jurisdiction, Venue and Related Procedural Problems, 145, 148, 191-94
  Pleading and Practice, 131-50, 152-62, 166, 168-73, 183-90, 193-95, 197-207
  Surveys, 115-16, 165-66, 203
  Trademarks, Trade Names and Service Marks, 133-36, 154-57, 173-75, 180-83, 221-24
  Unfair Competition, 144-46, 150-52, 163-69, 173-75, 186
    Appearance of Goods or Labels, 147, 156-57
    "Sears-Compco," 148
    Section 43(a) of the Lanham Act, 168-70, 173, 177-80, 190, 209-19

**Registration**
  Amendments and Corrections, 127
  Cancellations
    Pleading and Practice, 41, 84-87, 94-100, 161, 170
    Standing, 99
  Interferences, 152-53
  Oppositions
    Pleading and Practice, 5-7, 15, 43-47, 79-84
    Standing, 91

229

Trademark Law

**References are to pages**

**Registration—Cont.**
  Registrability
    Color, 142-43
    Consents, 76-77
    Configurations and Containers, 21-22
    Confusing Similarity, 34, 41, 43-47, 48-78
    Descriptiveness, 22-31
    Disclaimer, 26-27
    Disparage or Falsely Suggest (Connection with Persons or Institutions), 41-43
    Formalities, 122-24
      Description of Goods, 122-24
      Drawings, 124-25
      False Statements in Application, 15-16, 87-88, 170-71
    Geographical, 31-33, 91
    Letters and Numbers, 23
    "Mutilation," 34-35
    Ornamentation (Get-Up), 22-23
    Secondary Meaning, 27-28, 150-52, 158
    Service Marks, 35-36
    Supplemental Register, 39-40
    Surnames, 33-34

**Use and Ownership**
  Abandonment, 16-19, 161, 198-200
  Acquisition of Trademark Rights, 5-12, 196-97
  Affidavit of Use (Section 8), 87, 170, 197
  Assignment, 194-95
  Concurrent Use, 13-15, 100
  Incontestability (Section 15), 152-53, 157
  Licensing and Licenses, 12-13, 16, 171, 183-84
  Related Companies, 12-13, 125, 169
  Use and Use in Commerce, 8-12

# NOTES

# NOTES

# NOTES

# NOTES

# NOTES

# NOTES